"This book is both culture changing and life changing. ... ...g that Mark and Paul present is in their own words 'SIMPLE.' And it is what they claim it to be but it is also profound. If we can learn to adopt this solutions-focused way of approaching everyday situations we will transform our work and our lives in elegant and powerful ways. The book is packed with thought-provoking case studies. I love it."

Sue Knight, author of NLP at Work

"Before I saw this eminently useful and inspiring book for solution-focused work in organizational contexts I'd not have believed that there are sometimes even easier approaches than those already developed by the Milwaukee practitioners. Although 'simple' doesn't mean 'easy,' Jackson and McKergow manage to provide a usable approach for everybody doing practical work in and with organizations."

Matthias Varga von Kibéd, University of Munich Institute for Philosophy, Logic and Epistemology, SySt Institute for Systemic Training and Research

"The Solutions Focus introduces a concept that is both elegant and powerful in its simplicity. For too long, business has wasted time focusing on the blocks to progress rather than finding the routes to success—The Solutions Focus gives you the opportunity to find the routes to success. Don't be fooled, this process is simple but it is far from simplistic!"

Chris Howe, managing director, Cchange group and global change consultant

"Easy to read, pragmatic, well laid out and elegantly simple. The approach is nicely uncomplicated, the SIMPLE structure and mnemonic helps to think positively about the problem. I also loved the diagram that visually takes you through the steps that will get you to go from the problem to the future perfect. I know that my copy will probably become well worn as I read and refer to it many times and show it to other people too!"

Barbara Adamson, Executive Coach, Loxwood Interactive Ltd

Praise for
The Solutions Focus

"All good coaches focus on potential, affirmation and solutions. This book is a must. It is simple, easy to read and filled with illustrative examples."
Sir John Whitmore, author of Coaching for Performance

"A focus on solution construction is the core of great coaching. This is a beautifully crafted, elegantly simple approach to applying the power of solutions to organizations—a must-read for coaches and consultants looking for truly effective tools."
Anthony M. Grant, Director, Coaching Psychology Unit, School of Psychology, University of Sydney, Australia

"A classic: the most exciting and applicable approach since Fisher and Ury's Getting to Yes. The logic and ethics of the approach are refreshing and unfortunately all too rare in the corporate world where I do most of my work. It makes so much sense to identify and work with what works."
Nancy Caldwell, negotiation consultant, USA

"I look for a book to in some way help improve my personal performance. The great thing with The Solutions Focus is that every time I picked it up it caused me to momentarily stop and think about how I operate and in particular how I could take a more solution-focused approach in my work. Great value from a small book."
Mick Cope, author The Seven Cs of Consulting

The Solutions Focus

Second edition

The Solutions Focus

Making Coaching and Change
SIMPLE

Second edition

Paul Z Jackson &
Mark McKergow

n*b*

NICHOLAS BREALEY
INTERNATIONAL

LONDON · BOSTON

This second edition first published in 2007 by Nicholas Brealey International
An imprint of John Murray Press

An Hachette company

14

First edition published in 2002
Copyright © Paul Z Jackson & Mark McKergow 2002, 2007

The right of Paul Z Jackson & Mark McKergow to be identified as the Authors of the Work
has been asserted by them in accordance with the Copyright, Designs and Patents Act 1988.

British Library Cataloguing-in-Publication Data
A catalogue record for this book is available from the British Library.

ISBN 978-1-904838-06-7
eBook (UK) ISBN 978-1-90483-831-9
eBook (US) ISBN 978-1-47364-509-7

Printed and bound by Clays Ltd, Elcograf S.p.A

John Murray Press policy is to use papers that are natural, renewable and
recyclable products and made from wood grown in sustainable forests. The logging
and manufacturing processes are expected to conform to the environmental
regulations of the country of origin.

Nicholas Brealey Publishing
John Murray Press
Carmelite House
50 Victoria Embankment
London, EC4Y 0DZ, UK
Tel: 020 3122 6000

Nicholas Brealey Publishing
Hachette Book Group
Market Place Center, 53 State Street
Boston, MA 02109, USA
Tel: (617) 523 3801

www.nicholasbrealey.com
www.thesolutionsfocus.com

Contents

Preface to the Second Edition   xv

1   **Small Changes—and a Big Idea**   1
Problem focus or solutions focus?   2
The Solutions Focus model   3
Benefits of the Solutions Focus   6
Ways to use the Solutions Focus   7
A theory of no theory   7
Your own solutions   8

2   **Staying SIMPLE**   9
The power of simplicity   12
Change the doing or change the viewing   15
Introducing the solutions tools   17
Many routes to success   19
Strategy, tactics and pitfalls   19

3   **Solutions not Problems**   21
Problem talk and solution talk   23
Amplifying useful change   25
Potential pitfalls: Too much problem talk   27
    No customer for change   28
    Trying to solve an "unsolvable" problem   31

4   Inbetween—The Action Is in the Interaction   **36**
Systems thinking   38
Systems synthesis: The interactional view   42
Organizations as interactional systems   43
Potential pitfall: Finding the "cause" of the problem   47
Behavior emerges unpredictably   49
Potential pitfall: Whose fault is it anyway?   51

5   Make Use of What's There   **55**
Everything is a useful gift   56
Counters   58
When does the situation—or part of it—happen already?   59
Making use of skills and resources   62
Potential pitfall: Focusing on deficits   64
Build cooperation—or expect resistance   65
Potential pitfall: Expecting "resistance to change"   66

6   Possibilities—Past, Present and Future   **69**
Possibilities are central to progress   70
Possibilities from the past   72
Potential pitfall: Accusatory explanations   74
Possibilities present   77
Affirming and offering compliments   80
Resources   81
Potential pitfall: Using unresourceful words   82
Future possibilities   83
Potential pitfall: Explanations with no way forward   85

7   Language—Simply Said   **88**
Words matter   89
Potential pitfall: Bewitched by words   90
Scaling   94
Potential pitfalls: Words are personal   95
    Words are not the world   99

8   **Every Case Is Different**   **103**
        Finding enough fit   105
        Small actions   106
        After the small steps—finding more counters   111
        Potential pitfalls: Applying ill-fitting theories 112
            "Knowing" too much   117
            Relying on "experts"   122
            Acting "solution forced," not solution focused 123

9   **The Complete Toolkit**   **126**
        Reviewing the tools   128
        All the tools in action   130
        Practical applications   136

10 **Coaching Solutions**   **137**
        Meet OSKAR   138
        A coaching conversation   145
        The role of the coach—optimism and pessimism   154

11 **Managers Coach Their People to Solutions**   **157**
        Coaching for excellence, not for punishment   159
        Taking solutions-focused coaching into training programs 159
        Introducing a coaching program to an organization 161
        How much expertise does the coach need in the
            performer's topic?   163
        Contrasting internal managers with external coaches 165
        Deft use of the coaching tools   166
        What the organization needs to consider when
            introducing coaching   176

12 **Team Coaching**   **178**
        What's your role in the team?   178
        Working with teams   179
        Platform with teams   183

Future perfect with teams   185
Scaling with teams   188
Counters with teams   190
Affirms with teams   192
Small actions with teams   193
Guerrilla SF   194
Celebrating success—what's better and why?   195
Applying SIMPLE principles to coaching   198

13   Organizational Solutions   201
Consulting models   201
Finding what's working in organizations—every case is
    different   206
Growing and expanding businesses   210
Building solutions between organizations in conflict   214
Positive deviance   217
More ways to find counters in organizations   219
Toward the solutions-focused organization?   223
Conclusions   225

14   The Solutions Artist and Scientist   226
The solutions artist   227
The solutions scientist   228
Keep on keeping on   229
And finally...   229

15   How We Reached Here   230
Anthropology and systems   230
The Mental Research Institute   232
From problem to solution   234
Mark McKergow   237
Paul Z Jackson   239

Acknowledgments 243
References 245
Bibliography 251
Index 257
About the Authors 265

Preface to the Second Edition

Since we wrote the first edition of *The Solutions Focus* there has been a great growth in the application of its ideas within organizations. In this new edition we report on the most significant and interesting cases that we have encountered in our own work and those of other solutions-focused practitioners around the world.

What is the Solutions Focus?

The Solutions Focus is a powerful, practical and proven approach to positive change with people, teams and organizations.

With this approach of radical simplicity, you sidestep the often fruitless search for the causes of problems, take the direct route forwards, and simply head straight for the solution. The focus on solutions (not problems), strengths (not weaknesses), and on what's going well (rather than what's gone wrong) leads to a positive and pragmatic way of making progress.

What is so radical about it? Focusing on solutions (that is, defining and acting on what is wanted and what is better) rejects conventional approaches that share the widespread assumption that focusing on problems (by analyzing, reacting to and talking about them) is the best way to solve them.

William James, the father of modern psychology, said, "The art of being wise is the art of knowing what to overlook." The art of the coach, manager, or consultant using a solutions-focused approach is as much about the disciplines of what you *don't* do—delving into problems that are more usefully overlooked, for example—as it is about the solutions that you *do* focus on.

This book reveals how you—as a coach, leader, facilitator or manager—can apply a set of fundamental principles and an elegant box of tools to transform how you approach and deliver change.

Whether you are dealing with difficult people at work, aiming to get the best from a team or unraveling tricky strategic issues within your organization, the book will show you how to:

✔ Define solutions in ways to help you move directly toward them.
✔ Spot and use helpful events and resources around you.
✔ Avoid major pitfalls and obstacles along the route.
✔ Define and take small steps with the maximum chance of success.
✔ Keep things as simple as possible, but no simpler.

As Gregory Bateson, anthropologist and a founder of systems thinking, put it, "Change is happening all the time; our role is to identify useful change and amplify it." Drawing on the systems heritage, its development in complexity theory and social constructionist thinking, *The Solutions Focus* can be thought of as the new wave of change technology.

Along with appreciative inquiry, narrative and other strands of positive psychological approaches to organizations and people, *The Solutions Focus* is the application of sophisticated ideas about how the world works to the ordinary and extraordinary challenges and problems that face modern organizations.

Solutions that fit

This book offers you a bespoke method of finding ways forward with people and organizations. Whether you are already tackling a major problem or are merely vaguely aware that things could be better, you can start to make progress. And just like a Savile Row tailor, you'll be relying on careful observation and adjustment to ensure the right fit for your particular situation.

Making positive changes with a Solutions Focus is simple:

✔ Don't fix what isn't broken.
✔ Find what works, and do more of it.
✔ Stop doing what doesn't work, and do something else.

This may be simple, but it is not always easy. Organizations and people are complex and dynamic, and identifying what works is a subtle business requiring careful action and observation. As you will see from the many examples drawn from around the world in this book, involving organizations from a great variety of sectors and sizes, this means taking a systemic view and recognizing the multiple and interlinked ways in which people interact.

Fundamentals of the Solutions Focus

There are a few fundamental assumptions and principles that underpin solutions-focused work:

✔ Change is happening all the time: Our job is to identify and amplify useful change.
✔ There is no one "right" way of looking at things: Different views may fit the facts just as well.
✔ Detailed understanding of the "problem" is usually little help in arriving at the solution.

✔ No "problem" happens all the time: The direct route lies in identifying what happens when it does not happen.

✔ Clues to the solution are right there in front of you: You just need to recognize them.

✔ Small changes in the right direction can be amplified to great effect.

✔ It is important to stay solutions focused, not solutions forced.

Some of these principles may appear surprising at first. The idea that detailed understanding of a problem is of little help in making progress goes against the grain of much modern thinking, for example.

Conventionally, in many fields a huge amount of time and effort is spent on analyzing problems and often this is rewarded with success. A software engineer improving a wordprocessing program may analyze problems to sort out the bugs; a mechanic typically employs problem-solving skills to fix a machine.

Much of the success of modern medicine is founded on the great problem-analysis method known as diagnosis. If you have a painful leg, you expect the doctor to search for the cause and apply the appropriate treatment: a cast for a break, bandages and rest for a sprain.

In fact, a problem focus has been so successful in so many arenas that it is the automatic response for many experts when faced with any difficult situation. You may think that detailed understanding of a problem is essential to work out what to do next. The more certain you are of this, the more you are likely to be locked into a problem-focused mode of thought.

Yet while this problem focus has its place in many domains, it is less useful when the issue involves interactions between people. The Solutions Focus offers a more direct route to what works.

The new material for this edition

Most of the new material is in Chapters 10–13, revealing the myriad ways consultants, coaches, managers and facilitators are making use of solutions-focused tools and techniques. The case studies demonstrate how coaching can dramatically increase performance, with success stories from different organizational sectors.

In Chapter 10 you meet OSKAR, our original coaching model, developed for an organization that chose to drive performance by encouraging all its managers to be better coaches. There's a full-length transcript of an executive coaching session, complete with commentary, illuminating the twists and turns of applying the OSKAR model in practice with a real case. We consider the role of the coach as optimist and cheerleader.

The manager as coach is the topic of Chapter 11, illustrating cases of managers getting improved performance from their direct reports in industrial, educational and service settings.

Chapter 12 explores how to apply SIMPLE principles when you want to work as coach to a team. The case studies range from applying the techniques to a British team desperately needing remotivation, to a German industry example, to developing a brighter future for a group of Australian physiotherapists.

Chapter 13 shows how a solutions-focused approach compares to other methodologies with a positive psychological background, such as appreciative inquiry (AI). We see how immense change is possible when a consultant acts as a coach to an entire organization (or, in the case of the Australian fruit growers, the flying foxes and the environmentalists, to a multi-stakeholder set of organizations). This chapter also contains examples from Japan and Canada.

We discovered some of these new cases at the annual SOL conference (Solutions in Organisations Linkup, www.solworld.org), which convened twice in Bristol, then moved on to Stockholm, Interlaken and Vienna. Others we found at gatherings of the EDGe (Executive Development Groups), currently established in the UK, Canada, Singapore and New Zealand, where solutions-focused practitioners meet to network, develop their skills, and share current issues. We are excited at the many ways in which the Solutions Focus ideas are proving useful around the world.

These are all completely new chapters, reflecting not only the most recent information but also the growing emphasis on coaching as a transformational tool within organizations.

The earlier chapters, by contrast, are virtually unchanged. These deal with the principles underpinning solutions-focused practice and the tools with which you can immediately start to apply those principles. Principles are not supposed to change (or not by much), and we are happy to stand by what we have written.

Paul Z Jackson and Mark McKergow
November 2006

1

Small Changes—and a Big Idea

There are three simple, elegant and radical ideas at the heart of any solutions-focused change:

❑ One is to be as clear as possible about what's wanted—this is the "solution" on which we focus.
❑ Another is to harness what is already in place and use these positive forces to influence the emerging future in the direction of the solution.
❑ The third is to take a direct route to what works by overlooking pitfalls and excursions, such as delving into problems and what's not working.

So, if you are the sort of person who likes to be clear about where you are heading, you will find tools in here to help you clarify your vision and those of the people around you.

If you prefer change in your workplace to be as simple and straightforward as possible, and you see the sense in capitalizing on what's already going well, then this book invites you to join a growing worldwide community who are enjoying great results from these pragmatic notions.

And if you are keen to do more with less and make the best use of your resources, this book will start you moving toward a fundamental reshaping of the way you think about and deal with people.

Be warned: This book can change your thinking. At first sight, the ideas may seem obvious. Who would rather be problem focused than solutions focused, given the choice? Yet many people are, without even recognizing it.

Others mistake the principles for simplistic positive thinking. The Solutions Focus involves much more than thinking, such as new skills for questioning or acting in adversity, and a rigorous process for choosing precisely what to do, in often mind-bogglingly tricky circumstances.

It takes skill and practice. But if you are willing to master it, then the Solutions Focus allows you to devise steps that involve you and your colleagues or clients in changing your setup as little as necessary. It means being absolutely clear about what you want, discovering what is already working well, then encouraging the processes that strengthen these positive forces. This approach is now being used by many companies and organizations around the world, in the US and Canada, in the UK and across the rest of Europe and in Japan, Singapore and Australasia, as the basis for change and progress in challenging situations.

When asked which force he thought had the greatest power to shape history, Theodore White said, "The idea." You will engage here with ideas capable of delivering an immense amount of progress—fast. From proven roots in psychiatry and health through to developments in education and organizations, these ideas are transforming ways of working with people and their problems.

In contrast to the "big ideas" of the 1990s such as business process reengineering and downsizing—with their attendant negative effects and disruption—the Solutions Focus is a big idea about small steps.

Problem focus or solutions focus?

What are the most important differences between a problem focus and a solutions focus?

PROBLEM FOCUS	**SOLUTIONS FOCUS**
What's wrong	What's wanted
What needs fixing	What's working
Blame	Progress
Control	Influence
Causes in the past	"Counters" in the past
The expert knows best	Collaboration
Deficits and weaknesses	Resources and strengths
Complications	Simplicity
Definitions	Actions

The Solutions Focus model

In the diagram below, time is represented along the horizontal axis. The dot in the middle stands for the current situation. The P on the left is the problem—with its causes in the past and its continuation toward the "dreaded future." By contrast, the fluffy cloud on the right is the future perfect—an ideal state in which current problems have vanished.

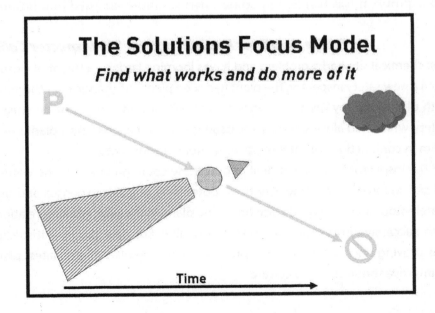

The Solutions Focus Model
Find what works and do more of it

Time

Conventionally, we assume that learning about the problem will help with working toward a solution. But here, we can see that the problem axis and solution axis are different and independent. Finding out about the problem makes us experts on the *problem*, which is best overlooked.

The idea of knowing where we want to be is familiar to any strategist, who takes an interest in where we are now and where we want to go. But while the conventional strategist's next step is to devise a plan to get us from here to there, the Solutions Focus practitioner takes a different route, knowing that any long-term plan is likely to be out of date before it has left the publisher, a prime candidate for derailment by unexpected events.

Instead, we look back in time to find what has been happening in our organization that is *already* taking us in the direction we want to go. This rich body of skills, resources and examples provides the fuel, the encouragement, the motivation and the sense of possibility to choose what small step to take next: a step in the direction of the future perfect.

Once we do more of what we already know works, we can notice its impact and choose to do more of it if it proves useful.

The following real-life example illustrates how a challenging workplace problem was handled by some smart solutions-focused questioning.

The Solutions Focus in action: "An Inspector Calls"

The chemical site had a problem and it was looming larger—a threat of closure from a new safety inspector. The plant had seen plenty of change over the years, with old machinery decommissioned and new processes brought on stream. Safety, which had always been a key issue, was now managed by a plant safety team in conjunction with the safety regulator's site inspector.

The inspector had a great deal of power: He could go wherever he wanted on site, enforce improvement notices (potentially at great expense), and ultimately stop operations and close down the plant. In the past, working relations with successive inspectors had been reasonable. But now the new inspector was proving uncooperative when presented with the plant team's latest plans to improve the site's safety culture.

The team members had been expecting support from the regulator and were surprised by his officious attitude: He wanted to see every piece of paper and was reluctant to engage in the customary informal exchanges with managers.

The team tried all the regular good tactics for getting along, but to no avail. As stories spread—"You can't get a straight answer out of him"; "He's not interested in anything except the paperwork"; "He's out of his depth, you know"; "He won't stop till he's found something wrong"—a sense of despondency gripped the site.

The safety team knew the essence of the problem: The inspector was stopping them from making progress with their safety culture plans and a worsening impasse would threaten the very future of the site, with appalling knock-on effects for their parent company.

Traditional problem-focused ways of approaching the situation might include:

❑ An examination of why the inspector wouldn't see sense.
❑ A "barrier analysis" of what was impeding matters.
❑ A psychological profile of the inspector, to establish the cause of his behavior.
❑ Attacking the inspector by official complaints to his seniors.
❑ A workshop with the inspector to firm up the nature of his concerns.
❑ Writing off the time and money invested in the safety culture project and starting again.

The safety team brought us in to help, perhaps suspecting that we would begin by setting up mediation between them and the inspector.

Instead, we took a solutions focus, asking them to rate their encounters with him on a scale of 0–10. One manager quickly snorted, "Zero!" We paused and waited. "Apart from once, when it was a 3 for 20 seconds..."

Suddenly there was a glimmer of hope. The crux of the solution, we figured, would be in those few seconds; not in any of the traditional approaches, and not even requiring conscious action from the inspector. The solution was not going to center on him as an individual, with all his "flaws, failings and difficulties," but on the interactions between him and the safety team. We needed to know more.

When we asked the manager what he had done to bring about this dramatic, if brief, improvement, he said, "I suppose I stopped pushing him for a moment and gave him time to think."

The mood of the meeting palpably changed. The team outlined the parts they had individually played in their own best exchanges with the inspector, and from these strands drew out a list of 14 actions they could do quickly, simply and cheaply to move just one point up the scale.

These included bringing fewer people to meet the inspector, wearing name badges at meetings and giving him more notice of impending questions and issues. The individual who had most contact with the inspector was given the task of noticing what was working best.

Instead of gloom at their lack of options, the managers said they now felt refreshed to be analyzing what was going well instead of what was going badly.

When we followed up some weeks later, matters were much improved. The threat of an improvement notice had been lifted and the project was back on track. One manager said that she know they were making real progress when the "impersonal" inspector inquired about her recent holiday!

Benefits of the Solutions Focus

Discovering what works and doing more of it is generally a positive, enjoyable and empowering activity for all concerned. Whether you are a manager with problems to solve, a coach, leader, consultant or facilitator, you will reap benefits from the Solutions Focus for your clients, your colleagues and yourself.

By cultivating what is already happening as the seeds of change, you nurture growth through small initiating events. Changing as little as possible has benefits in time, cost and effort. This form of change takes the path of least resistance.

Asking "When does success happen already?" generates a different kind of conversation from "When do we go wrong?" Energy, enthusiasm and cooperation are frequent and welcome side effects.

These benefits—along with many measurably improved results in sales, customer satisfaction, work attendance, processes and staff satisfaction surveys—account for the rapid growth of solutions-focused work in organizations ranging from blue-chip companies to campaigning pressure groups. From the mid-1980s onward, the solutions-focused approach has proved itself many times over and chimed intuitively with forward-thinking managers, coaches and business leaders. The work takes various guises, including solutions-focused strategy workshops, team-building sessions, problem-solving training, stress management, telephone counseling and systemic coaching for an entire company workforce.

Managers and consultants in Europe, the US, Canada, Australia, Japan, Singapore and elsewhere are deploying these ideas as an important ingredient in their work with public and private-sector organizations, accountants and consultancies, local authorities, government institutions, hospitals, educational establishments and banks.

Ways to use the Solutions Focus

Suppose you want your business to grow. You could buy a book that is a collection of ideas about building your business. These ideas would be assembled from other people's experiences of developing their businesses. What worked for these other people might work for you—or it might not.

Missing from that book will be many other good solutions that proved useful when applied to completely different types of problem. The elements for growing your business may be significantly different from other people's. Your ways of conducting yourself, your knowledge, your particular setting, offer you extra possibilities that the people in the books didn't have. A solutions focus *fits you and your situation today.*

A theory of no theory

To practice the Solutions Focus you need very little theory, most of which can be summed up by describing it as "the theory of no theory." It is an approach that allows solutions and techniques to be invented afresh each time, according to what is actually happening in an organization.

Your own solutions

The Solutions Focus has many virtues and has proved its worth in many different contexts. However, it is not:

❑ A recipe.
❑ A guarantee of success first time, every time.
❑ A surefire means to understand what is going on in tricky situations.
❑ A stick with which to beat people.
❑ A "way of life" to be adopted and lived at all times.

Nor is it simply positive thinking. The Solutions Focus is an approach, including specific forms of questioning, leading to action. The approach is often positive, but it is not necessarily so. Thinking is a vital element, but is rarely sufficient.

The Solutions Focus is also considerably different from "best practice" or even "modeling," which consists essentially of finding top performers and copying their methods. The differences between your personal makeup and that of other top performers may be just significant enough to make it harder to replicate their results than to produce your own.

We encourage you to focus on your own practices, identifying the aspects of you, your team and your organization that will speed your progress. Discover your own solutions that fit—even if they aren't in the textbooks. Or on the curriculum at business school. Or known to you— yet.

2

Staying SIMPLE

"Everything should be made as simple as possible, but no simpler."
Albert Einstein

While problems may be complex, the solution-focused approach to solving them is simple. The SIMPLE model encompasses all the ideas that account for the unique effectiveness of this way of working.

In this chapter we introduce the SIMPLE principles and the full set of solutions tools, noting why it is advantageous to aim for simplicity. Along with a robust definition of positive change, this sets the scene for expanding and illustrating these ideas through the rest of the book.

SIMPLE is a distillation of countless hours of practical experience and some radical breakthroughs in how people have comprehended the workings of the world. Understanding each element of SIMPLE will give you the grounding you need to practice the Solutions Focus in almost any circumstances:

Solutions not problems
Inbetween—the action is in the interaction
Make use of what's there
Possibilities—past, present and future
Language—simply said
Every case is different

Let us look in a little more detail at the propositions that make up this approach.

Solutions not problems

Amazing as it may seem, there is not necessarily a logical connection between the problem and the solution. By focusing on solutions, we avoid wasting time on problem talk. This may sound easy and perhaps even obvious, but it is rare for managers to maintain an intensive, exclusive heading toward solutions. In the chemical factory example in the previous chapter, the problem talk was all about the difficulty—or even the impossibility—of dealing with the safety inspector. By focusing instead on how the inspector worked (or might work) constructively, all sorts of possibilities appeared.

Inbetween

Many aspects of a solution are most helpfully thought of as being inbetween the people involved, rather than isolated or belonging only to one party. Empowerment, for example, is not something you give me or I give you; we co-construct it between us by the actions each of us takes. This interactional view is a link into systems thinking: The system has properties that exist outside any of the individual components.

Organizations are complex interactional systems, subject to some of the same phenomena as ants in a nest, cars in a traffic system, and the molecules of air that make up the weather. The findings from complexity—the study of such systems—throw light on to many of the issues facing organizations.

*M*ake use of what's there

The seeds of the solution are almost always present in the form of various Counters, parts of the solution that have been happening occasionally before, or in part or in embryo. These help make up the Platform for the solution that is going to emerge (there is more on Counters and Platforms later in the chapter). Our search for what is there that is useful can be forensic, in contrast to methods that quickly get into worrying about what is not there or what "ought" to be there.

*P*ossibilities

We mine the past, present and future for resources and possibilities that will take us toward the solution. Any useful story of the past, explanation (of what is happening in the present) or vision (of the future) will contain possibilities—the skill lies in recognizing and applying them. Unhelpful stories, explanations or predictions are often notable for their lack of possibility.

*L*anguage

Big words can make matters more complicated. To stay simple it is better to keep the language simple. Use $5 words rather than $5,000 words. Reflecting a customer's language in preference to an expert's jargon is also preferable: These words are already defined by the person who needs them.

*E*very case is different

The Solutions Focus is an approach to change, not a set of prefigured methods to fit every case. It offers a pragmatic route to find out what works in this instance, with these people, with this problem. Start afresh every time and construct new, bespoke solutions that fit each situation perfectly.

It is a flexible way of working, unlike many change disciplines in which the same methodology is applied to organizations irrespective of their differences. We are guided to any interventions by the different characteristics and quirks of each case.

The power of simplicity

Each individual facet of SIMPLE matters, but the choice of acronym is clearly not accidental. There is a cutting power to simplicity itself.

> *"The ability to simplify means to eliminate the unnecessary so that the necessary may speak."*
> Hans Hofmann
> (artist and painter, in The Search for the Real, 1967)

Why is it important to be simple? And what is simple enough? Our quest is for what works. If we discover a particular way to make something work, then there is no point in adopting any more complicated method.

Yet there are many complicated ways in which people and organizations do go about trying to make changes. Perhaps they are seduced by impressive-sounding models or led astray by customs and habits. The fact remains that it is both possible and desirable to be more direct, more simple and more effective in many instances.

Occam's Razor

The quest for simplicity has a distinguished history. William of Occam, a figure from fourteenth-century Surrey, England, railed against fellow philosophers who were building more and more complicated explanations to account for the circumstances of their world. It appeared that whoever came up with the most complicated was deemed the cleverest and therefore spoke the truth.

Occam's most famous statement is:

Entia non sunt multiplicanda praeter necessitatem. (Entities ought not to be multiplied except from necessity.)

He was saying that it is vain to assume more in philosophical matters when it is possible to assume less. In his quest to assume no more than he had to, he dissected every issue as if with a razor.

The vanity to which Occam refers applies in both meanings of the word. It is vain in the sense of futile: The extra elements add nothing to our understanding or to our ability to change matters. And it is vain in the sense of conceited: Elaborate models—in instances when simpler ones apply—are sustained only by puffery or hype.

There are three areas where it is worth taking particular care to stay simple:

❑ *Theory*—setting aside theories and assumptions that are not confirmed in this particular case.
❑ *Language*—tackling vague language that can obscure useful details.
❑ *Imagination*—avoiding using our imagination to infer hidden (and unhelpful) facets beyond those we observe.

When we do anything more complex than is necessary, we may be serving an interesting theory, but we are doing a disservice to the people involved in the issue.

We prefer straightforward words, stories and viewpoints that illuminate what works in a particular case. The rest is ignored. Although this may sound obvious it is far from common practice—and, as the following story reveals, is probably not even our natural inclination.

Bewitched by the complicated: The Bavelas experiment

In a classic psychological experiment first conducted by Dr. Alex Bavelas,[1] sets of two volunteers are asked to work out the differences between healthy cells and sick cells. They go to separate rooms and volunteer A—let us call him Adam—is shown slides of cells, with the instruction that he must learn to distinguish the sick from the healthy by trial and error. After each guess, the experimenter gives Adam a signal, letting him know whether the guess was right or wrong.

Adam receives true feedback: The signals from the experimenter correctly tell him how he is doing. After a while, Adam (and the other As) learn to distinguish the cells and generally score about 80 percent.

Meanwhile, in the other room, volunteer B, whom we shall call Brian, is also guessing whether each cell is healthy or not. But his feedback is independent of his own guesses since he receives exactly the same signal as A; that is, his feedback depends on A's guess. This means that B is in fact incapable of discovering the order he seeks.

A and B cannot see each other's trials and they are unable to communicate with one another until they are eventually invited to discuss their findings.

A's rules are simple, based on his sensory observations and the feedback he receives. B, however, offers a much more complicated theory based on his tenuous and contradictory hunches. At this point something curious occurs.

A does not shrug off B's ideas as unnecessarily complicated or plain absurd. He is impressed by the subtlety and complexity of B's theory and evaluates his own as naïvely simple and inferior by comparison. Before taking a second test with new slides, the subjects are asked to say who will improve most over the first test results. All Bs and most As say that B will.

In fact B shows hardly any improvement, but A, who has taken on at least some of B's complicated theories, performs significantly worse the second time around.

This experiment not only shows that simplicity can be good, but also demonstrates the attraction of complication. While you will aim to keep the routes of the Solutions Focus as simple as possible, you will encounter many lures to make your task far from easy.

One of the temptations along the way is to assume an "expert mind," choosing from a few possibilities, with a pretty sure idea in advance of what is going to work. Too often this is how organizational experts work, and too often the results are disappointing because the approach misses the significant differences in the particular cases.

There is, for example, no one "right" way of looking at organizations: Different views may fit the facts just as well. To discover what works in complex territory, it is helpful to adopt the beginner mind so as to entertain a variety of views of the situation.

This isn't always easy because we can be distracted from our search by theories, complicated language and metaphors—the means by which we naturally talk and think—which draw our attention into arid areas. Just like the Bavelas experiment volunteers, we can also be distracted by people who arrive with an "expert" label and a persuasive way of telling you just how complicated your organization must be. The sorry story of the failure of "reengineering organizations" is one recent widescale example.

Change the doing or change the viewing

The SIMPLE suppositions and the solutions tools (see below) are applied with one aim: to find the way to the solutions that people want. Whatever that may be, it always involves change.

As with many much-debated concepts, change is an area where language often complicates matters. We shall take the following definition of change, which helps us to determine whether or not it has happened:

Change occurs when someone does something differently or looks at something differently.

The converse is also useful to remember. If no one does anything differently or looks at anything differently, there has been no change. It is a little like when someone goes on a training course and returns to the office enthusing about it, while continuing to do precisely what they have always done.

All change occurs from someone's point of view. A change from one viewpoint may look like status quo from another. For instance, the managers of an organization decide that they are going to change the culture. They begin by introducing a new logo. Those involved with the logo experience a radical shift into new territory. Others perceive no shift in the culture whatsoever. Both perspectives are valid.

What matters more is for you to define the changes you want and be aware of when they are happening. This is Gregory Bateson's idea of a difference that makes a difference. Bateson, a British anthropologist, is an influential voice in studies of social systems. He has suggested that in a complex system such as an organization, we can create change by making a small difference at one point, which reverberates through all the feedback mechanisms to make the larger kinds of differences we seek. This was an early version of the much discussed Butterfly Effect.

The direct route

The Solutions Focus pursues a direct route. The direct route to what works for a given person in a given context is to start defining the desired results and looking for them as quickly as possible. This derives from the idea that what we talk about can have a great influence on what we subsequently attend to and do. In particular, given any issue, we prefer to talk about the solutions associated with the issue rather than the problems.

As the next chapter explains, the route to the solution depends on what the solution is, not on what the problem is.

Problem talk is often a digression down a sidetrack, which may or may not produce useful material. This is directly at odds with a large part of conventional psychological wisdom, where "talking through the problem" is regarded as a key precursor to change. However, the latest evidence from research across a spectrum of people professions[2] is that the solutions approach produces as good or better results in less time. Chapter 14 describes the psychological background to the Solutions Focus.

Applying simplicity should produce major rewards with an economy of effort. By changing as little as possible, we usually avoid many of the pains of revolutionary turmoil, while harnessing existing trends and resources to drive events forward with perhaps only a few tweaks.

And that is all you need do, apart from taking care to avoid damaging interventions. When you watch people at the peak of their powers, whether it is a superb footballer, a market trader or a surgeon, there is often a paradox. They seem to have more time in which to function, and they appear to accomplish more by doing less. Much of their skill lies in a reserve of confidence, knowing they could do more if they had to; meanwhile, they follow an elegant, minimalist through-line.

SIMPLE and yet not easy

There are many simple yet wrong solutions around. Taking a Solutions Focus is not about finding a simple solution and sweepingly applying it, because if it doesn't work then it isn't, by our definition, a solution.

Taking an effective Solutions Focus is all about setting aside pre-conceptions and finding what works in each particular case. The approach is simple, but not simplistic. Although the range of activity may be relatively small and the methods of the Solutions Focus unexpectedly simple, its practice is not always easy, and it takes skill to exercise the craft masterfully. It appeals to those who like to engage their creativity, proceed flexibly and think afresh each time they encounter people or circumstances where change is wanted. And, *pace* Mencken, sometimes the solution is simple and right, and sometimes the right solution is more complex.

> *"For every complex problem there is a simple solution, and it's wrong."*
> H L Mencken, US humorist

Introducing the solutions tools

The next six chapters take each facet of SIMPLE in turn. As you read the book, you will also encounter the six solutions tools with which to apply the SIMPLE principles.

When you use the book to grapple with your own problems and solutions, it is these tools that you will deploy to ease your route to the outcomes you want.

Although there is no one fixed route that applies to every problem (remember, every case is different and each solution is conjured afresh), Figure 1 sets out one plausible path.

Figure 1 The solutions tools

We might sensibly begin with the **Platform**, which may be derived from the problem. This is where we are now, a point of departure for our process of searching for what works. We want to establish the platform early, to support the changes we are going to make.

   A spectacular leap of the imagination can launch us from the platform directly to the **Future Perfect**, the situation without the problem, the way the customer for change wants it to be. You can define this quickly and effectively. What if the problem went away overnight: How would you know?

   Next we might accumulate **Counters**: resources, skills, know–how and expertise that will count in getting us toward the solution. Counters come in various denominations. One of the most valuable is "When does the solution happen already?"

Our counters typically line up along a **Scale**, so that we can measure progress and identify differences that make a difference.

Whatever the people involved are already contributing toward the solution will be recognized, valued and **affirmed**.

A Solutions Focus cycle pivots around **small actions** that the participants take to help the world to move with them. It is often astonishing how small a well-chosen action can be and still make a big difference.

Naturally, you note any differences that the actions make, which is why the arrows in Figure 1 take you back into finding counters. Any progress is a further counter toward a solution, and allows a fresh visit into further affirmations and choices of the next small steps.

Many routes to success

Figure 1 illustrates one potential route toward solutions, but remember that you are not constrained. Every case is different and it often turns out that there are other equally fruitful routes.

In different cases, different elements will be more or less significant. In one, the definition of the future perfect might prove the crucial step. In another, you might first establish some basic confidence by finding counters. In a third, the art of scaling may provide a quick focus on what needs to happen next. Working out which areas are productive—and applying them—is a large part of the art of the Solutions Focus.

Strategy, tactics and pitfalls

After the following chapters describing the SIMPLE principles and the solutions tools, we present a series of stories and case studies in a discussion about the application of the Solutions Focus to different problems that are regularly encountered within organizations. One chapter features extended examples showing all the ideas and tools in action together. Three further chapters discuss the use of solutions methods in coaching, teams and organizations. These elaborate on an array of strategies that you might choose and a consideration of tactics, including advice on avoiding the many pits into which travelers may fall.

The book concludes with tips on how to be a solutions artist and scientist, and a history of the solutions movement, including a description of how it all began for us.

3

Solutions not Problems

"The solution of the problem of life is seen in the vanishing of the problem."
Ludwig Wittgenstein, Tractatus Logico-Philosophicus *6.521*

As the name implies, *The Solutions Focus* is about the many ways that focusing on solutions can help you. So the fact that our first maxim in staying SIMPLE is "Solutions not problems" should come as no surprise.

SOLUTIONS NOT PROBLEMS
Inbetween—the action is in the interaction
Make use of what's there
Possibilities—past, present and future
Language—simply said
Every case is different

In this chapter we explore how you can focus on solutions in your own situations, and alert you to potential pitfalls that can waylay you from a SIMPLE path. In focusing on solutions, you will:

✔ Encourage solution talk, while dealing sensitively with problem talk.
✔ Negotiate a solvable problem.
✔ Establish who are customers for change (it could be you!).

We will also examine two of the solutions tools described in Chapter 2, which help you focus on solutions rather than problems:

The platform—the starting point, containing useful and hopeful elements.

The future perfect—describing how life will be when the problem has vanished.

Solutions Focus in action: Under fire with the Israeli Army Home Front Command

One person who has discovered the benefits of encouraging a focus on solutions is Aryeh Keshet, a psychologist teaching Solution Focused Stress Management at the Technion-Israel Institute of Technology.

In his army reserve duty, he has been training Rescue Units' command personnel in the Israeli Home Front Command. Aryeh was responsible for providing scenario consultation and training in preparation for missile attacks.

He began by introducing the concepts of problem talk and solution talk as criteria for developing leadership solutions. Most of the commanders were habitually preoccupied with identifying and mapping problems such as obtaining and operating rescue equipment, and dealing with civilians' attempts to rescue their relatives.

By insisting on replacing "problem descriptions" with "solution development," a new pattern of responding evolved. Said Aryeh, "Some grasp it quickly. Others are in the grip of problem talk and keep jumping in with their problem descriptions. I tell them that sympathetic though I am to their mounting problems, the training time is for generating and delivering leadership solutions.

"If they insist on talking about problems, I suggest that we arrange a special session during another reserve duty call, to focus on finding and detailing all the 'trees' in the 'problem forest' that they started to describe."

In a program of team development training with a Rescue Battalion, he asked the commanding officers what they wanted to be different—considering that every problem can be described as a situation in need of improvement.

Translating problem descriptions into goals and objectives, he directed all the ensuing talk toward "What can we do about it?" "Officers who were exposed for the first time to this sort of thinking were coming to me spontaneously after a one-day workshop, telling me they wanted to apply the solutions principles to solve different problems with their soldiers, without waiting for another workshop to do it."

When Israel was attacked by missiles during the Gulf War, Aryeh was frustrated by the context created by the media and the professionals' habit of interviewing people only in a problem-focused way.

"The Gulf War was not active fighting, it was waiting passively for missiles. The whole population was the front line. The experts were interviewing perfectly normal people about their normal uncertainties and anxieties.

"And instead of inquiring about their strengths and ability to face the unpredictable dangers, they focused on identifying and defining normal anxiety symptoms and encouraging their full expression. In doing so, the media and the professionals end up by creating helplessness and passivity instead of resourcefulness and the taking of initiatives."

Aryeh arranged a transfer from his post as a mental health officer in the Medical Corps so that he could do something about this, and gained permission to set up a radio and TV program to interview civilians in a more solution-oriented fashion.

Because the main problems with a missile attack are not physical damages but the psychological stresses of uncertainty, Aryeh—in his new role as a Civilian Behavior Officer—concentrates on the creation of user-friendly contexts and solution-friendly contexts. He asks, for example, "What can be done to prevail?" and "How can you maintain high morale?"

These contexts achieve their impact by drawing people's attention to their coping skills, growth resources and creative possibilities.[1]

Problem talk and solution talk

If someone has a problem, one option is to talk about it. We call such discussions "problem talk." We enter problem talk when people:

❑ Tell us more about their problem.
❑ Say what they feel is causing it.

❏ Elaborate on when it is at its worst.
❏ Guess who is responsible.
❏ Describe the other difficulties it may be causing.

There is often a great temptation to take a route deep into problem talk with these and other questions.

Problem talk is natural: "If only I could understand the problem, or better still find the cause, then I might be able to begin to find a solution." This seems the obvious approach for many managers and strategists and it dominates the thinking of most business organizations, as well as informing the approach of specialist problem solvers, such as advisers and consultants.

To illustrate the apparent naturalness of a problem focus, here's just one typical example, from a report on a knowledge management project carried out by Cranfield and BT:

> *It has concentrated on answers to the question "Why, with all the facilities available, does knowledge not get transferred—where does it go wrong?"*

While this may seem an eminently sensible question, it is also completely problem focused. The tacit assumption is that if you know where it goes wrong, you will be better equipped to do something about it. We suggest the opposite: if you know where it goes wrong, you will know more about it going wrong. But how about if you knew more about where it had gone *right*?

Strangely, the more you talk about problems, the bigger and more difficult they seem to become. Solution-focused practitioners need discipline to resist asking some pretty natural-sounding questions, such as: "What do you think is the root cause of this problem?" Many managers ask these and similar problem-focused questions, which lead to an altogether different sort of discussion from "solution talk," discussing where and how the solution is already happening.

It is true that analysis of the problem can help in some circumstances. Engineers will want to analyze the weaknesses of a wobbly bridge; if an airplane crashes, the investigators will home in on what went wrong. Once the problems are described or understood in sufficient detail, they are ready to implement their solutions by, respectively, strengthening the bridge or fixing the fault in similar models of airplane to prevent further disasters. To a great extent, their expertise lies in knowing when they have found out enough about the problem, so that they can turn their attention to what makes a practical difference: putting the solution in place.

Such analyses are also often designed to allocate responsibility, so that criminals may be brought to court, for insurance claims to be settled fairly and to leave a feeling that justice has been done—all of which may be practically and psychologically important. Nonetheless, the attention in such matters is primarily retrospective, often with only an incidental impact on what will happen in future.

Traditionally, some of the most important problems in organizations are engineering problems, where diagnosis follows a logical, predictable path that will—with sufficient cleverness, effort and budget—inevitably produce a solution. Increasingly in organizations the most interesting and significant problems are about people: their difficulties in communicating with each other, in getting the team to pull in the same direction, in taking the organization as a whole into the territory they want it to enter.

Keeping it SIMPLE: Focus on the solution

Focus on the solution and the first signs of it appearing. This can shortcut many hours of fruitless delving into the problem.

With these sorts of issues, analysis of the problem rarely helps in finding the solution. What it does do is make you an expert in the problem. This may be illuminating or even entertaining, but understanding *why* things are how they are does little to help you decide what to do next.

Amplifying useful change

There is a story going around that it is difficult to make change happen, an uphill struggle to get it started, and nearly impossible to manage.

Organizations spend millions of dollars every year on change programs, often with disappointing results. In our own lives we have the same experiences again and again—we try to change, but end up feeling stuck.

We propose a different story. In this tale, change may be easier than you imagine, is starting all the time and can be guided if not completely controlled. From this perspective, key questions are:

✔ How can we best be primed to notice change?
✔ How can we identify which are the useful changes?
✔ How can we capitalize on the changes we notice?

Things do change—and if we believe that change is all around, then we are much more likely to spot it.

Some changes are broadly predictable, for example many of the physical changes we face as we grow older, or the progress of the seasons year after year. Yet even these expected changes contain unpredictable elements: the differences in severity of successive winters or the various ways in which time takes its toll on our bodies. In fact, unpredictability is an important feature of complex adaptive systems. We cannot tell exactly what the weather will be like more than a day or two ahead. We cannot be certain which horse will win the race, or which team will carry off the cup, but we do know that there will be changes from one event to the next.

Keeping it SIMPLE: Use what's already happening

By identifying useful parts of what is already there, we are closer to constructing a solution—the building blocks are in place. Trying to invent new items is likely to take longer and result in a more precarious edifice.

The Solutions Focus in action: Customer service on the slide

American solutions consultant Lynn Johnson explains how he used a solutions focus in his work.

"I was consulting with a ski school in the mountains above Salt Lake City. They asked me to train them in good customer service, so I posed a question:

"'Suppose you have feedback sheets from the last 100 students you have taught. Suppose that 90 percent of the evaluations are favorable and 10 percent are negative. You are going to follow up with in-depth interviews and can only talk to one group of people. Which group will you want to interview?'

"They replied, 'The 10 percent who aren't satisfied.'

"'I disagree,' I said. 'You want to interview the 90 percent who were pleased. Are you really sure you know what you did that helped the most in teaching skiing? Are you sure you understand what it is you did right? Could it be that you inadvertently did something that really pleased a student? Would you like to know what that was?'

"The ski school was excited by the 'look for what you are doing right' and in the next month I heard several inspirational stories about the retreat. One of the best: The training director of the ski school was giving a lesson to a well-known local media person. She asked him: 'What would you like to learn today?' He replied that he wanted to learn to ski the 'crud' or the chopped-up snow.

"She then asked, 'What was different about times when you did ski crud very well?' He pondered, grinned, and said, 'That is a really good question!' The lesson was a great success and the resort made a new friend in the media."

Potential pitfall: Too much problem talk

You may be familiar with the kinds of meetings where problem talk abounds and be wondering how to move the discussion toward solution talk. Remember that it is likely to be counter-productive to cut people off briskly and brusquely and impose your solutions ideas. Many like to start by outlining their problems and you can listen attentively, alert for useful elements appearing. We call this "building the platform."

> *"Just because I'm solution focused doesn't mean I'm problem phobic."*
> Insoo Kim Berg,
> Solution Focused Therapy pioneer

The platform is where we begin the journey in our quest for what works. It is a practical way of turning talk about a problem into talk that, though not yet about a solution, is gently leading that way.

These are helpful platform-building questions:

✔ What do you want to achieve today?
✔ How will you know that we have made some progress?
✔ What would be the payoff from solving this problem? What would it help us to get?
✔ How confident are you that something can be done about this?
✔ When you have tackled this kind of problem before, what was the most help? What skills and resources did you discover then?
✔ What in general has been going well for you?

This last question leads in the direction of "problem-free talk," which can produce evidence of resources, skills and positive events already happening. People frequently dismiss these as unrelated to the problem, yet they often contain the germ of a useful way forward. We discuss how to use these findings in Chapter 6.

Potential pitfall: No customer for change

Someone has to decide that it is time for a change. From the perspective of the Solutions Focus, it doesn't much matter who: Anyone can play. As well as making such a decision, this someone also needs to be prepared to do something about it. This person is a customer for change.

In your own organization your customer for change could be you. You can change other people's behavior, but you usually need to start by changing your own. If you're up for that, you're a customer.

For consultants, finding a customer in the organization is often one of the first tasks.

When Mark was consulting in Ukraine, the original assignment was to help the country's nuclear power ministry change into a commercial organization. When he arrived, he found that the ministry staff was preoccupied with crucial issues of cash flow and fuel supplies.

While they were keen to know the UK experience of privatizing utilities, they were not yet customers for the sorts of change you might have expected—for example conventional accounting procedures or even receiving money for electricity (they were still bartering it for goods).

They were not customers for change in our sense, as they already knew how to change themselves to the extent that they were ready, namely to barter their way into a healthier immediate position.

Consultants can, at times, act as their own customer and produce changes in people's organizations that haven't been requested. The question then is more one of ethics: "I know what's best for my client, even if they don't," you may think. However, our experience is that people do not like this once they figure out what's going on. We recommend that you deploy the Solutions Focus to help your clients get what they tell you *they* want.

"But someone else should do something..."

Sometimes people want something to be different, but believe that someone else ought to take action. This is a natural state, but it is difficult to imagine how to make the difference unless we are willing to play at least some part ourselves.

A customer is willing to do something differently, to start or to stop doing something. Beware the person who refuses to act—interactionally this is probably a blind alley.

You get a strong signal that you are up this alley when you hear many complaints about other participants in the system, how it's all someone else doing something wrong: "This museum would run brilliantly if it weren't for all the visitors," for example. When the company is full of people whose solution is for others to start making changes, without being prepared to do anything about that for themselves, little of use will shift.

A more rewarding tactic is to discover what, if anything, they would be prepared to do. In one case, where senior managers wanted their middle managers to change attitudes, we repositioned the senior managers as customers for change. They were customers for what *they* could do to

Keeping it SIMPLE: Who is the customer for change?

If someone is not interested in the changes you want to make, that's fine. It is possible to influence them in other ways, by taking action yourself. They may come around in the end or their lack of interest may not matter as much as you imagine.

influence the middle managers.

There are often several different customers in one case. There may be a conflict of interests, with sub-groups each having their own viewpoints to be taken into account. We consider how to manage this situation later in the book.

The Solutions Focus in action: Working with the "green" people

Safety management consultant Peter Ackroyd is frequently in tricky situations. Practical traditions run deep in industrial plants, and many of the workforce view safety enhancement as an inconvenient distraction from the comfortable status quo.

"I used to spend a lot of time trying to get the majority interested in safety," says Peter. "Then I realized that a useful shorthand was to think of people as 'green', 'amber' and 'red.' The 'green' people are always up for doing something different—they love to try out new ideas. The 'amber' people are cautious and sometimes uncommitted, but can be persuaded in time. The 'red' people seem to be against any change on principle."

Rather than spend time and energy trying to convince the "red" people—usually a futile task in practice—Peter now starts by working with the "green" people. Their energy and effort result in the "amber" ones joining in over time: "In the end the 'reds' usually cooperate—often peer pressure seems an effective lever." Of course, Peter does not tell the "reds" who he thinks they are. Instead of labeling, he notices and welcomes the changes that even the "reds" are making.

Peter has learnt the benefits of finding customers for change and working with them to start balls rolling and influence others in the same workplace.

Sometimes there are customers for change closer to home than you suppose. When you do spot them, it's usually worth getting them involved. This can apply even when you suppose that there is little to add, as the following example from the world of education illustrates.

The Solutions Focus in action: Involving the "problem" child

If a child attends a case conference, South Wales educational psychologist Ioan Rees will make a point of asking the child for their opinion about what should happen next, which contrasts with much typical discussion that will be about the child, but not directly value the child's input. The child is certainly part of the interactions and usually brings many useful gifts when invited. If they are ignored, the gifts of boredom, frustration and "messing about" may be much more challenging to use! The child often makes a useful comment and in any case appreciates being asked.

Potential pitfall: Trying to solve an unsolvable "problem"

"When the answer cannot be put into words, neither can the question be put into words."
Ludwig Wittgenstein, Tractatus Logico-Philosophicus 6.5

What is a solvable problem? This often strikes managers as a surprising and interesting question. For us a solvable problem is one for which you can define a solution in crisp, everyday terms. Many people are adept at describing problems that are potentially solvable, but are expressed in ways that disguise the fact. For example:

✗ The solution is described only in vague or fuzzy language.
✗ The problem is put in terms of what is not wanted.
✗ There will be no way of telling whether or not it has been solved.
✗ It is expressed without mention of the customer's own efforts.

This is where the future perfect tool comes into its own. The future perfect is a distinctive part of the Solutions Focus toolkit. To appreciate the concept, consider the following question:

Suppose that tonight you go to bed—and go to sleep as usual—and during the night a miracle happens—and the problem vanishes—and the issues that concern you are resolved—but you're asleep, so you don't know that the miracle has happened—so when you wake up tomorrow what will be the first things that will tell you that the miracle has happened? How will you know that the transformation has occurred?

The idea is to pitch ourselves into the future, in concrete terms. The concreteness is encouraged by asking what will be noticed *first*. These will be specific details, often small. They are sensory based: You ask what you would see and hear.

Goals are fine. The future perfect takes you *beyond* the goal. Assume that you have arrived and it is happening. The question is: "How will you know?"

Change requires a first step, so the sooner your customers for change try one the better.

The Solutions Focus is a stickler for the first step, ensuring among other things that it is taken in the right direction, always away from stuckness, and preferably toward the future perfect picture. It does so by presupposing that the miracle is already upon us, and that therefore the first step is inevitable. It may even have happened already, in which case you are considering an altogether easier proposition, such as a second step.

Note that the question asks about the immediate, not distant, future. If the miracle has occurred overnight, you are saying (for the moment) that the route there is of no concern right now. Your attention is directed exclusively to what is different. When you have sufficient detail, you will be in a position to work back from the differences to the methods or steps.

Building on the future perfect

Let's explore further some of the ways in which you might flesh out the future perfect description.

What will be different when the problems have vanished?
This is designed to elicit details of the solution. It includes what you might call central differences, those that the customer for change imagines are associated directly with the absence of the problem; and peripheral differences, other aspects that may also have changed, whether as a consequence or an impact of the main changes or as incidental changes.

At this stage you want to know them all, because it may turn out that the peripherals are more useful for the change process than the central differences. As any reader of mysteries will tell you, the most interesting murder cases rarely pivot on the state of the corpse—it is the odd clues on the fringes of the scene that matter.

When problems appear all-consuming, sufferers struggle to see beyond them to a vista without the problem. This question neatly bypasses the problem and opens up this new landscape, perhaps for its first extensive visit.

Suppose a miracle happened tonight?
The magical events happen both immediately and while we are asleep. So not only don't we know how it happened—as is generally the case with miracles—we do not even get to watch it. We wake up and bingo! There are the results. If you are thinking that's unlikely to happen, you are of course correct. This is a tool for beginning a process of change, not an expectation that the times of miracles are about to return.

What will you be doing?
You want to hear specifics at a behavioral level. "What you will be doing, what you will be saying?" "Who will be in the room and what will be the nature of the activity?" The description will resemble a play or film script, full of dialogue and physical directions. You are much more interested in what people will be doing than in what they will have stopped doing.

If their language seems vague, check that the action is important, concrete, specific and behavioral. Prompt for this degree of detail by asking: "What would other people notice was different?"

What will be the first small signs?

Often the preferred future can seem vastly different from the present. You are usually interested in the first small signs that the future has arrived. These provide initial steps, or inform your search for relevant counters.

Making problems more solvable

You could be asked to work on unsolvable problems. By this we mean problems whose solutions are unknowable. How will you know? And what do you do in these cases?

The solution is expressed in vague or fuzzy language

If the problem is couched in vague or fuzzy language, help the customer to define a solution in more precise terms. Try asking for "video talk," in which the customer describes the desired scene as if through a video camera. Their description is confined to specific visible and audible events.

The problem is put in terms of what is not wanted

Putting a problem in terms of what is not wanted is surprisingly common, and has similar disadvantages to going into a supermarket with a shopping list of products you would rather not buy—no eggs today, no washing powder—yet hoping to come home with a sensible shopping basket.

What helps here is a shift to another part of the platform, one from which you can see what the customer for change does want.

There will be no way of telling whether or not it has been solved
Another treacherous alleyway is when you are presented with a problem
for which there is no clear way of knowing later whether it is better or
not. It is far easier when there are benchmarks or milestones for checking how much progress has been made. If these are not already apparent,
then put them in place.

If a senior executive says "We need more spirit of innovation," a useful response is "Suppose that tomorrow, when you come into the office,
you had more spirit of
innovation—how would
you know?" When you hear
what is meant by spirit of
innovation, you steer in that
direction.

The task, then, is to
negotiate a solvable problem. Remember, a solvable
problem is one to which we
can define a solution. And
that solution will be co-
constructed in an inter-
actional way.

Solutions not problems—Summary

✔ Work on the solution, not on the problem.
✔ Encourage solution talk.
✔ Aim to amplify useful change.
✔ Building the platform is a good use of problem talk.
✔ Find and involve the customers for change.
✔ Describe the future perfect: Suppose that the problem vanishes overnight,
  how will you know tomorrow that the transformation has happened?

4

Inbetween–The Action Is in the Interaction

"We used to think that if we knew one, we knew two, because one and one are two. We are finding that we must learn a great deal more about 'and.'"
Arthur Eddington, astronomer, 1882–1944

Solutions not problems
INBETWEEN—THE ACTION IS IN THE INTERACTION
Make use of what's there
Possibilities—past, present and future
Language—simply said
Every case is different

Many of the aspects of a solution are most helpfully thought about as being inbetween the people involved, rather than isolated or belonging only to one party. Leadership, for example, is not something you give me or I decide to take; we co-construct it between us by both our behaviors.

In this chapter we examine organizations and people interactionally. This systemic approach, first written about more than a quarter of a century ago, offers a simple and pragmatic framework. Systems have properties that are inbetween their component parts. It is the interactions between the parts that define the system.

This leads us to explore human problems and solutions in inter-actional terms—who does what, with whom, and when—rather than in the psychological terms of what may or may not be going on inside the heads of the participants. It is probably more useful to deal directly with John gossiping maliciously about his boss—if that is what seems to be the trouble—than it is to fret about John's nasty personality, which some might take to be the underlying cause. In this way, complexity science— the pertinent edge of systems theory—provides a useful adjunct to solutions-focused practice.

Complexity science also offers the phenomenon of emergence, the finding that relevant events are occurring all the time, in great number and unpredictably. This means that it makes more sense to look out for occasions when the solution—the set of circumstances for which we are aiming—happens anyway than to seek to understand the system by analysis or to force a solution by working against the grain. If you get better days when the boss offers John more responsibility, then the simple route (in the first instance) is for the boss to offer John more responsibility on more days. If that works, it doesn't matter if no one knows why.

Studying causes and postulating explanations is often unhelpful when seeking solutions. It is better to search for fragments of the solutions we want. When searching, look widely as well as narrowly to locate the helpful interactions. To look more widely, you might research how other managers have handled John successfully, for example.

Everything needed to produce the solution is there already, right on the surface. If something is important, it will appear on the surface sooner or later. There is no need to assume that hidden factors are at play or that "deeper" methods have anything to add.

The benefits of thinking inbetween are:

✔ You don't end up isolating and blaming individuals for failings that are to do with the system as a whole.
✔ You obtain a more plausible model of the way organizations work.
✔ There is a wider platform from which to launch the solution. You don't spend time and energy narrowing down "the" cause.
✔ Because the system has properties that exist outside any of the individual components, you can most usefully operate by directly applying

interventions to the system, not by analyzing or guessing what might happen.

In this chapter, the interactional view radically simplifies our quest for solutions. It also takes us around these pitfalls:

X Investigating causes, rather than searching for evidence of useful difference.

X Locating the "problem" with one party or another—either with me or with them—rather than exploring the interactions inbetween people that offer better prospects for progress.

The Solutions Focus in action: Crumbs!

For many years, Mark's partner Jenny used to fret about the crumbs Mark left after cutting a loaf of bread. She kept asking for no crumbs, and Mark continued to leave crumbs. Although this issue was seemingly small, Jenny was determined to rectify it. She was attending various personal development programs at the time and experimented during them on the crumbs problem. She had visualized the crumbs not being there; she had set her outcome; she had examined her inner child—but nothing seemed to help.

Matters came to a head one evening. Jenny asked Mark once again not to leave crumbs and Mark, fed up, exploded, "OK, I give up! I defy you to show me how to cut bread without making crumbs!" Jenny demonstrated not the impossible task of cutting bread without crumbs, but the simple task of clearing the crumbs up afterwards. "Oh," said Mark—and crumbs were never a problem again. A change of interaction had made the long-standing "problem" vanish in an instant.

Systems thinking

Interactional systems have been investigated both mathematically and in organizations. The idea of systems thinking in organizations was popularized by Peter Senge in his book *The Fifth Discipline*. Senge recently[1] outlined two main traditions of systems thinking relating to organizations:

system design or system dynamics, developed from the work of Jay Forrester and others; and emergence, relating to the study of complex systems.

System dynamics

In the system dynamics approach, the prime task is to examine the system, mapping how the interactions between the components produce the observed results. The intention is to intervene in some way and deliberately change some interactions, with a view to changing what is going on for the better. System dynamicists also tell us that the very act of attempting to map the system can itself stimulate useful debate and sharing of knowledge among those involved.

Senge says that the use of system dynamics in organizational change is based on certain premises:

❑ Managers have responsibility for the enterprise.
❑ Managers act as designers—establishing formal rules, strategies, policies and structures to enable the organization to achieve its goals.

At first sight these seem reasonable enough. However, there are some recognized problems with this approach:

❑ The attention of the managers/designers is distracted by day-to-day issues.
❑ Managers do not have the skills to be effective designers.
❑ In consequence, the organization has fragmented, "non-systemic" structures and policies.

The main strategy for change is therefore to focus on the learning of the CEO and the management team.

Senge points out that his work has been based on this philosophy for several decades. However, there is another tradition of working with systems that has been gaining momentum over the past ten years or so: emergence.

Emergent systems

You may be familiar with the complex system of world weather, in which there is a mixture of unpredictability and emerging patterns. As we all know, it is impossible to predict the weather accurately even a few days ahead, although we sometimes know enough to hazard a good guess.

In the emergent paradigm, systems are again characterized by interactions between the component parts. But rather than being inherently designable, these interactions are of a complex, interweaving, and selfreferential nature, which means that the net effect of all the interactions is impossible to predict accurately in advance. So it is said that the future of the system "emerges" from the interactions. Such systems are referred to as complex systems (or sometimes complex adaptive systems, although the terminology is still not universally settled). We shall examine some examples below.

Many kinds of interactional, complex adaptive systems have been identified in the real world. Examples include:

❑ Ants in a nest.
❑ Birds in a flock.
❑ Cars in a traffic system.
❑ People in organizations.

In his book *Butterfly Economics*, British economist Paul Ormerod writes about discontinuities of change, which he observes in various economic, political and social settings. These include phenomena such as sudden changes in the rate of crime, some films becoming blockbusters while others fail, or superior goods not always dominating a market. All may be seen as examples of complex adaptive systems at work.

These results are counter-intuitive to those brought up on the reductionist assumption that knowing all about the parts will enable us to understand the whole. We expect that knowing the innermost details about one element of a system—a person, for example—means that we know how that person will respond in a given situation.

In a complex system, the whole shows behaviors that can't be gleaned by examining the parts alone. The interactions between the parts are crucial, and produce phenomena such as self-organization and adaptation.

For example in the film market, if you want to predict smash hits it is not enough to know which movies are favorably reviewed in the media and which a certain number of early-in-the-run filmgoers choose to see. As the choice of film that one viewer makes depends on the choices other viewers have made (which is a pretty reasonable assumption given that the first viewers are likely to offer their opinions to their friends), you cannot tell in advance which of two or more potential candidates will be the blockbuster. (We note that this has not stopped major consultancy firms attempting to develop methodologies to do just this.)

In short, we can know everything about the rules of what appears to be a relatively simple system, yet it can still be unpredictable and surprising.

Emergence in organizations

In a review of emergence as it applies to management, Peter Senge summarized the premise of the emergent approach:

❏ Structures in social systems are enacted by their members through their day-to-day activities.
❏ Informal structures dominate formal: People know "how to really get things done around here."

It is interesting to note that nobody designed the informal structures—they emerged from people "just" doing things together. Senge went on to point out the problems with the emergent view:

❏ Change processes are messy and difficult to manage.
❏ Individual actors lack the perspective to see the larger system.

The consequence is fragmented, messy, informal structures that no one designed: They emerged. Patterns of behavior (known by some as corporate culture) emerge in an organization, despite the fact that no one individual wants them or sets out to design them.

Systems synthesis: The interactional view

Both the basic systems approaches described above have shortcomings in practice. The design view would be attractive if it worked, but it fails to show real results. The emergent view offers a better description of our everyday experience, but it seems to lack anything to grab hold of to use; after all, if the future is indeterminate, what chance do we have?

The Solutions Focus offers a way of synthesizing and building on these two traditions, by developing ways of working that seek to identify and amplify helpful interactions within defined contexts.

Interactions and people

In exploring complex interactions between people, there is a useful maxim to follow:

The action is in the interaction.

What happens in the world—events that affect us, our surroundings, and other people—happens on the outside. We see, hear, feel, smell and taste these events. All the wonderful simultaneous occurrences in our minds— our private world of thoughts, internal feelings and sensations, mental images, intuitions, and so on—can only get into the action by getting into the interaction.

There are all sorts of ways in which this can happen, both consciously and otherwise. A thought might trigger us to an action. A sportsperson visualizing success can help bring success closer, but only if they then go and do the sport. A feeling may alert us to some concern, which we may then talk about or act on.

The main route to the world treating us differently is for us to initiate a different way of treating the world. This is why we have the maxim
of changing the doing and changing the viewing, rather than merely
changing the thinking. The doing gets amplified and comes back to us
from a different world.

This version of the interactional view offers a more plausible model
of the way organizations work, enabling us to make more sense of our
interventions and take more successful routes to the changes we want.

Organizations as interactional systems

An organization works by people interacting: coming to work, doing
things and talking to each other. On the linguistic front, people converse,
give orders, discuss what to do and how to do it, debate strategy, produce
marketing plans and so on. The way
they talk is part of what shapes how   *"People are people through other*
events happen. And of course they   *people."*
talk in response to one another,   *Xhosa proverb*
which creates a system-like feel:
Each response amplifies or damps down the information conveyed by the
previous speaker, to create looping, circular processes.

Everything in an organization is interdependent with everything else:
That's the assumption of a systems approach. This means that as change
agents we are wary about attributing causality to any one particular
aspect. A client may say, "Oh, the managing director is causing the workforce to have low morale." Perhaps he is, but the morale—whatever that
may be—is also contributed to by the workforce. And because the morale
affects the MD as well, we should remain aware of the reverse links.

The Solutions Focus in action: Slower and faster

Most of us have experienced being stuck in a jam of slow-moving cars, which
suddenly dissipates without revealing any obvious cause for the jam—crashed
cars or roadworks, for example. So how did the jam arise?

Studies of fast-moving traffic flows[2] have shown that these "phantom" jams arise by accident. One car changes lane abruptly, causing those behind it to brake hurriedly. In fast flows of traffic, with short distances between vehicles, the braking snowballs back along the road, with drivers braking harder and harder to prevent themselves hitting the one in the front.

Eventually, the traffic toward the back is at a standstill, even though that is not what any of the drivers wanted.

If we wanted, we could trace the origins of the jam back to the driver who originally changed lanes. This would be fruitless, because he would be unaffected by the braking behind and be well away up the road. We might lecture him on not changing lanes. We might get him to promise never to change lanes abruptly ever again. Would this prevent the same thing happening? No— there are millions of drivers on the road, any of whom could do this and, in any case, such sharp driving maneuvers are often rapid reflex responses to approaching junctions, hazards and other road users.

The solution—as applied on London's legendarily packed M25 motorway— comes from examining when these jams don't happen. This is when drivers have enough time and space to react to other road users (interactionally, of course) by braking or maneuvering without forcing the vehicle behind to take evasive action and precipitate a jam.

This happens when the roads are quiet, or when the traffic is moving slower and drivers have more time to react. The solution for the traffic authority is to bring in lower speed limits at busy times, which bizarrely allows more traffic along the motorway than do higher speed limits and the jams that accompany them.

Note that this does not address the "cause" of the problem—abrupt actions—at all. It simply allows them to happen without undesirable consequences.

Unintended consequences and helpful accidents

Some unintended consequences can be helpful, others less so. It is often better to instigate a change and then reap the consequences (with forethought) than to remain feeling stuck.

A scheme in West Yorkshire was launched to help reduce the dangers faced by prostitutes. Police deployed extra patrols to arrest kerb crawlers, who had the option of attending a re-education program.[3]

Because men were getting caught more often on the well-lit streets, the trade retreated to the poorly lit back streets, where it was more difficult for the women to view potential clients to judge how safe they might be and more difficult for them to stay close together to watch out for each other's safety. Incidents of violence went up.

The scheme resulted in unintended negative consequences, but it may still have been worth making the effort, because there was no way of knowing what the consequences were going to be. (Except, perhaps, with the wonderful benefit of hindsight.) It might just as easily have turned out to provide the solution. Now the police have more detail about a strategy that doesn't work and can either stop doing it, or amend it in some way by keeping the useful elements yet making it different enough to constitute another step toward a solution.

This is the thinking that informs "blame-free" work environments. The idea is to allow people to take fresh decisions and to experiment, without fear of blame if the consequences are not entirely positive.

The difficulty, of course, is that so many of us are locked into the old mode of thinking that we automatically leap to the conclusion that any negative consequences are indeed the fault of the person who took the initiative.

Systems do not respect organizational boundaries

"When we try to pick out something by itself, we find it hitched to everything else in the universe."
John Muir, father of the US National Parks

Because all the elements of a system are interrelated, you should look more widely if your first efforts are not making the differences you want. When feeling stuck, ask: "What else is associated with this?" If the solution does not appear here, maybe it is lurking close by.

A computer software sales team was facing difficulties. The managers were upset with the salesforce, who persistently dropped prices at the end of each quarter, which meant that revenue was lower than expected. They wondered how they could prevent salespeople from doing this.

Meanwhile, in another part of the interaction, the salespeople were anxious to meet the quarterly quotas, based on sales volumes, set by the managers. So they dropped the prices each quarter.

To complicate matters the customers, many of whom regularly dealt with this company, noticed that the prices dropped at the quarter end and so delayed placing orders until the last moment.

This is a good example of an interlinked set of behaviors, each maintaining the others. In principle, a change at any point in the series of interactions is possible, which could create a new way forward. But which one? It depends on other aspects of the organization and you would need to ask a few more questions to find out.

In this case, it transpired that the managers and sales staff agreed to let customers know that prices would not be dropped at the end of each quarter, a measure that brought greater stability to the sales cycle.

Foxes and rabbits

The case above is an organizational example of Lotka–Volterra cycles, familiar to ecologists. These cycles are found in the natural variation over time of fox and rabbit populations, for example. If the population of foxes in a rabbit-rich area is examined in isolation, it may show remarkably large swings, both up and down. Similarly, the rabbit population will show variations, but not in step with the foxes.

It is only when foxes and rabbits are compared that we see the fuller picture. When the fox population increases, they eat more rabbits. The rabbit population shrinks. The foxes, now deprived of food, begin to die off in larger numbers. The fact that there are fewer foxes allows the rabbit population to increase once again. And finally, the greater availability of food provides support for a larger fox population.

In both the organizational and ecological examples, the message is the importance of looking widely for the systemic links, and at the same time recognizing what is important. In taking an interactional view, there may be chances for positive action in places that are not apparently related to the problem. These may well be in different parts of the organization or in very different activities.

In the example above, the behaviors of the managers, the salesforce and the customers were all connected. You may be encouraged that there are so many entry points for possible solutions.

Aaron and the argument

In an old Chassidic story, Aaron, brother of Moses, is visited by two friends who want him to resolve a bitter dispute. Unable to solve the argument, he sends them away and then visits each individually. He tells each in turn that the other has had enough of the argument, but is too embarrassed to make the first move to end it. He arranges for them to meet each other accidentally. Of course, they fall into each other's arms, each aiming to spare the other embarrassment.

This is a grand example of an interactional intervention. Aaron knows what his friends would like to have happen and, by imagining it in detail, perhaps he has the idea of supposing that some elements are happening already. He is himself part of their interactional system and is presumably aware of the impact that he is likely to have.

Potential pitfall: Finding the "cause" of the problem

As mentioned in Chapter 2, one distinct strand of the Solutions Focus is the realization that arriving at a detailed understanding of the problem by analyzing its causes is often little help in discovering a solution. In many situations, the causes of a problem interweave. Attempting to identify "the" cause is then an exercise in applied futility.

The world is literally unpredictable. Even if some kinds of cause can be identified, the future remains clouded in uncertainty.

In some cases, the circumstances are simply an accident of history, not the result of anyone making a conscious choice or for any beneficial reason.

Many causes, little illumination

Have you ever been kept waiting on a plane when the pilot informs you that the delay is due to the late arrival of the previous flight? This does nothing to speed our journey, but we feel comforted by apparently knowing the cause. While apparent causes can be persuasive, they may nevertheless stop us from seeking other answers.

The western scientific mind cries out for explanations and is tempted to consider results invalid unless we can explain the how, the mechanism by which they happen.

In his book *Lifelines*, biologist Steven Rose examines the legitimacy of claims that our genes determine our behavior. Five biologists gather by a pond. A frog leaps into the pond to escape a snake. The five then offer their "explanations" of what "caused" the frog to jump into the pond.

❑ The physiologist says that it is because the muscles in the frog's legs contract, following nerve impulses from the frog's brain.
❑ The animal behavior scientist says that it is because the frog wants to avoid the snake and is pursuing a goal.
❑ The developmental biologist explains that the way the muscles and brain have become "wired up" during its life make these jumping actions happen when danger approaches.
❑ An evolutionary biologist says that it is the result of adaptations during history, when the frog's ancestors were selected by their ability to escape from snakes.
❑ The molecular biologist steps up and, smiling sweetly, says that the other four are all wrong. The frog jumps because of the biochemical properties of its muscles.

These various explanations are all accurate, in their own fashion. But which is right? Well, as Celia Molestrangler used to say to ageing juvenile Binky Huckaback in the 1960s radio comedy *Round the Horne*, all of them and yet none of them—in isolation. Rose points out that biologists need all five explanations and probably others besides.

To speak of one of the causes—any one—as "right" is to miss the point. And that's just the biologists; goodness only knows what Freud would have made of this snake-related situation.

Now imagine that five business consultants join the biologists.

❑ The organizational psychologist says that the snake exerts power over the frog to make it jump.
❑ The business process reengineering consultant wonders whether the frog really needs to wait for the snake to arrive before jumping.
❑ The change consultant points out that the frog is simply following the usual "change curve," where things get worse before they get better.
❑ The health and safety adviser notes that the frog's jump was caused by its not wearing snake-resistant clothing.
❑ And finally, the organizational culture guru points out that the frog is simply following cultural norms.

The moral is simple: if you want an explanation, get a suitable expert to provide one. It may be less helpful than you hoped for making positive change.

The biologists need all five or more explanations because the task of biology is to explain biological phenomena as thoroughly as possible. The task of organizational change agents, by contrast, is to produce change—and if it so happens that nothing is gained from pursuing thorough explanations of change, that pursuit can safely be abandoned.

Keeping it SIMPLE: Reasons to be cheerful

Beware people asserting that their explanation is the right one. If it is not helping you reach your destination, then find another or, better still, hunt for signs of change without one.

Behavior emerges unpredictably

Classical philosophers reckoned that whatever higher-level properties emerged from the interaction of lower-level units, they were always

> *"The significant problems we face cannot be solved by the same level of thinking that created them."*
> Albert Einstein

somehow secondary to the lower-level units. Parts come before wholes. Bricks make walls; walls add up to buildings; buildings aggregate into streets.

On the other hand, in the interactional view, we see properties emerging that cannot be inferred simply by examining the lower-level parts in isolation. Steven Rose points out, for example, that the science of physiology is not simply derivable from biochemistry or chemistry.[4]

In the interactional view in organizations, we usually take the lower level to be individuals; the emergent properties at higher levels are the behaviors, relationships and results that those people generate in their interactions.

However much we know about each individual in isolation, we couldn't accurately predict how they will interact. The whole cannot be reduced to the sum of the parts. The interaction has an apparent life of its own. And if you want to change things, you can do so by helping any of the actors in the system to change their behavior. This can be done with their willing cooperation, because we assume that the individuals are basically capable of doing what they want to do, of functioning normally and productively. The action, for a solutionist, is in the interaction.

An accident of history: Time gentlemen please!

The British pub licensing laws were introduced during the First World War (1914–18) to stop munitions workers getting drunk and not working. These laws controlled the opening hours, and particularly the closing times, of all bars and pubs. As any Brit will tell you, the rush to buy a huge final round of drinks before closing time was inevitably followed by the rush of inebriated clients on to the street, and the ensuing fracas became a feature of many town centers on a Saturday night. That was how it was always done.

It stands to reason, doesn't it, that limited pub opening time cuts down on the amount people drink? Obviously, if the pubs were open all day, people would drink more. That's not in fact the case. In an experiment starting in

Scotland in the 1980s, pubs were allowed to open all day and to choose differ-ent times to close. The result was less drunkenness. Given more choice about when to drink, pub goers were treating their outing more like a social gathering and less like a how-much-can-we-get-down-before-closing-time competition. And fighting in the street was reduced because the varied closing times meant that people exited at different times, reducing the chances of confrontation. Indeed, the law was finally relaxed across the UK in 2005.

The Solutions Focus in action: The headteacher and the parents' association

A school in the west of England had suffered for a long time from the lack of a strong parents' association. Such associations in neighboring schools were pro-lific fundraisers and did much to enhance the life of their school in extra-curricular activities for pupils and social events for the adults.

In this school, however, while parents were willing to participate, many had been put off by their individual encounters with the headteacher, who was an acknowledged expert at communicating with children, but lacked skills in inter-personal dealings with adults. In a sense, the headteacher's poor communica-tion was the "underlying cause" of the problem.

The solution in this case, nevertheless, did not involve working on the head-teacher. Instead, a group of parents grew increasingly active in helping the sports master to organize the school sports day. That group then decided that they should hold a social event for parents after the sports were finished. The social event went well, and they were encouraged to organize other successful activities—and so they became a parents' association in all but name.

Potential pitfall: Whose fault is it anyway?

Another temptation is to place the problem "inside" a person. The per-son is presented as the sole owner of the problem or in extreme cases is spoken about as the problem: "The problem here is Andrew."

"We have the ability to construct our own futures, albeit in circumstances not of our own choosing."
Steven Rose, Lifelines: Biology, Freedom, Determinism

When we think about problems inside a person, rather than inter-actionally, we fall into the same trap as those who assume that DNA pre-determines our lives. Leading scientists, including neuroscientist and Royal Institution director Susan Greenfield, point out that the stories about genes for aspects of personality—an "aggression gene," for example—are missing a vital point.

Organisms—birds, ants, people—exist as parts of their environment. To abstract the ant from the nest, or the sales director from the company, is a reductionist step that will "always mislead."[5] Nor are these organisms pas-sive responders to their environments: They act to change them, con-sciously or otherwise. We are not at the mercy of genes and fate, we are active players in our own futures.

Distinguished geneticist and author Professor Steve Jones once said that he is not well disposed to red wine.[6] Some kind of genetic inheri-tance meant that when he drank red wine, even a moderate amount, he had severe headaches.

We asked him whether there was anything he could do about it and his reply was simple: "Of course! I don't drink red wine." Jones knew what worked and acted prudently on that information. He was also exer-cising control over his environment to help himself.

If, as a single person, you live in what visitors might call a tip, perhaps you are the victim of a "slob" gene. A way of exercising control over the environment is to hire a cleaner once a week and stop berating yourself. Similarly, in an organiza-tion, suppose you are a manager rather too prone to losing your temper when negotiating. A sim-ple solution might be to invite someone else to negotiate for you.

Keeping it SIMPLE:
Think interactions

The solution may lie in the way you interact with your surroundings—not simply inside you. The problem is nothing personal.

In each case, the key is to stop following the losing, blame-ridden path and to do something different.

In at the shallow end

In talking about problems and solutions, people often use metaphors to illustrate their points. "The sky's the limit" or "Getting things done here is like walking through treacle" are two that we have heard recently. Metaphors can be powerful in helping to construct solutions, but sometimes they muddy the waters. In particular, there is a whole class of metaphors that have amassed in the psychological

> "The uncreative mind can spot wrong answers, but it takes a creative mind to spot wrong questions."
> Antony Jay, Management and Machiavelli

world about the *depth* of problems that are misleading and unhelpful.

For example, someone might refer to an "underlying problem." We all understand what an underlying problem may be: a significant issue, one that may have a wide effect, one that has possibly been around for some time.

If by "underlying" the person describing the issue means that one problem is encompassed or preceded by another, then we can explore both the issues—as long as we are not seduced into supposing that we are more likely to find the solution in the underlying one than the overlying. Neither takes automatic precedence or priority.

Another danger with the description "underlying" is that it may lead us to suppose that a cause is underneath something, and is therefore not directly visible. Indeed, it may only be visible to a few "farsighted" managers or—if it is "buried"—to those equipped to "dig," who in the worst case turn out to be only their consultants.

Remembering that change happens when somebody does or looks at something differently, it makes good sense to work at the level of who does what and says what. This means that everything

Keeping it SIMPLE: Stay at the surface

Stay at the surface—work with what you find. There is plenty there to work with. If other elements are important they will appear in due course.

important is, by definition, directly available to our senses: tangible, visible or audible. It is on the surface. What appears is what we work with. Underlying aspects, if they are invisible, can stay there until either they put in an appearance (and so become visible), or they turn out not to have mattered. This is one important way of staying as simple as possible, but no simpler.

Sometimes people mistake this focus on simplicity for simplemindedness. Yet it is surprisingly difficult to stay simple, ask simple questions, remain focused and keep noticing what is working.

Inbetween—the action is in the interaction—Summary

✔ The Solutions Focus is a systemic approach, building on the traditions of system dynamics and emergence.

✔ People act in contexts created by their interactions and those of others.

✔ View organizational problems in interactional terms—the action is in the interaction.

✔ Promoting helpful interactions can produce widescale changes quickly and sustainably.

✔ Causes and explanations may tell us much, but rarely what to do next. Treat them with caution.

✔ The key interactions may not be related to the "problem"—they may involve seemingly unrelated people.

✔ It is all there at the surface. Postulating hidden or deep properties, particularly if they are unhelpful, is to complicate needlessly.

5

Make Use of What's There

"The way out is through the door. Why is it that no one will use this method?"

Confucius

Making use of what's there is an important part of the Solutions Focus. We are trying to discover what works and there are often clues right in front of us—if only we can find and recognize them.

Solutions not problems
Inbetween—the action is in the interaction
MAKE USE OF WHAT'S THERE
Possibilities—past, present and future
Language—simply said
Every case is different

If we can do that, we increase our chances of keeping it SIMPLE.

The benefits of working with what's there:

✔ What is there is probably relevant.
✔ The process of identification involves looking and listening, which may help others feel valued.
✔ It gives us a positive and relatively easy way to begin the search for solutions.

✔ We avoid imagining things that are not there—temptations to go astray.

✔ Our solution will be rooted in the reality of this particular set of circumstances.

Not everything that is there will automatically be useful, however. The usefulness depends to an extent on what it is we are seeking. In any search, you are more likely to find what you are looking for than what you are not. You will be alert and primed to notice those treasures.

The alternative to working with what's there is to concentrate on what isn't there, for example deficits, shortcomings, weaknesses, lack of cooperation from others. Spending time on these aspects is not usually a helpful way to start, nor is it a necessary precursor to change.

Particularly where people are concerned, we sympathize with Marcus Buckingham and Donald O Clifton, the authors of *Now, Find Your Strengths*:

Most organizations take their employees' strengths for granted and focus on minimizing their weaknesses. They become expert in those areas where their employees struggle, delicately rename these "skill gaps" or "areas of opportunity," and then pack them off to training classes so the weakness can be fixed. This approach is occasionally necessary: If an employee always alienates those around him, some sensitivity training can help; likewise, a remedial communication class can benefit an employee who happens to be smart but inarticulate. But this isn't development, it's damage control. And by itself damage control is a poor strategy for elevating either the employee or the organization to world-class performance.

Everything is a useful gift

Those of us interested in change can stay on track with even difficult situations or people who give us grief by adopting the attitude: "Everything is a useful gift." This principle of utilization enables us to expect value from anything the circumstances may offer. For example, suppose you are a manager within an organization whose boss appears brusque and stubborn and will only see you for five minutes at a time. If we are taking the attitude that everything is a useful gift, this could be framed as a boss who has precise and concentrated time-keeping qualities, and these attributes may well be valuable for the solution that you construct later on.

"Everything is a useful gift" is a process tip—a resourceful attitude that helps you remain constructive and resilient, so that you can keep others constructive and resilient in their search for solutions. And just because everything may be a useful gift does not mean that you have to use everything: You will be alert to all that is offered and then choose the ones that strike you as most helpful.

Milton Erickson: Master of utilization

In therapy, Milton Erickson was an acknowledged master of utilization, using whatever his clients brought—much of which could have been described as pathologies, weaknesses, rigid beliefs and resistance—as part of their treatment.

For example, Erickson was treating a young man who lacked self-confidence. The man had recently started a job in a bank and sometimes made mistakes in his work. Erickson showed great interest in the young man's descriptions of his work, particularly the mistakes. Each time a mistake came up, Erickson asked about the ways in which the mistake had been rectified, never about how he made the error. By helping the young man to find out how he made corrections, Erickson was utilizing the mistakes to help build his self-confidence.[1]

Erickson's list of useful gifts

"All aspects of the patient or the environment. This...includes both conscious and unconscious offerings, resources, strengths, experiences, abilities (or disabilities), relationships, attitudes, problems, symptoms, deficits, environment, vocations, hobbies, aversions, emotions... the list is endless, but the concept is simple. If it's part of the patient's life, it may be useful in achieving a therapeutic goal, and if the patient brings it, it's probably more potent than anything the therapist can introduce to the situation."[2]

Similarly, if you are a manager, you could take a solution-focused approach to your direct reports when they make mistakes. Instead of blaming or even "helpfully" seeking causes, you could ask about how they have made corrections or plan to make them. Or you could investigate when they don't make mistakes and learn from those times.

The Solutions Focus in action: Learning how learning happens

American solutions exponent Linda Metcalf sometimes works in school settings, helping teachers to notice how children with low IQ scores learn to make their way in the world.

"We developed a form that helped the teachers determine what particular skills were desired for kids with some limits. For example, if a child could not read at age ten, we asked what reading would do for him if he could. The answers included 'read a job application, read a stop sign, etc.'

"From that, we looked at how the student could do certain things and developed a plan from that. For example, the student always knew when recess was, when lunch was, etc. How did he learn that? These new exceptions gave way to techniques that were a bit unusual yet hopeful."

Counters

> *"Counter: small disc of metal, ivory, etc; thing used in bargaining; opposed or opposite; parry, countermove."* (Concise Oxford Dictionary)

Let us examine our next solutions tool, counters.

Counters make up a "what's there" stack that is tremendously likely to prove useful in the building of solutions. They include:

✔ Examples of the solution happening already—gold dust!
✔ Evidence of parts of the solution happening—good building materials.
✔ Skills and resources that will help to create the solution.
✔ Cooperation from others involved.

You will want to collect as many counters as possible to help in the search for what works—and they are usually right there in front of you.

If you were to take a problem focus, however, you might stumble over the pitfalls preventing you from keeping it SIMPLE. These include:

X Looking for difficulties and obstacles.
X Focusing on deficits and shortcomings.
X Finding (and generating) resistance to change among those with whom you work.

When does the solution—or part of it—happen already?

William Bateson (Gregory Bateson's father, a distinguished geneticist who was the first to use the word "genetics") once said:

> Treasure your exceptions! When there are none, the work gets so dull that no one cares to carry it further. Keep them always uncovered and in sight. Exceptions are like the rough brickwork of a growing building which tell you there is more to come and shows where the next construction will be.

The most helpful kind of counter is the kind where you discover that the solution is already happening anyway—right under your nose—although for some reason you hadn't recognized it as such. This sounds rather unlikely, perhaps, but this is one of the central tenets of solutions-focused work.

No problem happens all the time: There are times when things are better or less bad. These are times when something is working. The key to making progress and finding what works therefore lies in these instances.

Questions for counters

When you have as clear and detailed a future perfect picture as possible you search for counters, parts of this picture that are already happening or have already happened. You ask:

✔ When does the future perfect happen? Even a little bit?
✔ When do parts of the future perfect happen already?
✔ When do resemblances to the future perfect happen already?
✔ What do you suppose you did to make that happen?
✔ How did you do that?
✔ What else?

If you do not yet have a description of a preferred future, ask:

✔ When is the problem not so bad?
✔ Think about the most recent time the problem didn't happen—what transpired instead?

The discovery of counters serves as immediate evidence that what the customer for change wants is possible (at least to some extent). One counter may not be conclusive proof, but it is a shard of evidence and often in itself convincingly suggests a prospect of change in this situation.

In organizations or groups, for example, counters are often greeted as bright symbols of desired change and lend a motivational boost to any change project.

If neither of the above routes produces anything (a rare occurrence in our experience), you hunt for the third sort of counter:

✔ How have you managed to get this far?
✔ How have you been handling the situation?
✔ What have you been doing to prevent matters being even worse?

You may also notice customers deploying skills and resources, particularly away from the "problem" situation.

The Solutions Focus in action: Safety in the shade

Safety is vital in chemical plants. Personal safety is particularly important, and it is a legal requirement for firms to provide personal protective equipment, such as overalls, helmets, gloves, and safety glasses, for their workers. Getting people to wear this equipment is another matter, however. Often after many years operating the plants, workers have stopped noticing the risks around them.

One such chemical plant was jointly run by Zeneca in Italy. The managers (and the law) wanted people to wear safety glasses. The workers were nevertheless reluctant. The solution emerged when someone asked themselves, "When does this future perfect even partially occur? When do our people wear glasses anyway, even when they don't strictly need to?" We're talking Italian men here. When do Italian men wear glasses when they don't need to? When they are cool, fashionable sunglasses!

So they commissioned a set of safety glasses with mirror shades, and offered them to operators on the factory floor. And a miracle did happen: The workers instantly began wearing them most of the time, even outside the chemically hazardous areas. From just a small change in the design came this significant change in behavior.

The firm could have chosen a problem focus instead: It could have studied the reasons for people not wearing the old safety glasses, their motivations for risking themselves and their health, or the underlying causes of accidents around the world. Would this solution have emerged from such an inquiry? We guess not.

One of the features of solutions derived in this way is that once started they are usually self-driving. When the right track has been found, progress is made and supported by people taking the kinds of actions they take in any case (whatever they enjoy or have decided to do), without large-scale cajoling from managers or outsiders.

The Solutions Focus in action: Scooting along with Honda

Honda entered the US motor cycle market in the 1960s. It became famous for its small, user-friendly motorcycles in a market dominated by large British and American machines. Was this a brilliant strategy, hatched with fiendish cunning in a Japanese boardroom? Not according to the view of strategy guru Richard Pascale.

In Japan, Honda produced a range of motorcycles. Its strategy for the US was to enter the market with big motorcycles, as these were dominating the US market then. It therefore imported, advertised and did indeed try to take on the market with big bikes, and failed miserably. However, while that was going on, by accident it discovered the popularity of small bikes: Honda's staff had imported some for their own use, and people kept asking where they could buy one. Fortunately, someone noticed and they began to sell them in the US.

The Solutions Focus in action: Small differences can matter

Counters have often gone unnoticed, even though they are significant. Even the slightest hint of an element of the future perfect can be enough to prompt progress. We were coaching a manager who wanted her team to take more ownership of the work. Asked when they took ownership at the moment, she replied, "Oh, they take very little ownership."

There is an important difference between very little and none, so we asked about the little ownership that they did take. Immediately the manager realized that she knew a way to increase the team's ownership of their work and work area.

As soon as attention is directed toward the appropriate topic, change can happen fast. The manager here knew right away what she had to do and her clue had been present, although unnoticed, from the outset. She finished the session in complete confidence, suddenly realizing that the intractable problem had indeed vanished.

Managers sometimes feel like kicking themselves once they discover what works and begin applying solutions. It seems so obvious with hind-sight. When you take a solutions focus, you quickly start noticing what is helpful, useful and important. What is equally striking is how rarely those counters are apparent when you take a more problem-focused approach.

Making use of skills and resources

Another way of making use of what's there is to uncover evidence of skills and resources that have been used to make progress in the past. These can appear as stories of success or as examples of cooperation and people working together.

This also highlights two more potential pitfalls: focusing on deficits and difficulties; and focusing on resistance to change in the target audience.

Finding strengths

Examining how you have successfully tackled situations similar to the present one is a great way of unearthing strengths. By examining how you have risen to a challenge, you can pinpoint a wealth of useful ideas and resources about yourself that you can deploy now or later. Compare this to a problem focus, when you list the mistakes and missed opportunities arising from how you mishandled situations. In that way, you continue to risk missing the point about everything you did cleverly, intelligently and in the right spirit—all of which you could easily repeat.

The Solutions Focus in action: Pressure management at Marks & Spencer

The stress management program at Marks & Spencer, called "Managing Pressure," was adapted to include elements of the solution-focused approach. Noel McElearney, occupational physician at the company, and well-known organizational psychologist Steve Williams were influenced by the results that their M&S colleague Claire Thormod was having in a clinical setting using solution-focused therapy and were struck by the simplicity and elegance of the approach.

However, Noel comments: "You can't do mass therapy on a bunch of managers who didn't even know they needed it. We translated the therapeutic approach into a management tool, we were honest and told them that the approach had its roots in family therapy and they too knew that it didn't help to explore just what was wrong.

"On one course, 12 managers from the same department took the opportunity to spend some time together and escape the office. Things had not been going well.

"Problems had arisen from rapid expansion: There was inadequate infrastructure; computer glitches had allowed them to sell stocks that had never even been manufactured; their managers were remote in terms of both geography and attitude; and there was pressure from home over long hours they had to put in at work. They were also concerned that the employees they had inherited were simply not up to the new circumstances.

"The conventional approach would be to break each of these problem areas into small packages, offer fixes for each one and then somehow put them together again. But in this case we decided to shelve their problem list.

"What we did instead was to ask them to come up with an example of a large problem that they have successfully tackled. At first they could not think of any occasion when they felt they had got it really right. In the end, we reminded them of when they had handled an emergency situation. (Fortunately, we had been briefed.)

"Grudgingly at first, the managers talked about how they had responded, what they had done differently and how it had felt. We helped them to analyse what they had actually done that was different. They identified key areas of management behaviour that, previously, we would have lectured them on. They stated what they thought would be possible in other circumstances.

"We asked them to identify what would be happening in their world of work that would tell them when things were getting better. We asked them to assess where they were at the time and to identify what marginal improvement looked like. Success is seldom total, and they identified a need to keep working at it as a team.

"Many months later the managers have made themselves less pressured and they use the techniques in team meetings to transform new problems. And, by the way, most days they go home on time."[3]

Potential pitfall: Focusing on deficits

It is sometimes tempting to focus on deficits, particularly the deficits of other people. It is particularly tempting to envisage solutions where the people become instantly transformed and nothing else around them is changed. From your consideration of "inbetween" you are more aware that people often change what they do when their surroundings also change.

However, sometimes it is possible to reach solutions that rely on people *not* changing. Rather than identifying what people are doing wrong, wonder what might happen if you banked on them continuing their current practices.

The Solutions Focus in action: When the chips are down

Many years ago, a catering company was trying to implement portion control in its canteens. Profit margins were carefully calculated and serving too much food to each customer would have an adverse effect on the bottom line. However, the managers had reckoned without the dinner ladies.

The cost accountants had worked out that one scoop of chips was the "right" portion: enough to eat and profitable at the price charged. The dinner ladies, being cheerful and generous souls, always made sure their customers were well provided for, and gave them a scoop and a bit extra. Whatever the company tried—training, reminders, threats—customers continued to receive their extra chips.

Finally, the managers decided to work with what was there. The ladies could not be prevented from giving out a scoop and a bit. In fact, they could probably be relied on to do so. The solution to portion control was simple: a smaller scoop. This was easy and cheap to supply, and the dinner ladies could still feel good about giving the hungry workers a bit extra.

Build cooperation—or expect resistance

In taking a solutions focus, you are playing a kind of cooperation game. Your move is to invite other people to bring their ways of cooperating with you to create the solution. You might receive instant cooperation and scarcely notice you've done it; on other occasions it takes more effort.

In seeking to make use of what's there, we go beyond listening that merely shows an interest. The extra step is to assume (initially at least) that whatever is said to us is fact. We may or may not maintain this position, but a good first response is often, "Yes" or "OK." It is rarely "No! You're wrong about that"—even if they appear to be.

Suppose that you are shown a workplace that is tatty and ill-kept. There is oil on the floor and the bins are overflowing. Nonetheless, the foreman states with pride that this is a tidy place. If you are taking a solutions focus, you do not fall about laughing or mutter about delusions: You accept it, for now. You will be interested in what leads him to assert that it's tidy, how it used to be, what has been done to improve it. In the end, all may agree that it could be a lot better—or worse. But to do other than accept what is given at face value is to stray from the SIMPLE path.

Potential pitfall: Expecting "resistance to change"

Managers, colleagues and other observers sometimes talk about people who are resistant to change. Strangely, we have rarely met a member of the resistance. Believing that people resist change is like wading upstream in a river and cursing the resistance of the water. Perhaps any apparent resistance is a message that this is not the most efficacious way. Climbing out of the river and walking along the bank or finding a boat to drift downstream might be better methods of achieving your ends.

Here is our view of resistance: If someone starts to resist what you are doing, it is a sign that you have not yet found the best way to cooperate with them. The resistance, in fact, is a useful gift, another angle that you may be able to utilize.

It can be a matter of pace: If people feel that they are being forced along at too great a pace, they may dig their heels in and resist. In that case, slow down.

If they imagine that you have not heard what they have to say, or if you are failing to take account of what they want, they may resist. Your best move is to listen and demonstrate that you have done so, perhaps by employing active listening techniques, summarizing their position and so forth.

Remember the interactional world. It takes two to tango, and so either of you can stop doing what doesn't work and do something else.

The Solutions Focus in action: Avoiding resistance at British Airways

Engineering staff in one division of British Airways were refusing to use a new set of computers to access and record data.

Instead of tackling the problem head on, confronting the trade union or delving more deeply into the reasons why they didn't want to use the machines, one bright engineering manager took a solution-focused approach and gained permission to place one of the computers in the staff's restroom for a couple of weeks.

He began using the machine himself during his breaks: He tracked the flight loadings, the information that revealed the number of spare seats on the planes. He suspected that his colleagues would be interested in his findings as they were generally keen to take up offers of reduced air fares, which were available to them on flights with low loads. They were permitted to make late bookings on flights with spare seats. Hot holiday destinations were the most popular and also the most scarce.

Soon the staff were watching over the engineer's shoulder, asking him to look up the loadings on flights to their preferred destinations. After a few days he stopped looking up the information for them, posted the instructions on the wall and let them take their own turn. Queues formed at break times to take advantage of this popular service.

Then two weeks later he removed the terminal. As they protested, he told them that management could not justify this use of resources simply for them to book their own discount flights. Of course, he added, the management might be interested if staff were willing to learn to use the system and incorporate it into their work, but they were not currently expecting it because the union were apparently opposed. Within two more weeks, the staff had persuaded their union to take a different view, and the terminals were reinstated under a new agreement.

Make use of what's there—Summary

✔ Work with what's there, not what isn't.

✔ Everything is (or can be viewed as) a useful gift.

✔ Find counters, examples of the solution happening already, complete or in part, and evidence of strengths, skills and resources that could be relevant.

✔ Avoid focusing on deficits—aim first to utilize what's there.

✔ If you encounter "resistance" to change, suspect that you are generating it and ask what you could do instead.

6

Possibilities—Past, Present and Future

"If you treat an individual as he is, he will stay as he is, but if you treat him as if he were what he ought to be and could be, he will become what he ought to be and could be."

Goethe

In adopting the Solutions Focus you will always work with possibilities—in the past, the present, or the future. This may sound puzzling. We are accustomed to hearing about possibilities with respect to the future. This is most important for the Solutions Focus as we explore preferred futures, how life will be when the problem has vanished. But what of present and past possibilities?

Solutions not problems
Inbetween—the action is in the interaction
Make use of what's there
POSSIBILITIES—PAST, PRESENT AND FUTURE
Language—simply said
Every case is different

The idea of possibilities in the present refers to uncovering and highlighting current resources—"possibility machines"—and favoring conversations leading to topics, strands and directions that generate feelings of possibility. Solution-focused conversations are frequently characterized by an atmosphere suggesting that matters can and will be different.

These possibilities are present, even if they have so far been neglected or unused.

The past can also be a source of possibilities. Used in one way, the past serves to reduce possibilities: when we look for single causes, apportion blame and recount unhelpful happenings and experiences. Alternatively, it can produce possibilities: when we tell resource-laden stories about ourselves and each other, and when there is future-oriented learning to be gleaned from the ways we explain what happened. We seek to link the past and present to the future.

Possibilities are central to progress

Let's consider what happens when we don't work with possibilities. A future without possibilities is a future without hope, one in which neither we nor anyone else can make a difference. Experience shows that hope is a great motivator. Expectations and hope are vital in lighting a forward path.

Suppose, for example, that there was a disease called workaholism, in which sufferers always did too much work, to the detriment of their home or social lives. Suppose, too, that it was an incurable disease (perhaps with a genetic cause). Any workaholic would thus have no hope for a future in which work took a back seat. Perhaps it would be preferable simply to be someone who was currently working too hard, as this would leave room for at least two hopes: one, that you might not work so hard in the future; the other, that there was no incurable disease called workaholism.

Often, no hope for the future is connected to stories from the past. Nothing we have tried has worked, nothing made any difference, it never happened for me. While we may all experience feelings like this from time to time, that does not make them any more valid or any more logically connected to what will happen next than feelings that everything always goes right. We note, however, that our feelings and attitudes can make a difference to how matters turn out, particularly where our agency is involved; that is, when our actions will have an impact on the situation.

In those cases, optimism and pessimism do play pragmatic—though not always entirely logical—roles.

Our interpretations of the present may be rooted in the stories we remember from the past. While some parts of what happened remain with us, the stories we tell about them may certainly be changed. The company picnic may have been so rowdy and ill-behaved, they say, that there's a new policy: There will be no further picnics, on the basis that the staff just can't be trusted. Or the story can be changed: The picnic was high spirited, illustrating the urgent need for staff to have the opportunity to let their hair down, and so there will be more frequent picnics and social events in future.

The benefits of possibilities

The benefits of working with possibilities include the sense of hope and motivation that this invariably engenders. The alternative—working from certainty of the future and precise knowledge of how unhelpful the past has been—offers a direct route to stuckness and accusation. The pessimistic fatalist is rarely the first to spring into action. Focusing on how and why things are bad is considerably less helpful than directing attention to how matters could be different.

The Solutions Focus in action: Not born in the USA?

There was a business school exam question in the late 1970s that asked whether Honda should enter the global automobile business. To the MBA students the answer was obviously not, because there was already an efficient, competitive and saturated market. Honda had little experience with cars and no distribution system.

Nonetheless, perhaps failing to read the exam answers, Honda successfully entered the market, and the academics later admitted that they had not taken sufficient account of the energy of a company determined to succeed.[1]

In this chapter you will discover how to find possibilities in the past, in the present and in the future. You'll also collect the solutions tool of

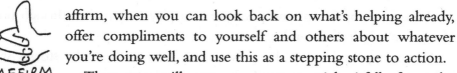

AFFIRM

affirm, when you can look back on what's helping already, offer compliments to yourself and others about whatever you're doing well, and use this as a stepping stone to action.

Then you will survey some potential pitfalls from the SIMPLE path. Relating to the past, you may drift toward "accusatory explanation." Relating to the present, you face the danger of using unresourceful words, which may have more impact than you suppose. Looking to the future, appreciate the differences between explanations that lend a sense of possibility and those that impose a varnish of dead-end finality.

Possibilities from the past

As well as holding different attitudes about the future, we each tell different stories variously interpreting the past and the present.

Some tales are full of villains and evil deeds, others stress the hero and concentrate on resources. One version of British industrial history will say that the unions were the winners, another awards the laurels to management. There is an old saying that the winners write the history. In fact, anyone around to tell a tale can write their own history. And this is something many of us do much of the time.

The resultant stories carry great power within the organization; just think of the influence wielded by the office gossip. Solution seekers tell stories about their successes, from the early triumphs of the founders to the most recent turning points. These create a kind of corporate mythology, which helps make up what insiders experience as the organizational culture.

One of the most potent organizational stories is Hewlett-Packard's fable (which is not to say that it is untrue) of Dave and Bill launching the computer company from their garage workshop in California. It is such a vital touchstone of the corporation's identity that following a major reshuffle, they told the tale again in a series of television and newspaper adverts, while also reincorporating it internally to emphasize to the staff the company's preferred values and behaviors.

As every enterprise starts small, and all successful film scripts and nov-els begin life on the back of an envelope or equivalent, so there will be a similar "miracle of creative endeavor" story in the history of any organization.

Executives from Walkers Snack Foods were fascinated when, as outside consultants, we told them the story of how their colleagues within the PepsiCo group, in the Frito-Lay company, had cemented their reputation in America by the heroic efforts of their drivers, who ensured that deliv-eries always got through no matter what the weather. This fundamental tale of reliability and success was ready for retransmission to a branch of the organization eager to share in the corporate mythology.[2]

Personal stories

At the personal level, it makes a big difference whether an executive describes him- or herself as a resourceful character who has dealt capably with the challenges faced, or as a somewhat inept bumbler to whom fate routinely deals a losing hand. As colleagues, we can encourage our exec-utives to tell those versions of events that will prove helpful for present and future tasks. Ben Furman, a solution-focused colleague from the therapy field, put it neatly in his book title: *It's Never too Late to Have a Happy Childhood*.

Whatever stories we may tell, we are going to encounter some tough times. As Winston Churchill is reputed to have said, "Life is one damn thing after another," and it is not as if we can go through life without dif-ficulties. We are faced with challenges all the time. The particular prob-lems to tackle are when life becomes the same damn thing over and over—the ones when we feel stuck.

It is in these sorts of circumstances that the solution-focused approach is so valuable. And the process often begins with a salutary surprise to the sufferer. They learn that whatever they are experiencing as the block or the problem may be the key to the solution. And, conversely, their cur-rent efforts to solve the problem may only be exacerbating the situation.

Potential pitfall: Accusatory explanations

One of the greatest temptations toward going astray in the search for solutions is to hunt for the cause of a problem in the past, crying, "You started it!" The corollary is usually, "So—you do something!" Even if they did start it (which may or may not be the case), the likely riposte to your view is their view, in which they say, "Nonsense, it would all have been fine if you hadn't acted up earlier." An impasse results.

Ben Furman calls such exchanges "accusatory explanation." Although accusatory explanation presents an illusion of progress, it is unhelpful and saps energy.

First, memories are flawed, and you cannot even be sure that your memory of the past is accurate, let alone that others would agree with you. Second, perception is selective: You tend to notice what you look for, or what your attention is directed to.

Put three holidaymakers into the Amazon jungle and ask them what they saw. The botanist will tell you about the variety of exotic plants, the ethnologist will describe how migrant populations are changing the area, while the package holidaymaker will complain how awful it was not to be able to get a decent cup of tea.

These people all experienced the same trip—so who was right? It is an unhelpful question, as each viewpoint is valid. Better to ask the botanist if you want to know about the plants.

Suppose we are trying to improve communications between a research department and a marketing department. The cause(s) of the poor communications might be well known; say, the two mistrust each other after some farrago five years before. Now we know the cause, we are straight on to the solution, right? Wrong: We can't go back five years in a time machine and sort out the farrago. We need to deal with this problem now, not five years ago. We begin with the present and link to the future, or we mine the past for elements that may prove useful now.

The Solutions Focus in action: Focus or firefight?

At a strategy workshop for an industrial services company's training team, the problem was that they had lost focus, were not sure how they were doing as a team, and experienced life as constant firefighting.

We asked how they were measuring up to their targets. It turned out that they were doing well, even under pressure, delivering most of the training required to high standards.

The parts that they were missing seemed significantly more manageable after they appreciated how much they were achieving. Moreover, the remedies were apparent, as they were founded on the organizational and personal resources that the participants were already using to do what they were doing.

They left reinvigorated, changed very little, and continued to flourish as a training delivery department and as a team that enjoyed working together. A month later, they were delighted that what had seemed like small changes to them had resulted in much larger changes in the wider organization—not least in the growth of their reputation.

Keeping it SIMPLE: Focus on futures, not causes

It is usually simple to start with how the future might be, then look for help from the past. Starting with the past may quickly complicate matters.

As we saw in Chapters 3 and 4, the Solutions Focus does not seek the causes of problems: Instead, we are much more interested in the causes of solutions. These are to do more of what works and stop doing what doesn't work. People who want change want to know what to do. They need practical action, not academic analysis.

Also, knowing the cause may predispose you to looking for the solution in certain areas, which may well not be the most fertile. How we define the problem has a big impact on how we try to define the solution. We want to define the problem in a way that is solvable. A good way to do this is to define the solution—and then to examine the situation to assess what can help. There is no need to restrict yourself to a limited view just so that you can spend a long time "defining" (and potentially building and expanding) the problem.

Cigarettes and unintended consequences

We may not know how to reduce the number of people killed each year from cigarette-related diseases, but we do know how ineffectual is the "obvious" route of banning cigarette advertising, based on the premise that advertising leads to smoking. All sorts of factors lead to smoking, and advertising is only one part of the complex interrelationships between the tobacco companies and their targets.

As the director of Britain's anti-smoking campaign group ASH put it, "The regulation to date has actually been counter-productive. It has fuelled a creative arms race and forced tobacco companies into innovative ground-breaking approaches."[3] In Malaysia, for example, where cigarette advertising is illegal, B&H has rebranded itself as a chain of bistros and a blended coffee. The sophisticated image turned out to have a particular appeal to children, and smoking among teenagers rose rapidly.

This is not to say—if your aim is to reduce smoking—that banning advertising is necessarily a bad tactic. It does mean that it should be only one tactic in a broader strategy. Once the consequences are apparent, you will need to take other actions as well, which may usefully include redefining the preferred future, perhaps in terms of health, awareness and personal choice.

Cause and correlation

Another potentially distracting track is to confuse cause with correlation. When you have a cold and your nose runs, the cold is not caused by nasal mucus. If you have a headache, you can alleviate the pain by taking aspirin, but it does not follow that the cause of the headache is too little aspirin in the brain.[4]

Peters and Waterman may have encouraged readers to wander down this route in their classic book *In Search of Excellence*. They found many common factors between successful businesses and may have created the impression that these *caused* excellence in the businesses. Complex systems are more complicated than that, and while there were many fine ideas and insights in their book, it does not always work to derive advice for your organization from descriptions of excellence elsewhere.

What works for some organizations may or may not work for others. What works for you is likely to be unique, and a solutions focus helps you discover what that is as quickly and easily as possible.

Possibilities present

You can use language to suggest that there will be remedies for current problems. By saying "You may be finding this difficult at first" or looking forward to "when you realize you are making useful changes," you presuppose that it will get better.

It is true that you cannot be absolutely certain of improvement, but it is a more helpful working assumption than any alternative.

"A powerful question alters all thinking and behaving that occurs afterwards."
Marilee Goldberg, The Art of the Question

There is nothing to lose and plenty to gain by adopting such an attitude and incorporating positive presuppositions. Also, if you don't fundamentally believe that you can improve your own situation or help others in theirs, you may be ill-advised to take on such a challenge in the first place.

"Suppose that you and your team are working really well on Monday. How will you know?" is a variant on presupposing. It pitches the mind into the future, with the suggestion of a topic headed "working really well."

Some aspects of this attitude are conveyed by the phrase "positive thinking." Another important aspect, which is particularly characteristic of the Solutions Focus, is the sense that the positive future is founded primarily on evidence that exists in the present.

Presuppose that success is not only possible but inevitable

Presupposing that what we want to happen will happen is a powerful weapon in our linguistic armory, helping us to create a context where success becomes more possible in practice. In particular, we always presuppose that the solution can be found. Compare the following questions:

❏ *Do any parts of your future perfect happen at the moment?* (The answer to this may be swift, instinctive and decisive, and could well be "no.")
❏ *Which parts of your future perfect happen at the moment?* (The answer to this sometimes begins with a long pause and "hmmm…")

In solution-focused work, design your inquiries to produce helpful answers. People are generally good at answering the questions they are asked, which makes it reasonably straightforward to construct conversations and stories that assist us in reaching our goals.

Sometimes even the simplest questions produce useful answers. We enjoyed the story of the mother who asked her child: "How many times do I have to tell you put your toys away?" The child responded, after some thought: "Four times."

Co-creating solutions

One part of working with others in a solutions-focused way is that by talking and acting together we co-construct conversations and stories. These stories help shape the future. A conversation about resourcefulness in the face of adversity may develop into a different story from one about a delivery being late once again, even if the underlying events were the same.

The questions that we ask ourselves and others help to shape the story. So we practice eliciting responses that lead to our desired endings.

If you are employing a solutions focus with someone else, then both you and that customer for change are jointly responsible for the outcomes. Rather than leading from the front, it is sometimes easier to lead from one step behind and give people a tap on the shoulder with a good question.

Solution-focused and problem-focused conversations

When devising solutions, examine the differences between times when the problem happens and other times (particularly times when the solution happens). Remember, this is different from examining the cause of the problem. When prompted, people readily recall examples of different things happening—unusually, accidentally, randomly, whatever—and there they may hold the seeds of the solution.

Let's examine the differences between solution-focused and problem-focused approaches to a typical personal work problem.

SOLUTION FOCUSED	PROBLEM FOCUSED
I want to find time to write an important report.	I can't find time to write an important report.
When do you spend an hour or so writing each day?	*When is writing a problem?*
When I do it first, before doing my post and email.	I seem to get sidetracked by the post and email—there's always so much to do.
So, how to write the report?	*So, what's the cause of this lack of ability to focus on your work?*
Write for an hour or two first thing. Delay doing post and email.	Well, I've always been easily distracted and I'm a great procrastinator!
What else?	*So it will be difficult to write this report then?*
Arrange meetings for the afternoon, when possible. Keep the first part of each morning free. That sounds great, I'll try it tomorrow.	Yes, I guess so. Maybe I should shelve the project for a while until I've learned to become more disciplined.

The difference is clear: The solution-focused questions lead to a story of possibility, while the problem-focused questions lead to this "small" difficulty turning into a much larger and less tractable issue about character.

Affirming and offering compliments

AFFIRM

Another way to work with what's there and consider possibilities is to offer compliments, which allow us to ascribe positive worth to aspects that we have noticed, even if others have not yet realized their importance.

Giving compliments is one of the most underrated tools in the box. Compliments in the solution-focused sense are specifically for identifying and highlighting resources and progress.

You can compliment others on aspects that they have recognized themselves and you can bring other achievements to their attention. You can compliment yourself for your own efforts, achievements and qualities.

In this context, compliments are feedback on people's qualities, skills, capabilities and attitudes, based on what you have *directly* observed. Why directly? If you can say "I was impressed with this and I've seen you do it," it is incontrovertible in a way that "I was impressed with this, which I'm imagining from something or other" isn't.

Compliments are so underused that it is often also helpful to show people how to use them themselves with other members of their teams. For traditional British managers, for example, both giving and receiving compliments can be tricky at first.

It seems that Brits are stronger at spotting mistakes and homing in on what is wrong or not so good. "That's a nice jacket," says one computer programmer. "Oh, I got it from a charity shop," replies his colleague. Encourage him to say "Thank you" instead—or at least to add it.

Within the organization, anything that has worked well or is novel will form the basis for a compliment. For a solution-focused facilitator, the quest is to catch people doing things well and quietly mention them: "I liked the way you did that," "I enjoyed your work on…"

In order for compliments to become common currency, people need to accept them as well as give them. You could supply "compliment fish." This isn't to get people fishing for compliments exactly: Each time anyone gives a compliment they also hand over a cardboard cutout fish. Everyone can keep track of their balance between giving and receiving.

One managing director wondered what would happen if he gave too many compliments to staff within his company. We told him that it was an interesting question, but it had never yet been tried.

How to do compliments

It is always possible to identify something that people are doing well— the trick is to express this acceptably and sincerely, without patronizing.

One method of avoiding patronization is to wrap the compliment inside a question, by asking: "How are you doing this so well?" This opens a route to exploring how to do more such activities, and to begin making the connections between those and the customer's preferred future. All by working with what's there.

Resources

Helping people to uncover their resources is crucial in solution-focused work. The resources you are interested in are not merely financial, though these matter too. You want to know what people have achieved in their work and outside, what resources they have at their disposal to fuel their pursuit of solutions. Problem talk typically ignores these strengths.

It is amazing to discover just how much people have achieved outside of work: climbing mountains, bringing up families, accomplishing all manner of social and personal goals. And it is equally amazing that they are then asked to sit at a desk and leave most of their resources behind. You may wonder whether companies are really tapping into the resources of their people.

If people are acting successfully, moreover, there may be seeds of solutions there for other aspects of their lives or work. For example, we know an engineer who is terrific at managing projects, but complains of lack of self-confidence. Her project management skills may come in handy in what we might call her "confidence project." Hobbies, interests and past successes are good hunting grounds for what works.

When team members get together and investigate their collective resources, they begin to appreciate just how much they can achieve together. A Solutions Focus teambuilding event, with this awareness of resources, has a radically different flavor from the deficit-based approach, which typically asks about gaps and team behaviors that are missing.

You may start to unearth resources with questions like:

✔ When you've faced tough situations before, how have you handled them?
✔ When you've faced situations like this one before, what did you do?
✔ What are your particular ways of getting through a crisis?

The Solutions Focus in action: What are your talents?

A team of telephone receptionists, security staff and their immediate line managers were performing badly. Morale was low and in danger of sinking ever lower in a vicious circle of recriminations.

The turning point for the team was when they shared descriptions of their individual resources. They revealed that their talents included computer skills, parenting, dowsing and the restoration of vintage cars. They agreed that if they harnessed the qualities needed for their achievements outside work, they could achieve whatever they wanted within the organization. Immediately, their morale and performance improved.

Potential pitfall: Using unresourceful words

Keeping it SIMPLE: The easy way to resourceful words
By asking solution-focused questions, we engage in conversations featuring many resourceful words. These words are particularly effective when they come from the customer for change.

The legendary therapist Milton Erickson was a master at suggesting to his clients what he wanted them to think about, usually the outcomes they wanted for themselves. He constructed his sentences to use the relevant positive and resourceful words, even if the grammar suffered.

Simply using resourceful words seems to help, and by using the Solutions Focus you will talk resourceful talk quite naturally whatever the situation. On the other hand, if you start talking to people about problems, the grammar will shift around to include problem-focused words, which are often unresourceful.

The Solutions Focus in action: Increase your word power

Recent research by Jeffrey Hausdorf and Becca Levy has shown that elderly people briefly exposed to negative age-related words like "senile," "forgetful" and "diseased" walked more slowly, performed worse on a memory test, and under-rated their own abilities, in contrast to similar people exposed to positive words like "wise," "astute," and "accomplished."[5]

Future possibilities

"What do you want to have happen? And how will you know when it has?" The answers to these questions provide a simple definition of the future perfect.

This preferred future is devised and elaborated by the customer for change. If there are several customers, there may be several preferred futures. This sense that something could be different runs through solution-focused work. And if there is a way forward, it always starts from here (wherever we are now).

If we do not seek possibilities—for example by creating a clear description of the future perfect—there is a greatly reduced chance of:

❑ Reaching the outcomes we want.
❑ Knowing what we want.
❑ Recognizing when it is happening.
❑ Taking the steps necessary to make these prefigured events occur.

Expectations

The impact of positive expectations—sometimes called the Pygmalion effect after Ovid's story of the sculptor whose prayers were answered when his statue of his ideal woman came to life—has long been known. The Solutions Focus aims to harness the effect to the fullest possible extent.

The work of Robert Rosenthal in the 1960s and 1970s drew attention to the wide and often unconscious effects of our expectations. Rosenthal famously worked with the expectations of schoolteachers. In one experiment, he conducted an IQ test in an elementary school, then randomly selected 20 percent of each class and informed the teachers that these students were likely to be showing signs of a spurt in intellectual growth and could be expected to outperform the others. A year later he returned and repeated the test, and found that the selected groups showed significantly greater improvement than the others. In all grades from first to sixth, the improvements were significant, with an average 12.22 percent IQ point gain.

The positive expectations of the teachers had entered the interactions: When the students performed particularly well, this confirmed the teachers' expectations and reinforced their behavior. This in turn reinforced the achievement of the students.[6]

In the workplace this same phenomenon has many forms: the "unmotivated" person who is never set a challenge because we all know he wouldn't rise to it; the anxious presenter who makes herself more anxious by worrying about her anxiety as well as her next presentation. In applying the Solutions Focus you want to have expectations working for you.

Although Rosenthal was working in the 1960s, the business world had already produced its own examples of the effect of positive expectations and self-fulfilling prophecies. A well-documented study[7] concerns the Hollerith tabulating machine installed at the New York census office in 1890. This machine, similar to a typewriter in operation, required its operators to learn a new skill. The inventor reckoned the skill somewhat complicated and estimated an upper limit of 550 cards processed per worker per day. After the initial training and a practice period, the workers could indeed produce 550 cards per day. After more experience the number increased slightly, but only at great emotional cost. However, when 200 new workers joined up, they knew nothing of the machine or the difficulty of the task. While the original workers were straining themselves to process 700 cards in a day, the new group soon began tabulating 2,100 per day with no ill effects.

When you expect there to be a way forward, one presents itself. If you expect trouble, you will usually encounter it. When we run sessions on the topic of creative problem solving, the participants often make their breakthroughs on certain challenges only after we assure them that there is a solution. Their confidence that there is a solution lends them an almost magical transformative power. If they made that assumption for themselves, clearly they could solve their problems a great deal faster.

> **Keeping it SIMPLE: Expect the best**
> The biggest predictor of US college students' grades is not SAT tests, or school exams, but the extent to which they expect to do well.[8]

Helpful explanations

There is something in all of us that seems to enjoy a good explanation and sometimes we meet people who really want one as part of their satisfactory solution. So what makes one and what role does explanation play in the change process?

Chilean scientist Humberto Maturana came close when he said: "An explanation is something that the receiver accepts as an explanation."

Potential pitfall: Explanations with no way forward

Part of a good explanation is that it is accepted by those who want one. Another aspect is that the explanation should allow some way forward for the customer. For example, the explanation given to generations of underachieving school students—"You have low IQ"—is particularly pernicious. It purports to explain the poor performance without offering any hope that matters could be different.

Explanations have what is sometimes called "explanatory power," in that the nub of the explanation sometimes prompts a new action. Thus it makes sense to ensure that the explanations we accept have a positive explanatory power.

Keeping it SIMPLE: Find a helpful explanation

If you must find an explanation, make sure it is a helpful one: one with possibilities and accepted by those involved.

On the question of IQ, there are preferable, more recent suggestions—for example Howard Gardner's ideas about multiple intelligences—that offer explanations and at the same time alternatives. In brief, he opens up vistas in which there are many and varied signs of people displaying intelligence, and many ways in which their intelligences—if wisely deployed—will enable them to learn.

How important is it that we have an explanation? It is perhaps less important than many people believe. If change is sought, and change is available, then we go for that change first and, afterwards (if we must), develop an explanation that suits us. If we crave an explanation from the present or the past, let us seek one that offers some possibility of our preferred future.

British science writer Jack Cohen put it neatly: "We can explain everything, but we can't understand anything. The really dangerous people are those who are certain they know what they're doing."

Possibilities—past, present, and future—Summary

✔ Possibility plays a primary role in determining what happens next.
✔ Offer compliments and affirm whatever is already working well for you.
✔ Possibilities can be found in the past, in stories and evidence of resources.
✔ Avoid "accusatory explanation."
✔ Possibilities in the present can be generated by the words you choose and the ways you interpret what's there in front of you.
✔ Avoid using unresourceful words with people.
✔ Generate hope and positive expectations for the future from events that have happened or are yet to happen.

7

Language–Simply Said

"It is inherent in our intellectual activity that we seek to imprison reality in our description of it. Soon, long before we realise it, it is we who become the prisoners of the description. From that point on, our ideas degenerate into a kind of folklore that we pass on to each other, fondly thinking we are still talking of the reality around us."

Aneurin Bevan, British statesman

Solutions not problems
Inbetween—the action is in the interaction
Make use of what's there
Possibilities—past, present and future
LANGUAGE—SIMPLY SAID
Every case is different

Bevan says that language imprisons us. For the solution-focused mind, it can also be a liberator.

You have seen (in Chapter 6) how to use words to generate either a sense of possibility and resources, or a sense of stuckness and futility. This chapter examines language from a different perspective, revealing how language can complicate matters and distract you in your search for solutions.

In organizational settings, problems can be considered as the result of people discussing matters in certain ways that build things up into what they call "problems," with all that implies. Instead, it is possible to think and speak as if you are dealing with either stuck patterns that can be moved, or situations with untapped potential. Try discussing your problem as a set of circumstances in which the right way forward has yet to materialize.

In taking a Solutions Focus, pay fresh attention to language, deploying it to navigate through the SIMPLE route to find what works. The benefit of simpler language is that it allows us more easily to reach solutions that work here and now. In addition, it leads to:

✔ More chance of the participants in the change process communicating effectively and understanding each other.
✔ Faster and more precise communication.
✔ A reduction in impressive-sounding nonsense.

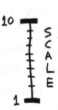

In this chapter you will meet the solutions tool of scaling. This unreasonably effective method is an easy way of moving toward helpful and specific language. Scaling has a variety of uses in solution-focused work, which you'll explore here and later on.

Keeping language SIMPLE helps you skirt around many pitfalls. Among those we shall address here are:

❑ Bewitchment by words—big words often impede progress.
❑ Not using people's own words—people know and like what they say.
❑ Words are not the world—the dangers of generalities and unhelpful labels.

Words matter

Language does more than merely describe. It also influences the way others form their opinions. Words allow us to communicate, express ourselves, convey our thoughts and

"While language structures reality, questions help structure language."
Marilee Goldberg, The Art of the Question

feelings to others, initiate action, entertain ourselves, make people laugh or cry. Sigmund Freud, musing on the origins of language in his introductory lecture in psychoanalysis in 1915, wrote, "Words were originally magic and to this day words have retained much of their ancient magical power."

On many occasions the richness of language is a source of inspiration. Yet when we feel stuck and are grasping for an elusive solution, it can be an obstruction. This happens, for example, when different people describe the same subject in different ways, and the different descriptions lead to frustratingly dead-end conversations and actions.

The Solutions Focus in action: "Electronic transformers"

The senior team of one electronic component manufacturer had decided that the company was short of transformational leaders, managers who were innovative, tenacious, prepared to countenance and implement radical new methods. They wanted managers who were unafraid of unpopularity and who wouldn't take "no" for an answer.

As they discussed the issues, members of the senior team also mentioned they had another problem: Some of the staff were awkward, obstructive and outspoken toward existing company initiatives, and went around telling anyone who would listen that they had better ideas.

Hoping to resolve their various difficulties, the senior team set about simplifying their language, replacing judgmental adjectives with descriptions of what people were doing.

It turned out that one person's transformational leader was another's obstructive manager and, once this was recognized, our senior team was in a position to make clear choices about whether or not they wanted to encourage the transformational/obstructive behaviors.

Potential pitfall: Bewitched by words

You might hear in a boardroom the question: "What are the real problems facing this organization?" The way the question is phrased wraps in an assumption: that there are "real" problems, which perhaps could be visited, explored, photographed or excised.

Yet it is usually more useful to conceptualize problems as socially constructed by groups of people. Problems viewed in this way are interactions between people. We place problems in a different epistemological category from items with a tangible form—trees, cars and machines, for instance—and so are ready to talk about them in a different way. There are significant differences—linguistically as well as practically—between fixing a photocopier and fixing a leadership crisis.

Ludwig Wittgenstein, in his book Philosophical Investigations, *argued that language is a poison that can be used to seduce, mislead and bewitch us. But it can also heal, as when we speak truly. When we are bewitched, we tend to stare the hypnotic gaze. We then tend to see illusory essences, which rise out of pictures embedded in language, but which seem to lie deep in the mind or the world. Distinctions and differences are missed, the eye is dazzled by the ideal. And all this leads to us talking disguised nonsense.*[1]

Language sometimes relates to the world directly, describing precisely what happens, and sometimes its relationship is more abstract. Truth does not exist in the world in same way as objects, but we sometimes talk as if abstracts were concrete, which often causes confusion and unproductive effort.

In pygmy societies, the pygmies say that emotions are the only truth. We may use language to attempt to convey our emotional and other experiences—to get us closer to communicating these sorts of truths—but it is also important to accept that in the end at least some experiences can be known only to the person who experiences them. There will always be a gap between experience and language. The solution-focused practitioner will respect the experience and accept it as valid for the person who experiences it.

As well as indicating presuppositions, attitudes and emotions, language often complicates matters. The Solutions Focus encourages us to wield Occam's Razor and seek the simplest solutions, using the most precise language.

$5 and $5,000 words

Solutions pioneer Insoo Kim Berg finds practical value in simplicity and draws the distinction between $5 words and $5,000 words. The latter are

"There is a time for specificity and a time for abstractions, and a great deal of nonsense is generated by people who do not know what time it is."

Neil Postman

the words used to baffle and aggrandize. They are the words that put issues into expert territory. Only experts can wield them with sufficient skill; and, of course, they will charge you handsomely to do so. French scientist Alan Sokal, in his book *Intellectual Impostures*, describes

an extreme example, when he wrote an article for a postmodernist journal using long and scientific words in a deliberately meaningless way. The paper, "Transgressing the boundaries: Towards a transformative hermeneutics of quantum gravity," was nonetheless accepted and published.

Organizationally, you may have encountered examples like these:

❑ "This organization needs a paradigm shift."
❑ "Stakeholder wealth creation can be enhanced by focusing on the value chain."
❑ "Knowledge management is key in leveraging our intellectual property."

Yet in many cases the $5,000 words would translate into simpler, everyday $5 words, which could be arranged to achieve exactly the same ends. For example:

❑ "We want to respond differently to certain events."
❑ "We can make more money by examining what we do and changing it."
❑ "We can make the most of what we know by sharing it around the organization."

If your solution-seeking conversations are foundering on too many labels, judgments, abstract concepts or $5,000 words, encourage people to simplify their descriptions by asking how other people would describe the situation, perhaps

Keeping it SIMPLE: Use $5 words

$5 words are usually positive, detailed, and describe observable events and objects. They are often seen as the low-rent end of language, but they can be devastatingly practical.

people with a less flowery vocabulary. "How would a mechanic describe it?" or "What would a new recruit say was going on here?" Get specific. Say it in $5 words.

Sometimes people ask us what we have against long words. The answer is absolutely nothing—as long as they don't get in the way. If people are using long words and no one wants anything different, that's your prerogative. When you're after change, that's a good time to check out those big words.

First tiny signs

One quick and easy way of switching from bewitching language to specific and detailed language is to speak about "the first signs of progress."

The Solutions Focus in action: Working under par

The local operations manager was at his wits' end. He was overworked, his office was a mess, and he had no idea what he was supposed to be doing today as his diary was out of date. All in all, he said gravely, "My spiritual health is suffering badly."

Without claiming any expertise in either health or in spirituality, it was difficult to know what to say. There seemed little point in trying to warn him of the linguistic confusion into which he might be falling. Fortunately, there was no need. Instead, the question was, "Hmmm, your spiritual health. What would be the first tiny signs that your spiritual health was improving?"

"Um," replied the manager. "I'd be organized enough to fix up a game of golf on Saturday. I always used to play golf and relax, and I haven't had the chance recently." So he agreed that whatever else he did that day he was to be sure to organize the game. He duly did, and his office arrangements somehow began to improve as well as his "spiritual health."

Scaling

Scaling is an effective way of measuring how close you are to the desired outcomes of any change program. It is also a tool for encouraging and assessing progress toward the futures described by those involved in change.

Scales offer an intuitive logic that is readily accessible. Most people find it reasonably easy to establish a scale. They know for themselves the meaning of some of the points, and they are often able to tell you what a point represents for them.

Your task is to elicit descriptions of various points along a scale. When you discover what the small changes along the way look like, you have your primary guide to the next step in the change process. This is to suggest that the customer for change takes the actions that they have identified will:

✔ Take them one step up the scale; or
✔ Be those they will be taking when they are one step up the scale.

If you can do the latter, there is no need for the former. Any transitions will be automatically taken care of by the very fact of arrival.

Let's imagine a scale. The scale runs from 0 to 10, and 10 represents the state of affairs when you have reached your future perfect or desired outcome. Zero stands for when none of the things that you want is happening (or when the problem is at its worst). Where are you now?

Note that this is a subjective and personal scale. It is not a full and objective rating: It's much more useful than that!

Suppose you place yourself at 3. This is a surprisingly useful piece of information. First, it implies you are already some distance along the scale. You could ponder on questions such as: "How come I am at 3, rather than 1 or 2? What am I already doing that's helping?"

A great deal of information about counters and existing parts of the future perfect can be gleaned here, and it is a prime opportunity for you to boost confidence and self-esteem. Whatever is raising you to the current point on the scale is a resource that you can deploy to sustain and fuel the next step.

The next questions are: "What would the next small step up the scale look like? What would you need to do to get to 4?"

What is crucial here is that you are discussing a small step. If you knew how to get to 10 you would probably have done so already. So you coax descriptions of small differences that can be appreciated as step changes, and then descriptions of the actions that might lead to those results.

Most people readily pick up the idea of scaling and use it to amplify their awareness of what's already helping, and what needs to happen next, in language that is positive, detailed and specific—in $5 words.

Professor Andrew Derrington, professor of psychology at the University of Nottingham, has experienced the power of scaling for himself:

> *The second question, known as the scaling question, is simpler. It asks clients to put a number on how they feel, where 0 is the worst they have ever felt, and 10 is the way they feel the morning after the miracle. The sequel to the scaling question is to ask clients to imagine what they might be able to do to move themselves half a point up the happiness scale. Whenever I have a dose of the glums I ask myself this question. The thing that amazes me, and convinces me that I shall never need therapy, is that I always know the answer. Try it yourself. You will put your therapist out of business.* [2]

Potential pitfall: Words are personal

In the film *Annie Hall*, Woody Allen and Diane Keaton's characters talk to their respective therapists about their lovemaking frequency. He says, "Hardly ever—three times a week." She says, "Constantly—three times a week!" So we have to distinguish between statements like "constantly," a personal viewpoint, and "three times a week," verifiable at least in principle. Woody and Diane are talking about the same phenomenon here, but each has a different emotional perspective. A feeling of stuckness could easily arise if they conducted a debate centered on "constantly" versus "hardly ever."

Taking what people say at face value does not imply disapproval or dislike: It is a discipline for staying both simple and neutral, until significant links or contrasts present themselves as pointers that might prove pertinent for change.

Let's assume that everyone probably has a good reason for saying what they say but that need not concern us, and we can usually leave it at that. We are not interested in anything unless it will help or hinder the speaker on the route toward the desired change.

The labels "freedom fighter" and "terrorist," for example, may refer to the same person engaged in the same activities. However, the two labels lead to different interpretations of actions, intentions and worthiness. In many contexts, different terms with varying degrees of applied approval, emotional kick and presuppositions have an important role to play. Does your organization champion "imaginative creators" or harrass "idle daydreamers"?

Stay alert for occasions when the language that you or your fellow customers for change choose—the words and labels selected—leads in unhelpful directions.

One difficulty with $5,000 words is their tendency to mean different things to different people, who then generate confusion and nonsense among themselves. If you are involved in a negotiation, for example, it is a good idea to check out what people mean, by asking them to rephrase their statements in $5 terms of who is doing what.

Accept the words first, then clarify rather than challenge

By accepting the words of the customer for change (in the first instance), you are well placed to receive the "useful gift" of the emotions or attitudes that those words convey. The speaker is more likely to feel that they have been listened to with respect and empathy. Later, you have the chance to redescribe the same phenomena so as to allow for constructive change.

Solvable problems and SIMPLE words

The aim is to focus on what's possible and changeable, rather than what's impossible and intractable. Instead of wasting time arguing about perspectives, we agree on what we want to have happen. Our first preference is to describe a solution. If we cannot describe a solution, it is possible that there isn't a problem—we may merely be debating fruitlessly without criteria.

If, for example, John is making a presentation and Roger thinks his style is terrific while Jane argues it is poor, the debate will progress only when Roger and Jane describe what they mean by "terrific" and "poor" *in this context*. If that turns out to mean certain points of style, or hinges on results such as the response of the audience (buying a product, agreeing to a new deal, or whatever), then we can picture a "solution" to John's presentational "problems": He must present as dictated by the style guide or deliver the results required.

If we have a problem and cannot fully describe a solution, we turn next to defining improvements on the current situation. For a problem to be susceptible to the Solutions Focus, it must offer scope for change for the better. And it is the solution-focused manager who has to deploy language skillfully to define matters so that change is perceived as possible—and preferably measurable.

Keeping it SIMPLE: Accept their words

When you are working with other people, accept and use their words as much as possible. They know what they mean.

Keeping it SIMPLE: Ask "What else?"

"What else?" is often a tremendous tool for digging out more details. Eliciting details about a particular aspect of a preferred future or counter is usually better than moving to the next point. Not asking "What else?" risks missing some vital aspect of the situation, leaving you with a large pile of half-baked ideas.

Let's see what that means in practice. People often wish that they had more time. They are capable of the most tremendous feats of imagination, energy and effort. Even so, it is difficult to imagine a time management solution that actually increases the number of seconds in the day. Deciding how to use the existing seconds is much more feasible and offers a practical route to managing time.

If the problem is that the organization doesn't have a customer-service culture, we need to be specific, asking for details about what people do or might be doing. We ask, "How would you know when you did have one? If you came in tomorrow and there was a tremendous customer-service culture, how would you recognize it? What else would indicate that there was one?"

Using key words

You can identify key words if you are talking with a customer for change by listening for their metaphors. Do they talk in terms of war, where everything is a battle, with winners, losers, campaigns, battle-grounds, casualties, combat, fighting, advances, retreats, strategy and tactics? Or are you in a garden, where the talk is of growth, nurturing, pruning, arranging, paths, borders, shoots and flowering?

If "war" and "gardening" are what one could call governing metaphors, you can usually select an appropriate image within any given governing metaphor to discuss helpful futures in phrases that the customer for change will readily understand. This is one way of using their language. Choosing helpful titles for the project and its associated activities may also be valuable. The "Cultivating care for the customer" project, for example, is clearly labeled and will help lead to the desired results, particularly if the name is chosen by those committed to making the changes happen.

Potential pitfall: Words are not the world

What do we mean when we talk about organizations? How we talk and think about organizations has implications for how we make efforts to work with them or change them.

As sociologist Gale Miller points out: "Most people (particularly sociologists) tend to use an overly static language in talking about organisations. They treat organisations as solid structures, not as processes and language games."[3]

When thinking about organizations as solid, we may be seduced into imagining rigid hierarchies, power flowing from the top down, supposing that everyone is working together and suspecting that huge efforts will be needed to make any changes—we may have to "shatter the frame," for example, or "reengineer the organization."

If, however, power flows in more ways than down, influence is exerted at many different points. If we start to perceive organizations as interactional systems—collections of people responding to each other—many possible starting and intervention points appear. You may recall the benefits of taking this interactional view.

Will the true "teamwork" please stand up?

There is a suspicion that $5,000 words are on the market whenever we encounter reification (itself a splendid $5,000 word). Reification means converting a dynamic process into a static phenomenon. For example, teamwork, a noun, is used to describe some interactions: how the people in a team work, help and support each other (or not) to achieve results.

It is tempting to use fancy nouns to sound grander or more concrete than verbs, or to create a label for a bundle of individual events. While sometimes it is useful, at other times it obstructs problem solving.

Reification is often carried further. Teamwork becomes the word to describe all the various ways in which people work successfully (or not) together: a project team designing a motor car, a fast-food kitchen crew preparing burgers, a management team refraining from actual violence during a board meeting, and so on. So the idea that a team can work well together is transformed, linguistically, into a "thing" too fuzzy to prove useful in any individual problematic case.

Hours are devoted to arguing about what teamwork really is, and what are the best examples and metaphors. The same can be said for many words in the management lexicon; strategy, empowerment, culture and communication spring to mind, and you may well spot more.

If you are talking to a group about teamwork, your starting point is to relate it to the team you're working with. What do they think signifies good teamwork? How will it help them if they do more of it? When do they do it already? What are the resources they can use to do more of it? This is entirely in the context of this team, today. There are more ways in which groups of people, "teams," can work well together to achieve their goals than are captured by the neat models in management books.

By choosing a static word to describe a process and then searching elsewhere for knowledge of how to do it, we are in danger of missing two important angles. First, teamwork happens when people do "working as a team." It is not an object kept in a box in the corner of the room to be talked about at times of crisis. Secondly, this team has its own special fashion of doing good teamwork and it is our job to help its members realize it, rather than to insist that we know more about them operating as a team than they do.

> **Keeping it SIMPLE: What will be the first signs of progress?**
> When people start talking in $5,000 words, ask them about the first tiny signs of progress. This can easily and respectfully lead to $5 words. For example, the first steps toward "a more empowered culture" might be "I'll respond more positively to ideas that are offered by others, and they'll know I'm interested in their ideas."

"Culture"

The myriad ways in which any group organizes itself gives each its own "culture." In broad terms, the culture is the characteristic flavor that leads us to experience one company as bureaucratic, another as casual; one as modern, another as professional.

It is likely that an entrepreneur who barks out orders will tend to employ people who are quick to accept them and happy to work in a top-down hierarchy. Sets of behaviors are learnt or habituated, frequently unconsciously. When everyone is playing the same (perhaps unconscious) game, it is notoriously difficult to change it. The culture appears fixed.

However, culture—like a problem—is not concrete. Talk of culture is a way of summarizing what people do and how they interact. And it is in these interactions particular to any organization that the change seeker can pursue the easiest and most collaborative routes to solutions. So, if you wish to change your organization's "culture," a promising start is to select some $5 words to describe how people go about their affairs.

Language—simply said—Summary

✔ Language can be a great complicator and also a great aid in simplifying.

✔ Words were originally seen as magic—and they retain the power to bewitch.

✔ Break the spell by describing the situation in $5 words: positive, detailed, observable.

✔ Scaling is a useful tool for describing your situation in specific terms. On a scale from 1–10, where 10 is the future perfect, where are you now? What's helping you to reach that level already? What would take you a small step (say, one point) higher?

✔ Words are personal: We use them in our own ways and understandings.

✔ Words are not the world. Watch for $5,000 words masquerading as accurate descriptions in problem talk.

8

Every Case Is Different

"I think theories, at best, are useless... Among other things, a Theory offers explanations, when explanations are dubious and are not connected to solutions."

Steve de Shazer, Solutions Focused Therapy listserv, October 1998

"Every case is different" sounds like common sense. We all know that there are unexpected differences between people, between organizations and from one change project

Solutions not problems
Inbetween—the action is in the interaction
Make use of what's there
Possibilities—past, present and future
Language—simply said
EVERY CASE IS DIFFERENT

to the next. However, making it a central assumption unlocks some simple and surprising potential, as we contrast this tenet with the urge to follow theories and models whose power lies in the extent to which every case is the same.

Remember the primary maxim of the Solutions Focus:

Find what works and do more of it.

One application is to develop theories derived from previous cases that bear some similarities and to follow them. This can be effective, as long as the similarities are sufficient for the solutions to apply no matter what the differences between this case and the previous cases may be. Two dangers are:

❑ The differences are more salient than the similarities and so the solution fails.

❑ Attempting to fit every case to the theory or method: If you have only a hammer, there's a temptation to see every case as a nail.

Another application of the maxim is to examine what, in this particular case, we mean by "works" and which aspects of the present situation appear to be helping, sustaining and exemplifying this working. Then we try doing more of that and see if it is indeed what works here. If it isn't, we look again and in extremis invoke the second part of our maxim:

Stop doing what isn't working and do something different.

Either way, each case offers a new beginning, with the benefit that the solution—whatever it turns out to be—fits this particular situation. This leads to:

❑ An increased chance of achieving the desired results.

❑ A greater degree of relevance to the people concerned.

❑ More ownership of the actions required to achieve successful changes.

❑ Enthusiastic implementation as results occur quickly and are shared.

❑ Avoiding the blind alleys of inappropriate theories and models.

Another benefit is that the close attention required to begin again each time keeps your focus sharp, and shows the people you are working with that you are interested in their views. Indeed, you are interested, because you know that it is their viewing and their doing that will make the significant differences.

The approach entails clear-minded discipline and persistence. In this chapter we describe the distinctive aspects of a solution-focused approach that stem from the assumption that every case is different. And there is the last solutions tool, small actions—the small steps you take not only to make progress, but also to learn more about how this case is different.

You will also tour some potential pitfalls that can lead you off the SIMPLE path:

❑ Applying theories that do not fit this particular case and then blaming the case.

❑ Knowing too much and in the process missing something useful.

❑ Relying on experts, who themselves may know a lot and miss even more.

❑ Being solution forced rather than solution focused.

Art Tatum

Art Tatum, a great jazz pianist of the 1930s and 1940s, used to enjoy making bad pianos sound good. He would work out how the piano he was presented with at any club was different, then improvise to incorporate the odd and out-of-tune notes. People hugely enjoyed this skill and rarely left with the impression that he'd been playing a "bad" piano.

Just as each piano is different, so is each organization. The Art Tatum story illustrates how an attitude can shade into a skill: Without the "useful gift" attitude, it is unlikely that he would have developed that particular skill. Similarly in business, a "can do" attitude is a useful precursor of a "will do" set of results.

Finding enough fit

Imagine a lock and a key. Is there only one key that fits each lock? No: Some are "skeleton keys" that fit many different locks. If the fit is sufficient, the lock opens. And if even the skeleton key does not have enough fit, the lock stays shut.

In using the Solutions Focus, you are seeking actions that have enough "fit" to begin the desired change process—to unpick the lock. Usually you do not know in advance what these are; if you did know, you would probably have done them by now.

All the activities in the book so far are designed to help you to find what works in your particular situation. The next step is to try something and see what happens. You have some information about what might fit in this case: Now test a first key in the lock.

Small actions

 Take small actions—easy actions that don't require a frightening amount of effort. Note that these may or may not be the actions that bring about the desired change automatically. They are better seen as experiments with the territory. They are taken with the attitude: "Let's do this to find out what happens."

Of course, these may indeed be the actions that lead toward the solution. Sometimes this happens surprisingly quickly.

The actions at this stage are small: You do something slightly differently, vary a routine or introduce a new procedure. Remember, you are working with complex and indeterminate systems in which everything is interrelated. As with the leverage principle, a small change in one place can create large changes elsewhere. It is in this spirit that you plan the first steps.

Which small step?

There are various good choices of action flowing from a solution-focused approach:

✔ Doing more of what works:
  ❑ The most likely to succeed.
  ❑ The easiest.
  ❑ A random choice of what might work.
  ❑ Noticing what works.
  ❑ Acting "as if" the future perfect had arrived.
✔ Stopping doing what doesn't work and doing something else instead.

These are the fundamental criteria for successful solution-focused actions. They should be:

✔ Small.
✔ Actions that can be taken tomorrow.
✔ Seen as starting something, rather than stopping.
✔ Specific and clearly defined.
✔ For the customer for change to do.

Small

Why *small*? People are more likely to take small steps than large. There is often something daunting about a large action: It requires more effort and energy to do it. A small action, by contrast, can seem almost incidental. Yet, as we know in an interactional world, the right small action will make a big difference.

One small action can get you moving and then be followed by further small actions. This creates the possibility of making adjustments as you go along, rather than being irrevocably committed to one big action that may turn out to be unhelpful.

It can also be easier to come up with ideas for small actions. The range of possibilities from which the action is selected is closer to how matters are now—and inventing action ideas requires less of an imaginative leap.

Small steps

Golfers who want to hole a putt from 50 feet don't aim at the hole. They learn to aim at a point on the ground just a few feet ahead of the ball, on the line they want.

Similarly with businesses. A small start-up consultancy had ambitious plans for a multimillion-dollar turnover, blue-chip clients, and a large program of "good works" within the community—great thoughts, but hardly a project for an afternoon.

However, when asked about the first signs of these objectives happening, they changed perspective from the inspirational vision to the details of much smaller, more doable actions: letters they could send, meetings they could prepare for and arrange.

Describing the first signs of progress in a tricky situation prepares us to spot progress, provides a tool for feedback about what's working and—most of all—generates hope. However, you may sometimes meet people who know exactly what they need to do and still don't do it.

The Solutions Focus in action: The step so small it wasn't worth taking

John knew that both he and his team would work better if he spent more time with them, but he spent a long time away representing his firm to customers. As the business development director, he was keenly aware of his role representing the firm overseas—and also of his managerial responsibilities to the team back at base.

He realized he should engage with the team, but was easily seduced by the knowledge that there were only 30 minutes until his close-of-day gathering with the other directors. "No point doing it for 30 minutes: This is so important that it needs at least an hour," he said.

This happened again and again, while the team despaired of seeing him. It was only when he figured that the first sign might be that he showed up at all, if only for 10 minutes, that he finally made a move. He nervously went along to the team office, discovered that they weren't going to string him up for dereliction of duty, and had a productive discussion.

It is only by taking a first step that anyone starts a fresh interaction, by involving other people and taking the opportunity to set off some new futures.

Quick

Aim for *actions that can be taken tomorrow*—or within the next few days at the latest. Change is happening all the time and you want to hitch your ride on its bandwagon as soon as possible. A more immediate change gets us going: Personal inertia is broken and we enjoy the new feeling of impetus.

You will start seeing results—impacts of the actions—sooner rather than later.

Starting

Why *starting something rather than stopping*? It is often easier to start something new than to stop something. Anything that is a habit is by definition difficult to stop. And, if change is encouraged by positive reinforcement, it is much easier to be aware of when you are taking the reinforceable action than to know when you are not doing whatever it is that you want to give up. Is the crucial moment now or an hour ago—when is the moment to reinforce?

On the other hand, if you are doing something new, you know exactly when the reinforcement can take place and you have the bonus of mental reinforcement: You are pleased that you are engaging in the new behavior.

If stopping something happens to be an important part of a solution, decide what counts for you as the opposite of the unwanted behavior. Perhaps finding something to admire is the opposite of making a complaint: Finishing a task list is often the opposite of leaving work undone. A creative way to find opposites is to ask: "What would surprise people?"

Opposites may well be actions that the change seeker has taken before, forgotten about, and is more than willing and able to do again.

Taking new actions opens the door to celebration. Much of your most pleasurable solution-focused work will be identifying causes for celebration and choosing appropriate ways of celebrating the new actions that are helping people stay on track of their desired future.

Specific

The criteria *specific and clearly defined* will be familiar to many goal setters. We call an action specific in contrast to generic. If someone says that they will improve their communication with colleagues, they are making a generic pledge. To make a specific pledge, they would need to say which colleague or colleagues. They could make the pledge even more specific by saying when and by defining which form of communication they have in mind. So "I shall send an email to Harry by the end of tomorrow about stock levels on the third floor" is pretty specific.

Some action setters worry that by making this sort of commitment, they are missing all the other elements that the more general "improving communications" encompasses. After all, while Harry may get the message, he is the only one who will.

In practice, however, all the interactions engendered by the initial action tend to result in whatever it is that our action taker means by improved communication. Harry will respond and make changes to the stock level. Meanwhile, anyone else involved will be taking their carefully selected specific actions, and our change seeker will be alert to those changes that are most useful within the communication strand.

By contrast, a vague notion of improving communication, however well intentioned, leaves the option of no action at all—and quite possibly no sense of the absence of that action. In that case, nothing deliberate is done and nothing intentionally changes.

The more detail, the more specific. The more clearly defined a goal is, the easier it will be to know that the action has taken place or is happening.

The clearer the action, the more likely it is to occur for another reason: The owner of the action knows precisely what is entailed by their promise of action, and so does anyone else who has heard it. Both specifications act as motivators.

For the right people

The final criterion is that it is *for the action taker to do*. Again, this may appear obvious. If so, you would be amazed by how many people create actions to be taken by others—often their colleagues, and not infrequently their consultants. Such actions are fine, if that is what the colleagues or consultants want to do. But they are not solution-focused actions undertaken by the customer for change.

After the small steps—finding more counters

Although you hope that the agreed actions will be useful, your main intent is to find what works. What works may or may not be what you expected to
work—accidents, random events, special circumstances, aspects you hadn't noticed before can all produce interesting and vital results. So review the action by asking: "What's better? How did you do that?"

This question maintains the Solutions Focus by keeping clear of problem talk and staying with details of what is working. The idea is not that the task will work (though it may well have some beneficial effects), but that you use it to *enhance your knowledge of what does work.*

This is a vital point. The Solutions Focus is an iterative process, deliberately capitalizing on how the future emerges from the immensely complex set of interactions that is the present. We don't know what will happen, but we do know how to harness it, whatever it is.

Questions to ask about change that is happening:

✔ What's better?
✔ What did you do that made the change happen?
✔ What did others do?
✔ What effects have the changes had?
✔ Who has noticed?
✔ What do you think will change next?

The Solutions Focus in action: Is today a gold day?

Kevin was facing a problem familiar to many of us. His in-tray was always full, no matter how hard he worked. There was always something to do at work. That had been fine with him up to now, but he was spending less and less time at home in the early evenings—exactly when his young son was being bathed and preparing for bed. As a responsible dad, Kevin desperately wanted to be there to play with his son and help his wife.

At a solutions coaching session, Kevin identified various counters that might allow him to get away on time. But he was still unsure quite how it was all going to fit together. He agreed to simply note the days when he went home earlier and what happened on those days. These would be called his gold days. After two weeks he reviewed the gold days, wondering what was different about them. In this case, it seemed to help if he started the day with a firm idea about when he wanted to leave (not just "at a reasonable time"), worked with his secretary at certain times of the day (but not others) and remembered his paternal role (by looking at the photograph of his wife and child on his desk).

His subsequent task—predicting in advance whether this would be a gold day or not—was even more helpful in drawing his attention to his own methods of getting out of the office early enough to see his son before bedtime.

Now you have an even greater stock of counters, you define more small actions and refine the skeleton keys. Once you possess a key that fits your lock, hold on to it and keep inserting it when you need to.

Potential pitfall: Applying ill-fitting theories

"Laws" of physics—laws without exceptions (so far)

We build up knowledge from experience and experience can be generalized. In science, for example, observation and logic have led us to define "laws of physics" or "laws of nature." And "law of nature" has with good reason become an expression for anything that is always the case.

The law of gravity, for example, states the ways in which objects attract each other. These are utterly consistent and operate without exception.

The precise mechanism of attraction is not well understood and searches continue for gravity waves, but the attractive force itself is always there. If anyone can produce an exception—by demonstrating a situation in which gravity does not exert a force on an object—they will swiftly claim a Nobel Prize and worldwide fame.

Laws of economics—a step away

Classical economists, wanting to learn from and emulate science, set out to find similarly universal laws about how people interact with money. As economists soon realized, people are different from physical particles in that they make choices, sometimes rationally, sometimes not. The workings of choice are much more difficult to handle mathematically than particle interactions, and so economists hatched the idea of "rational agents," people who made only rational choices based on the information they had and who could see the impact of those choices infinitely into the future. This makes the mathematics easier, but at a cost of moving a step away from the world we live in. People don't have all the information at once, they cannot see far into the future, and even when they can they do not always make the rational choice.

As economics developed, economists increasingly worked with mathematics. In particular, they developed detailed models and conclusions based on the idea of rational agents. But the extent to which these models have led to a better understanding of the real world is debatable. Real-life interventions based on economic theories and models are also often controversial: Different economists subscribe to different models, and even within a particular model there are huge difficulties concerning measurements and quality of data.[1]

Management theories

In the field of management science there are also many theories. One business theory is that you will succeed if you are first to a market. Another, contrasting theory is that the first businesses to a market will fail: They are the most vulnerable and those that wait and learn from the mistakes of the brave pioneers will reap the greater rewards. Both theories are supported by a number of examples and are created by the logical step of induction: When events are observed to occur consistently, it is reasonable to assume they may continue to do so, and we can revise the theory if at some point this ceases to be the case.

This pair of theories, like all theories (the laws of physics aside), will have exceptions, times when the theory is not borne out in practice. Yet somehow it seems that the theories persist even in the face of many counter-examples. They take on a life of their own and can cause mischief long after their credibility should have vanished.

In organizations there are many pervasive theories. They may be implicit: guiding assumptions within the organization that are rarely if ever expressed. Sometimes you can spot them when you hear management by slogan. For example:

❏ All improvements have to be planned.
❏ If you cannot measure it, you cannot manage it.
❏ Strategic planning is always a waste of time.
❏ Strategic planning is always necessary.
❏ Underlying issues must be tackled in a structured way.
❏ People are motivated only by money.
❏ Lower prices mean higher sales.

Slogans are fine, but they are not always true. Sometimes they help and sometimes they get you stuck—and leave you no way out. For example, if you think improvements must always be planned, you may reject a useful unplanned improvement and hamper productive change.

You may have heard philosopher Alfred Korzybski's famous quote from his 1920 book *Science and Sanity*: "A map is not the territory." This draws the distinction between the map—the theory through which we understand what we observe—and the territory—the observations themselves.

Gurdjieff's ant story

Some ants feasted at a fabulous picnic, went back to the anthill, and drew a map for the other ants, showing how to get back to the picnic. Many ants visited and had a splendid meal. Soon many of them wanted copies of the map, and whoever had a copy was very important. Shrines were built around the copies. When the map sometimes failed to lead to a picnic, there were arguments about whether the ants concerned had understood the map correctly. But the map itself was never questioned, even though often those who followed it didn't find a picnic.[2]

Pledging allegiance to a theory is to risk ignoring cases contrary to the theory—for our purposes, the multitude of actions that real people take to change matters and improve their lives and their businesses.

Theories with exceptions

The management theories that have been hatched to help us understand common situations suffer from exceptions, instances when the theory doesn't apply in the real world. While there are no exceptions to our theories about gravity (yet), there are many occasions in other fields—in economics, the social sciences, psychology, management—where theory and practice don't add up.

Medicine: HIV in Africa

In medicine, for example, a widely held theory states that any individual who has sexual contact with someone with HIV is at high risk of contracting HIV themselves. Yet there is at least one exception. A small group of sex workers in Nairobi had not contracted HIV, even though they had been exposed many times. It transpires that they have a genetic mutation that makes them resistant.

Interestingly, this was not discovered by examining those with HIV (taking a problem focus). By taking a solutions focus and examining instances when the "problem" of HIV infection didn't occur—although it would have been expected to—a vital link was found. Genetics expert Professor Steve Jones says that this discovery does not as yet lead directly to a solution to the AIDS epidemic.

However, at the current rate of progress of human genome research, it would not surprise us if one day it did.

Economics: Mackerel in Scotland

One basic economic theory that governs the actions of many sales teams is that bringing down the price helps you sell more. But this didn't apply to selling mackerel in Scottish fishing villages, where the bottom-feeding mackerel were thought to be dirty in some way. People were reluctant to buy them even for their cats. Then the price was put up and suddenly mackerel was selling well as people began to take the fish seriously as food: "If that's the price, they must be worth something."

The many exceptions to theories might be considered a nuisance, as they prevent academics from convincing us that they have understood the world correctly. To others they are a boon, demonstrating how the richness of global experience harbors useful surprises.

Theory guides perception

We form theories in order to help us understand, which is a perfectly natural desire. The danger is when our supposed understanding blocks fresh evidence or tempts us to fit the facts to the theory instead of the theory to the facts.

According to one famous story, philosopher Karl Popper was working with deprived children in 1919. He was having difficulty with a case and went to the experienced Alfred Adler for supervision. Popper reported that he had presented the case to Adler, who had straightaway analyzed it according to his theory of inferiority feelings, even though he had not lain eyes on the child concerned. Slightly shocked, Popper asked him how he could be so sure on such small evidence. "Because of my thousand-fold experience," he said, to which Popper added, "And with this case, I suppose, your experience has become thousand-and-one-fold."[3]

In particular, beware of theories saying that things are not possible, even when they actually happen. One theory of alcoholism, for example, says that it is an incurable disease. Yet there are plenty of people who have drunk heavily for years, then stopped or reduced their drinking to a satisfactory level. The theory cannot account for this, except to say that they are in denial or remission, or that they weren't "really" alcoholics. A simpler explanation is to say that alcoholism is not always or necessarily a disease: Some people drink too much, and then stop drinking too much.

The mark of such theories is their all-encompassing nature, indicated here by the word "incurable." Watch out for theories including "always," "never," or their equivalents. Unless they are laws of physics, treat them with caution.

Note also that if many people are in thrall to a theory, this may give you—as a skeptic—a source of advantage, able to create results that shouldn't happen or shouldn't work, but do. Recall the story of the skeptical Dublin engineer who said of the newly opened Liffey bridge, "It's all very well in practice but it'll never work in theory."

Potential pitfall: "Knowing" too much

In applying a solutions focus you adopt a beginner mind, alert to what is happening and aiming to avoid prejudging what is important. As detective Sherlock Holmes says in *A Study in Scarlet*: "It is a capital mistake to theorise before you have all the evidence. It biases judgement."

If you have started with preconceptions, while you are following up your expectations and hunches, the vital information about what works can be streaming over your head, out of the window and into oblivion.

"We know what works"— Consulting firm advertisement seen at Newark Airport "You know what works and we can help you find it"—The Solutions Focus advertisement, location to be decided.

If we offer a theory, it is a theory about the general nature of change, not a theory about organizations. The trouble with theories about organizations is that the theories implicitly suggest the causes of the organization's problems, and distract from the solutions. If you come in with a theory about organizations, then everything is explained without the need for wondering what is significantly different here.

From theory to observation

When we have explanations, those explanations invite judgments. The explanation will be either right or wrong. Theories, too, operate in a realm of right and wrong: Contributors to the debate aim to prove or disprove their own and others' ideas. The energy is addressed to the debate, diverted from the solution. Kudos goes to the winner or the best arguer, not always to the deviser of the neatest or most practical resolution.

> *"We must do away with all explanation, and description alone must take its place."*
> *Ludwig Wittgenstein,*
> Philosophical Investigations
> *109*

In taking the Solutions Focus, resist the temptation to prove or disprove anything. Rather, seek to help with this case at this time. Observe carefully, pick up on events, remarks, actions and intentions that are helping the customer for change to reach their goal.

Here and now

The discipline of treating each case as different is closely allied to the requirement for an improvisational performer to be "here and now."[4] Alternatives to "now" are the past, in which you are remembering how something used to be or are making judgments based on the expectations that you brought to the situation; or the future, in which the mind is leaping ahead to the next question, next meeting, or another branch labeled "wishful thinking."

Sometimes we are invited to meet people and told about them in advance: "He's a pain, always moaning," or "She's very sensitive, take care." So the reputation of the person sets our expectations and we end up noticing and responding to what we've been told. Beware of dealing with the person's reputation rather than what you observe for yourself.

The Solutions Focus in action: Knowing what's what at SAS

Scandinavian Airlines (SAS) president and CEO Jan Carlzon offers an example of noticing and capitalizing on a useful change, switching policy from the previous problem-focused approach.

He tells how the airline proposed to solve the problems of elderly Swedish travelers, with their fear of traveling abroad, cranky stomachs, and aversion to sunbathing, by creating apartment-type suites, hosted by medically trained matrons.

When they invited a small group from a Stockholm retirement club to discuss the proposals, the senior citizens were unimpressed, saying that they preferred excitement, adventure and beaches on their travels. The airline launched their new suites anyway, and only abandoned them when the pensioners "didn't show up."

At last they listened to what the customers were saying, stopped trying to think about their problems—which were leading to unwanted "solutions"— and provided genuine solutions by servicing the new ambitions of a still lively clientele who knew what they wanted from the possibilities offered by a modern airline service.

Adopt a beginner mind

One useful idea in working with what's there and appreciating that every case is different is "not knowing." If we know beforehand what is important in solving a particular kind of problem, then we are already risking missing some vital elements of what makes this case different.

Solutions depend on your specific situation and on all the tiny details and factors that make you and your organization what you are. So instead of recipes or 1–2–3 routines for change, we offer a template for finding out for yourself what to do.

Although you may be an expert as a manager or in your technical field, when you aim to create useful

> *"In the mind of the expert, there are few possibilities. In the mind of the beginner there are many."*
> *Shunryu Suzuki*

change in complex circumstances, it is to your advantage to adopt a beginner mind and reap the benefit of additional possibilities. When a situation feels stuck, the obvious possibilities have probably already been tried and found wanting.

To see the most possibilities for change in a certain situation, it may help to know little or nothing about the generalities of the field concerned. Professor John Ziman has observed, "It is well known that major scientific progress often comes from scientists who have crossed conventional disciplinary boundaries, and have no more authority than a layman in an unfamiliar field."[5]

The Solutions Focus entails starting afresh with each assignment, listening, noticing and responding to everyone individually. Build up your ideas from scratch each time—partly to ensure that you are responding to this case rather than last week's, and partly because the solutions this time will be different and will stem from what you discover.

Jumping to assumptions

Part of not knowing about the situation is not to leap to judgments about what people are thinking. Instead, assume a more general positive intent. Let's assume that there may be a positive intent behind behavior that appears to be negative or unhelpful. For example, if someone is persistently late for work, steer clear of "Why are you late for work?" and instead ask something like "I'm sure you have a good reason for being late for work?" These two conversations head in two quite different directions and there are no prizes for guessing the more productive.

The more useful conversation benefits both from the tone that the participant with the beginner mind is likely to adopt and from the question's greater chance of uncovering resources rather than deficits.

Note that there is no element of wishful thinking or evasion of difficult facts. The person is late and that will be dealt with. What is different about a solution-focused approach is how the person is treated (in this case with respect rather than suspicion or blame) and how the lateness is investigated as a potential source of a solution (perhaps the late-comer has been doing something else during that time that is of immediate or potential benefit to the organization).

The physical position you adopt can also affect the relationship of expertise. A trainer can take a low–status position, for example by crouching at a flipchart to take notes while others explain the details of a pertinent situation. Or you might sit on the floor while a group of people are on chairs, if you want to underline their expertise and your position of not knowing. The person on the floor is demonstrating humility and it is surprising how it can ease the strain in tense group settings.

> *"To succeed in life you need two things: ignorance and confidence."*
> Mark Twain

The Solutions Focus in action: The value of not knowing

A solution-focused consultant was asked to work with British Aerospace on the repair and refitting of an aircraft that had fallen behind schedule. Understandably in the rush, there was insufficient time to arrange a full briefing before the series of workshops with the supervisory teams began, so she devoted one of the first sessions to analyzing and describing the issues.

She said, "I know very little about what's been happening on this project. You know every aspect, and I would appreciate it if you helped me to understand."

The participants split into two groups to compile a prioritized list of reasons to explain why the work was lagging. Attending the course meant time away from their project and they wanted to know—some of them asked aggressively—"What can you do?" The atmosphere was tense as they presumably waited for the consultant to offer an instant solution, which they would know they had either already tried or was way off beam.

When she stressed the absence of prefigured solutions, they seemed pleased that she was not claiming to have the answers, and they certainly did not mind her not knowing the details of a situation that they had been experiencing for many months.

The group relaxed and, in that atmosphere, the consultant exposed levers implied by their analyses. The purpose of having two groups was to provide each group with a second perspective—to enjoy the advantages of stereo over mono—and perhaps to discover some aspects that they didn't "know" or had not fully appreciated.

Because she did not know the details in advance, it was clear that she had not been briefed by senior management. She could present herself as being more on their side than that of senior management, which led easily to solutions rather than blame.

Potential pitfall: Relying on "experts"

The insistence on not knowing and setting aside theories does not mean abdicating the responsibility to provide expertise. Your expertise has a part to play. It puts you in the privileged position of being genuinely impressed by your customers: the ones with knowledge of the situation, those who have been trying to resolve the problem, whose efforts will lead to the solution this time.

You know that moment when the plumber looks at your water tank and takes a sharp intake of breath: "Phooow! Who put that in for you? What a cowboy! What on earth was he thinking of?" and so on. You might say instead: "Wow! How have you been managing with this system? You've been going short of hot water? That must have been difficult in the winter."

Being impressed by your customers for change is a shortcut to a good working relationship, even if the tank *has* been installed badly. This is not to deny any of the facts, it is to reorient ourselves.

Experts and their place

Ed Schein made important distinctions in his book *Process Consulting*. He described various relationships between consultants and their clients. Some clients want:

❑ To purchase expertise—like hiring a plumber to clear out a blocked drain.
❑ Problem diagnosis—such as an audit of a troublesome IT system.
❑ A way forward—for example a team wanting to work together better.

All of these are honorable reasons for hiring people to help you solve your problems. A solution-focused consultant, along with most facilitative methods, operates within the third category, which Schein calls process consulting. The consultant helps the client by taking them through a process.

> "Consultancy is two people talking, trying to figure out what the hell one of them wants."

However, most process consulting is, wittingly or not, problem focused. The consultant begins by examining the client's problem and even pointing out problems that they didn't know they had.

Solution-focused process consulting respects the client's knowledge of their own situations, does not second guess them and certainly does not invent problems from the consultant's perspective. We are aware that our own ideas may cloud the issue at this stage, when the primary aim is to learn the client's view about the client's way forward.

> "It's not that I don't care what the problem is. It's more that I don't think [the consultant] would know any better than I. And anyway, it's more important to identify the solution than to understand the problem."
> Professor Andrew Derrington[6]

Remember to keep it simple and work at the surface—everything you need is there.

Potential pitfall: Acting "solution forced," not solution focused

As you think and act in a solution-focused way, you may also need to note the varying degrees to which your colleagues (and if you're a consultant, your clients) feel the need to tell you about their problems. While some are ready immediately to join conversation about the solution, others want to spend more time telling you about their problems.

A vital part of taking seriously what people say is to allow them to say it—whatever it is. We should let them know that we have heard and comment on what they have said. Problems can appear big or insurmountable, particularly when the sufferer feels that no one has properly understood just how daunting they are.

In these situations, it is most important to:

Be solution focused—not solution forced.

Sometimes, in their excitement to deploy the Solutions Focus, people become over keen. Take this example, in which Jeff arrives in the office of Karen, his manager:

Jeff: "Sorry Karen. I'm afraid the monthly team report isn't ready yet."
Karen (fuming): "Again! That's three months in a row! Look Jeff, tell me about the times this doesn't happen! Huh."

While Karen commendably wants to apply the Solutions Focus here, she seems unlikely to get results. The Solutions Focus is a collaborative method, and Karen has better prospects of constructive responses from Jeff when the heat is lower. Meanwhile, she could ask herself the most basic of solution-focused questions:

❑ Is what I'm doing working?
❑ Am I getting the results I want?

Of course, if Jeff happens to respond with talk about when matters go better, then this is working, so carry on. If not, another approach might create different results. Now Karen is applying the Solutions Focus to herself, rather than to her and Jeff and the monthly team report.

So, when you're working with other people:

❑ Gently encourage people to focus on solutions.
❑ Beware of forcing people to focus on solutions when they want, for now, to do something else.

Every case is different—Summary

✔ Assume that every case is different and find what fits this particular case, with the elegance of a skeleton key.

✔ Small actions can quickly and easily shed light on what works.

✔ Avoid applying ill-fitting theories—look for the exceptions.

✔ If you "know" a lot, you may not look very hard—adopt a beginner mind.

✔ Use experts wisely and cautiously—you may know more about you than they do.

✔ Act solutions focused, not solutions forced.

9

The Complete Toolkit

You can apply the Solutions Focus anywhere you encounter a complex problem. Not only is the scope for applications huge, so is the number of variations for deploying the solutions tools.

Just as every case is different, so too is every practitioner of the Solutions Focus. As long as you are taking as direct a route as you can to find what works in your particular case, you are applying the Solutions Focus.

What you will not be doing is adopting methods that:

✗ Focus on problems rather than solutions.
✗ Apply a general recipe that someone else has defined as what works.
✗ Identify deficits, in teams or individuals.

You will recall the SIMPLE approach:

Solutions not problems
Inbetween—the action is in the interaction
Make use of what's there
Possibilities—past, present and future
Language—simply said
Every case is different

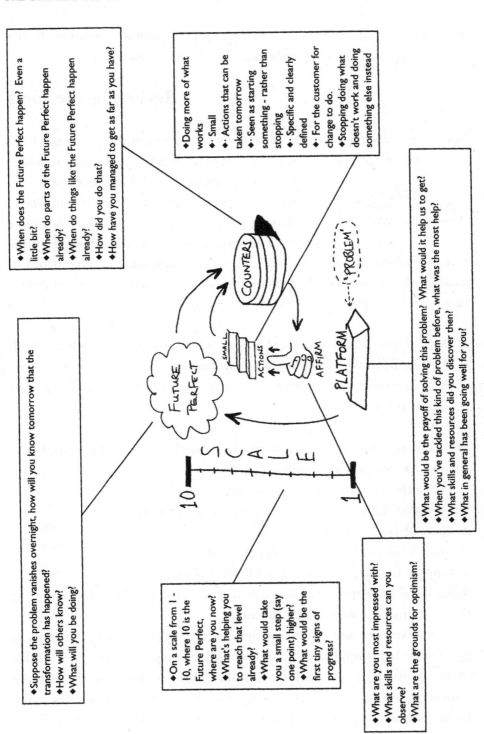

The simplicity of the Solutions Focus expresses itself in a set of tools that you can apply to each different case (see diagram opposite).

Reviewing the tools

You have encountered the tools one by one through the previous chapters. They are presented above in a typical order in which you might apply them when dealing with your problems.

Let's begin with the platform. *Establishing a platform* is the starting point for change. Typically, you have a problem or someone comes to you with one. By converting problem to platform you shift your perspective: The issue is not so much problematic as a set of circumstances that provides a point of departure. The word "platform" contains suggestions of:

✔ A solid structure that is there already, a foundation on which to build.
✔ A place from which horizons are visible.
✔ A departure point—at least a hope that a train, for example, may be about to leave.

We want to establish the platform early in the process, to support the changes we are going to make.

From the platform we shift our attention to the *future perfect*. This is the state of affairs desired and designated by the customer for change. It is how things will be without the problem. There is a way to suppose the future perfect quickly and effectively:
What if the problem went away overnight—what would be happening in the morning that would let you know?

Once we have some sense of the desired future, we seek elements of that future happening already, and identify the resources that will enable us to approach it; we may even realize that we have many of those resources already. Our next step then is to *find counters*: resources, skills, know-how and expertise that will count in getting us toward the solution.

Counters are:

✔ Aspects of the future perfect that are already happening or have happened before.
✔ Times when the problem is absent or less prominent.
✔ Resources and skills that have been helpful before or are likely to prove helpful soon.
✔ Ways in which matters are being handled well already.

They come in various denominations. One of the most valuable is: "When does the solution happen already?"

When you find counters, it usually helps to let those involved know what you have found and assure them that they are of value. There is a tendency to neglect and underestimate our resources in the face of daunting prob-lems and challenges. The next strategic step, then, is to *affirm what is helping*. One method is to offer compliments to draw atten-tion to resources and skills that people unearth during their solution seeking. Compliments, resources and skills are all counters—anything that counts.

Wielding these tools generates at least a sense of possible movement, and more often a long list of possible actions. One of the temptations along the way is to select an action too early in the process. Exciting though it may be suddenly to see a way out of a problem's gloom, it is good practice to wait until you can consider all the possible actions sug-gested while using these tools, and then select the *small actions* or set of actions that are most likely to bring the results you desire. It is often astonishing to note how small a well-chosen action can be and still make a big difference.

Naturally, you want to note the differences that the actions have made in progress toward a solution, which is why the arrows take you back into find-ing counters. Any progress is a further counter toward a solution, and allows a fresh visit into further affirmations and choices of the next small steps.

10 ⊤
  S
  C
  A
  L
  E
1 ⊥

Connecting all these elements is a *scale* running from 1—the problem at its worst—to 10—the future perfect realized in all its miraculous splendor. You apply the scale ingeniously to bring out the differences that make a difference, to measure progress and even to generate it.

The diagram on page 127 illustrates one route toward solutions, but we are not constrained. Every case is different and it often turns out that there are other routes through the elements, which can prove equally rewarding. In different cases, different elements will be more or less significant. In one case the definition of the future perfect will be a crucial step. In another the future perfect is left until you have established some basic confidence by identifying counters. In a third, the art of scaling may provide a quick focus on what needs to happen next. Calculating which areas are productive—and applying them—is a large part of the art of the Solutions Focus.

All the tools in action

The top team of the British division of an international medical supplies company wanted to create a strategy for change. It set aside two days to apply the Solutions Focus with the 12 participants, who included the managing director, the senior managers, account executives and the sales team. Another aim of the workshop was to improve team spirit.

Platform (1)

The platform was succinctly and uncontentiously described by the managing director. This was a successful company, growing at a satisfactory rate. The team generally worked well together, although there were tensions between office-based staff and the salesforce who were out on the road. Communication could be better and there was a lot of stress. Because there were several recent recruits, not everyone knew each other.

The two days began with personal introductions, aiming to break the ice, help people get to know each other and uncover more platform information. It was also a way to start the session with problem-free talk, avoiding any prospect of a depressing atmosphere of gloom or insurmountable difficulties.

As everyone knew that the main aim of the program was to work out a strategy, it made sense to delay supposing the future perfect in favor of an activity that could do the double duty of increasing the team's knowledge of each individual and uncovering personal counters that would almost certainly serve whatever strategy they decided later to adopt.

Counters: Resources

Members of the team described their achievements. One had climbed a challenging series of rocks to scale a big Spanish mountain. Her climbing group had roped themselves together to guard against falling. She was complimented on her ability to share and exhibit trust.

Another was involved in running two businesses, which prompted compliments regarding energy, drive and organizational abilities. Someone else had a passion for performing in musicals, exhibiting qualities of teamwork, presentation skills, and creative flair.

Even the less promising mentions of interest, such as shopping for shoes, allowed colleagues to note how smart the participant looked. Each compliment pointed out resources and created an atmosphere of sharing, and many discovered things they had not known about each other before, certainly not in such a positive, problem-free light.

Platform (2)

Then they described their work-life, by presenting a semi-improvised scenario of a typical day. From the performance and the discussion it sparked, they clearly demonstrated their feelings of being in two camps.

On the one side are the customer service staff, toiling in the office, pressured by telephones continually ringing, delivery deadlines, unreliable couriers, materials not arriving at hospitals, surgeons shouting at them. Everyone joins in the firefighting, which builds up a backlog of the scheduled tasks and further stress.

On the other side is the sales team, individuals isolated on the road, resentful when forced to call in during their busy periods to managers who didn't appear to want to hear from them just then.

And, apparently, each group had up to now been almost entirely unaware of the particular stresses of the other. In fact, far from displaying understanding of the other camp's problems, the office-based staff were expressing resentment at the potentially uneven splits of rewards and bonuses, with the sales staff raking in the cash when orders were booming; while on the other hand, the sales people envied the office team with their guaranteed salary no matter how tough the market conditions.

Affirming: Compliments

Even when presented with a challenging or potentially depressing picture, there is plenty of opportunity for compliments. Here the senior managers in a busy organization had impressively dedicated two days of their time to a joint quest for solutions, frankly portrayed rich details of their working lives and incisively identified several important, topical issues.

The future perfect

The first inkling of the preferred future was provided by their objectives, which they listed individually and discussed in pairs early in the workshop. They were saying they wanted:

❑ Clear business targets.
❑ The chance to raise issues.
❑ To learn about each other and from each other.
❑ To gain confidence.
❑ To identify where the newcomers would fit into the company.

In groups of four they drew poster-sized pictures of the future perfect. The drawings revealed a great deal more detail, including:

❑ Sales exceeding targets.
❑ More happy clients.
❑ A particular surgeon, Mr X, buying the 100th model of a certain machine (let's call it the one that goes ping).
❑ A network of sales locations covering a map of the UK, with a diagram of communication links.
❑ A team approximately twice the current size, depicted on an organization chart.

- ❑ A celebration of a couple of key promotions within the team.
- ❑ A hospital operation succeeding by using a recent item from their catalog.
- ❑ A newspaper headline awarding them a "company of the year" trophy.
- ❑ A series of sales training meetings, with each salesperson presenting to the others in turn.

Counters

There was plenty of vivid detail and it certainly looked like a future in which everything was going very well indeed—but was it too futuristic or too perfect to be true (or useful)? To elicit counters you simply ask how much of the vision is already happening. "We're doing a lot of that now," one of the team said.

For example their counters—aspects of the future perfect that had previously happened or were occurring now—included exceeding sales targets in consecutive periods. This was immediately heartening for the new sales recruits.

Times when their problems were absent or less prominent included their gaining confidence in using new skills. In one recent instance Helen, an experienced salesperson, had used a technique picked up during a training session to close a sale that had previously eluded her. Instead of asking the surgeon whether he would use the product soon, she had asked him when and where—which he told her, and then did.

They also built their stack of counters by listing their many currently successful methods. When a group faces great challenges, it helps if their counters are robust, and so the group played the part of skeptical inspectors to each other's claims. What would inspectors require? Evidence. Evidence in sufficient detail to convince them that the claim could be substantiated.

Compelling evidence for the build-up to the 100th sale, for example, was the story the sales manager told about when he had invited a prospective client to visit a hospital that had installed the machine: to watch it in action, talk to the engineer, ask questions and clinch a sale. Having done it once and found it worked well, he planned to do it again, with confidence.

Scaling

For other parts of the future perfect the counters were more scarce and the evidence skimpier and less compelling. The staff scaled each of their drawings to indicate the current position, proffering a wide range from picture to picture. The picture for selling the 100th machine, for example, they rated as 2, because they had sold only a few so far. Yet having noticed a counter that seemed a real breakthrough, they now felt there was good potential for racing up the scale.

The picture for sales training meetings rated 8, because it seemed only a small step from get-togethers that they already held when other issues formed the agenda.

Small actions

A number of skill-building activities during the two days instantly provided the team's first actions for moving closer toward the preferred future. They improved their interpersonal communications and continued to alert themselves to the resources that they would need for their quest. They told each other, for example, about their best experiences of teamwork, analyzed what had made these exceptional, and identified the part they had played in enabling that team to work well together.

One person, for instance, had coordinated the planning of a family wedding, successfully delegating many important tasks to the 40 people involved. Another had organized a charity dinner, finding this a meaningful activity that inspired and motivated the volunteers to give of their best.

Affirming

To explicitly build their resource bank, each participant told the others "What I bring to the company," to which the listeners added a selection of compliments. So when Clive, who had described himself earlier as stressed, now said that his contribution was "organization," he was pleased and surprised to hear others mention that he brought a good calming presence.

In one of the problem-solving team-building activities, they noted that all were keen to participate (no one volunteered to observe!), and they also noted an ability to listen to each other's ideas, valuing them before proceeding. Their competitive streak was manifest too: Once the others knew that one group had a solution to a puzzle, the others intensified their efforts to reach it. Interestingly, if a solution was assumed to be possible, they spent less time belaboring the problem and more time solution seeking.

More small actions

Making changes sometimes requires breaking habits. After an energizing activity in which participants experienced success by trying new ways of acting, there was a gleam of openness to change. Felicity had explained that she enjoyed the buzz of hearing her sales results the moment the order was confirmed at head office. And a colleague was proposing a new routine for telephone calls, for those who wanted it. Felicity said, "I'm a creature of habit, I want my results as they come in... Though actually I might try the new way soon, and see how it works out."

The team members discussed and proposed a number of changes. Everyone wanted a better system for telephone contact between customer services and the salespeople.

The regular evening calls from salespeople to head office were at the wrong time for both parties, covering information they didn't want (at that time) and missing bits they did want.

With the possible exception of Felicity, everyone was keen to experiment with a phone call from the office to the sales team, in the morning rather than the evening. These routine calls would be from base to field instead of the other way round, thus avoiding the busiest firefighting times at base.

The solution was so obvious, they wondered why they hadn't thought of it before. It transpired that the current system was based entirely on history and habit. It had started in the days before mobile phones, when there was only one salesperson, who of course had to call the office because there was no way of the office knowing her whereabouts. And the call was in the evening so that she could collect the day's messages left for her at the office.

They anticipated that the new system would ease the pressure considerably, creating more time for any genuinely urgent messages to be dealt with more promptly. Acknowledging that they knew more about one another's circumstances, and expressing an active willingness to help, they decided to hold a monthly meeting, with one sales representative and a set of procedures to enable everyone to have their say.

Among many other ideas, they would also learn more about one another's work by visiting one another's patches. They would eliminate unnecessary duplication of forms, and two office workers who needed to sort out their work share would meet to discuss the appropriate level of delegation.

Most of the elements of the preferred future were entirely within their own grasp and many were adopted within the week.

Follow-up

Within a month, the team members had taken most of the promised actions, delaying or slightly changing only a few when faced with the cold light of reality. "There's a good feeling," said the managing director. "The staff meeting went well, and we've scheduled another. People contributed to the meeting. Everyone is working on their action plans—they know the importance of getting things done.

"The salespeople have had positive calls, and the people in the office have gone ahead with their plans for delegation."

On every issue they had agreed to tackle, they were further up the scale toward their future perfect.

Practical applications

In the following chapters, we explore ways of applying the Solutions Focus to coaching, team leadership and organizational development, three popular strands of finding what works at work.

10

Coaching Solutions

Coaching is one of the most popular applications of solutions-focused work in organizations. The Solutions Focus has its roots in psychotherapy, which shares with coaching the common working ground of purposeful conversations. As with therapy, coaching conversations may be between two people or involve a small group.

Solutions-focused coaches are helping many individual managers and teams within companies to achieve more of their goals. Coaches in large industrial organizations, in smaller entrepreneurial enterprises, in higher education colleges, in schools and in the police force have been trained to apply solutions-focused coaching skills.

Coaching was already growing in popularity as a way of enhancing results within organizations; now, combined with solutions, there is an even more potent mix.

The traditional image of a coach, generally derived from sports, is where the coach is an expert at the sport, but is now perhaps a touch too old to compete any longer. You might imagine an ogre cycling along the riverbank hurling abuse at the rowing eight through a megaphone. Or maybe a football coach screaming from the touchline as the players strive to live up to his expectations.

Coaches in the twenty-first century act more like facilitators, helping clients to clarify their goals and ways to achieve them. The coach may act as a sounding board, as a focal point for discussions or even simply as a colleague showing an interest.

The modern coach—whether an independent practitioner working one to one with a series of clients, or a manager within an organization deliberately applying coaching as a means of handling the workload— needs a range of skills to succeed in helping a staff member or a team to improve their performance.

The various solutions tools can assist any coach in focusing a conversation and finding ways forward. Coaches are interested in helping the performer (the person being coached) to progress, and the organization is interested because that progress is almost certainly linked to results.

Coaches may or may not have expertise in the skill area applied by the performer; if they have, then another of their skills will be knowing how and when to use their expert knowledge. And any coach—whether solutions focused or not—will need to be a craftsperson, versed in techniques such as questioning and listening.

Meet OSKAR

OSKAR is a framework for solutions-focused coaching. We originally developed the model for the Coaching for Results program at Walkers Snackfoods (of which more in the next chapter) and it has since proved a versatile and flexible guideline for independent coaches as well as managers working as coaches. It is used in face-to-face and telephone coaching.

OSKAR is an acronym, standing for **O**utcome, **S**caling, **K**now-how, **A**ffirm and action, **R**eview.

When OSKAR is used as a process, we begin with *outcome*. This is the part of the conversation in which the coach discovers what the performer (the coachee) wants. We typically include both the platform and the future perfect tools when discovering an outcome. And it often makes sense to include some problem-free talk as part of your platform building.

OSKAR

1 OUTCOME
❑ What is the objective of this coaching?
❑ What do you want to achieve today?
❑ What do you want to achieve in the long term?
❑ How will you know this coaching has been of use to you?
❑ The future perfect.

2 SCALING
❑ On a scale of 0 to 10, with 10 representing the future perfect and 0 the worst it has ever been, where are you on that scale today?
❑ You are at n now: What did you do to get this far?
❑ How would you know you had got to $n+1$?

3 KNOW-HOW AND RESOURCES
❑ What helps you perform at n on the scale, rather than 0?
❑ When does the outcome already happen for you, even a little bit?
❑ What did you did to make that happen? How did you do that?
❑ What did you do differently?
❑ What would other people say you are doing well?

4 AFFIRM AND ACTION
❑ What's already going well?
❑ What is the next small step? What would you like to do personally, straight away?
❑ You are at n now, what would it take to get you to $n+1$?

5 REVIEW
❑ What's better?
❑ What did you do that made the change happen?
❑ What effects have the changes had?
❑ What do you think will change next?

Problem-free talk in coaching settings characteristically includes social chitchat, gentle resource spotting, and any context issues such as how long the session is going to last and making sure the room is comfortable or the phone line audible.

If there is to be a sequence of coaching sessions, then the outcome will include discussion of what the performer wants out of the coaching program; if it is a one-off meeting, then it is useful to discover what the performer wants from that meeting. Typical questions are "How will you know this coaching has been of use to you?" and "What has to happen for you to know the coaching has been worthwhile?" or "What has to happen in the next hour for you to know it has been time well spent?"

When the coach has grasped what the conversation is about and has a clear idea of the platform, it is often a good idea to find out the future perfect for that performer with respect to the platform topic.

This sets up a clear description of how the performer imagines matters without the problem (if there is a problem) or with them at their best, handling the issue. Benefits of creating this clear description include:

✔ A motivational pull toward it—it sounds good, so the performer wants it.
✔ The prospect of recognizing it when it happens or has happened.
✔ The prospect of selecting (from the larger description) parts of it happening now or in the future.

As ever, the future perfect is a direction setter. If a performer is clear about where they want to go, they are in position to appreciate how far they might already have come and to recognize what a step forward would be like.

One difference between coaching and therapy is that clients for therapy arrive with a problem, generally severe enough for them to be sent or to bring themselves for treatment. With organizational coaching, sometimes there's a problem—"I don't know how to deal with my lazy

colleague"—and sometimes there isn't. Instead, there may be an ambition—"I want promotion"—or a technical challenge—"I want to be
better at handling media interviews"—or even uncertainty about what's
wanted—"I've been given these sessions, but don't really have anything
in mind as yet."

We are sometimes asked if it is possible to coach someone if there is
no problem. The answer within the Solutions Focus is a very clear yes. It
is only because it is possible to create a solution with no necessary logical connection to a problem that the solutions-focused approach can
create a solution when there is a problem.

The next phase is often *scaling*. This is our familiar scaling
tool. The point here is for the performer to make a call
about where they are on the scale. It gives a sense of objec-
tivity to state a number. There is no need for the coach to
argue about the figure. The discussion is about how the performer got that high, and how they might get a step higher—a resourceful discussion about progress.

Scale numbers also open up opportunities for fruitful discussions
about differences. We might explore:

❏ Different figures from different moments in a client's life—"When
was it higher?"
❏ Different scales—perhaps for confidence and for commitment.
❏ Different perspectives—"Where would your customer put you on
that scale?"
❏ Different opinions, particularly with team coaching—"What is Dave
seeing to give this an 8, while most of you have given it a 5?"

Once we have established the appropriate scale, we can explore *know-
how*. Our interest is in what works here. And our assumption is that there
is a lot of know-how around. What can we discover about what the performer knows, what the coach might know, what others can add?

Know-how is about what works specifically in relation to the context.
It is important that the know-how fits, which is why it typically makes

sense to start with finding out what the performer knows—they are likely to have the clearest idea of the issue they are facing and the relevance of any potential know-how. Then we might look more widely.

For the performer to remain motivated, it also helps if they find the know-how for themselves—even if that means asking for it from the coach or someone else—rather than having it imposed on them (for example by having the coach tell them what to do because the coach knows best).

The search for know-how is much the same as the search for counters. We want to find out when the solution happens:

✔ When has the outcome happened already?
✔ When does the outcome happen in part, even a little?
✔ When have you had experience of something like the outcome?
✔ When did you achieve similar things before?
✔ Who else do you know who has achieved this?
✔ How did they do it?

And we want to find out what qualities and resources are available to help bring about progress:

✔ What other teams or organizations are good at this kind of thing?
✔ Where else can you find out more about what you need here?
✔ What resources are you bringing to the project?
✔ What qualities and experience do you have that are going to help you here?
✔ What did you do to make success happen?
✔ How did you do that? What did you do differently?

In short, the coach asks questions to create a sense of possibility and capability.

Then the coach sifts through the answers so as to be ready to offer *affirms*. The coach listens out for examples of what is going well, and what the performer has in their arsenal. The best of these can then be mentioned during the course of the conversation.

In the OSKAR process, a good time to reflect these experiences and qualities back to the performer is immediately before asking what action they might take to get closer to their outcome. Hearing about one's relevant, successful experiences and resourceful qualities seems as good a preparation as any for selecting a useful next step.

So the coach summarizes what has impressed them so far, then invites the performer to select a small action. This is for the performer to do personally, and is usually expressed as something they might do to take them one point up the scale:

❏ "What is the next small step for you to take personally?"
❏ "You are at n now, what would it take to get you to $n+1$?"
❏ "What's the first thing you will notice that tells you you are one point up the scale?"

The small steps are best based on what works or what is expected to work.

Choose from...
✔ The most likely to succeed
✔ The easiest
✔ A random choice
✔ Noticing what works

Choose things...
✔ To do tomorrow
✔ Concrete
✔ Starting, not stopping
✔ For the right people

In organizations, people are often used to action plans and taking pretty ambitious steps. If such a step or action plan point emerges from the coaching discussion, that is fine. However, it is not necessary. The small step in solutions-focused coaching is not a goal and not something that the performer will be tested on later. It is better thought of as a moment in a conversation, designating something that might lead to progress or unblock some stuckness. There is no particular virtue in its being large.

Indeed, it can be enough for the "action" to be along the lines of looking out for progress, a consideration of signs rather than steps. A useful question here is: "What will you notice that will tell you you are one step up the scale?"

This is clearly different from typical organizational action planning. There is, of course, a place for action planning and holding people to account for taking actions (or not taking them) and for their consequences. But that is another matter, perhaps for performance reviews or day-to-day discussions between managers and their reports, and not for OSKAR coaching.

The choice of small step is with the performer, not with the coach, though the coach will have an influence on the choice.

Once the performer has a clear sense of what they want to do (or look out for), the main purpose of the coaching session has been achieved. There may be some checking against the original platform, and the coach may add further affirms, if appropriate. If, as a coach, you have a concern that the small step is not well chosen by the performer, you might scale for confidence or commitment.

The R of OSKAR is for *review*, and refers to the start of the next session or the beginning of any subsequent session. (You might also call the checking process at the end of the first session a review.) Our interest in subsequent sessions is in what is better, what progress has been made. It also brings a cycle back to the start, to consider what might be next for the coach and performer to speak about.

✔ What's better?
✔ What did you do that made the change happen?
✔ What effects have the changes had?
✔ What do you think will change next?

The coach keeps the conversation focused on what works, looking for opportunities to give and share credit, and to find out what the client wants now. If positive results have occurred as a direct result of an action the performer took, that is fine and worthy of congratulation and exploration ("Wow, how did you do that?"). If the performer changed their mind and took actions other than those mentioned in the coaching session, that's fine too. Any progress is welcome, even if it appears to have nothing to do with any action by the performer. Better is better.

Let's consider an example of OSKAR in action, a conversation between an executive coach and a senior manager in a design and engineering company. Commentary on the conversation appears in brackets.

A coaching conversation

Coach: Hello Bridget.

Bridget: Hello, nice to meet you.

Coach: Thank you for seeing me. Perhaps you could say a bit about what it is you do.

(Invitation to problem-free talk and contextual background.)

Bridget: OK. I work for a medical device manufacturing and design company. We make devices that are used in intensive care units, and I am head of training in the company. We're an international company, our headquarters are based outside London, and I look after the training function there.

Coach: And what brings you here today?

(Continuing to build the platform as part of the outcome.)

Bridget: Well, I've been here a couple of years. It's a dynamic company, it's a great company. It's full of engineers and salespeople, and they don't seem to take training seriously. They just don't want to turn up to courses. As far as I'm concerned, training should be on the strategic map. For example, they're taking new products into the different countries, and they should be talking to us about these developments, but they don't. They see training as a jolly, a day out, something that they get sent on, and they don't turn up sometimes. And when they cancel they give us no notice. My staff are good people but they aren't getting themselves heard—they can't get their message out.

Coach: Sounds tough. You take training seriously and you'd like them to take training seriously.

(Attempting to summarize the platform. The tone of Bridget's voice indicates she is passionate and serious about her work. There is an element of affirming in the coach's comment.)

Bridget: Yes, I would.

Coach: You talk about your staff and about people who experience training. Say a little bit more about who your staff are.

Bridget: Well, I have four staff. I have an administrator, so she's the one who's pulling her hair out when these people are changing their dates. She tries to get in touch with them, but they don't call her back. And I have three other staff. One of them is very technical, he's an IT trainer; and the other two focus a lot more on sales, product information and the softer skills of management.

Coach: These three, they only deliver training?

Bridget: They deliver training and they'll go and sit down with the clients and find out a bit more about the customers, about the people, a bit of what they want, and they'll come up with other new stuff as well— it doesn't always have to be training courses.

Coach: So they assess training needs and they deliver what's needed.

Bridget: That's right.

Coach: And design?

Bridget: They do a little bit of design, and I get involved with that if they need me to help them.

Coach: Do you enjoy working with your team?

(We've established some practical resources—the team. Now the coach is wondering about what might be going well, another potential resource and area of know-how.)

Bridget: I do. I'm very fortunate. There's the odd thing that's not so good, but they're a good team. They're feeling a little bit demotivated at the moment. They think there's too much work, and the way it's received means they're not necessarily having a good time.

Coach: You'd like them to be feeling a bit more motivated?

(This sounds like another important part of the outcome.)

Bridget: Yeah, and I feel that myself, you know, it's hard for me. I'm feeling like we've put everything into this and we're not getting back what we'd like: some recognition, and for people to actually take us seriously.

(The platform seems pretty clear, so let's find out more detail about what she would like the situation to be—the future perfect, the solution.)

Coach: Right. I'm going to ask you a rather strange question, OK? Suppose we finish this conversation today, and you go off to do the rest of your work; then you go home, do what you do in the evening, and go to sleep... And while you're asleep, a miracle happens... you know, just like that... and the miracle is that all these problems go away and the training is happening the way you want it: You've got a motivated team, you're feeling the way you want to about it, and the recipients of the training are receiving it in the way you want them to. All of that happens in this miracle. But of course you're asleep, so you don't know the miracle has actually happened. When you get back into work the next day, how will you know?

(Bridget pauses to think and the coach waits.)

Bridget: How will I know? I'll get into work and the first thing I do is turn on my computer. I usually do that, and I'll still have that space for myself. I'll check my emails and... instead of the emails that say we can't do this, or the lack of response even to emails I've sent out, I'll get things coming from other people confirming that they are coming on courses. And they'll be requesting stuff.

Coach: Requesting stuff?

Bridget: Yes, you know, requesting training courses, or development for their teams. Or they'll be requesting one of my staff to work with them, and I'll be copied in on the things that are happening.

Coach: Such as?

Bridget: Well, we have reams of sales and profit information that can influence product development. They'd have copied me in on that. They'd have copied me in on some of the area manager meetings as well. So some of the bigger strategic stuff I'd be copied in on, but I'm not wishing myself huge emails here—just some of these documents. So my emails would be quite different.

Coach: Your emails would be different. And in particular, they'd be requesting training and development and there'd be other opportunities.

Bridget: Yes, and they would be coming from people like the directors of R&D and sales, from some of the different areas. I get quite a lot from operations at the moment, we've done OK there; but more from some of those other areas that aren't at the forefront at the moment.

Coach: What else?

(An invitation for the description of the future perfect to be expanded further. Bridget is getting into her stride. She has also mentioned some useful counters to note, such as the requests for training from the various departments.)

Bridget: I'd see my staff and they would be coming out of their offices telling me that they were very pleased, things were going smoothly, that they put a course on and people have turned up. They're coming to me with ideas of what they can do next, as opposed to getting depressed about what's happening now. They are talking to each other more as well. When we meet one to one we are definitely talking about the future of what could happen, rather than why we can't get bodies on this training course. It will be about who's been there, who's done what, how's it worked, where shall we go next, all those kinds of things.

Coach: Fantastic. How would other people in the organization know that this miracle had occurred? Your boss, for example?

(Enriching the description by asking for other perspectives, making it more interactional.)

Bridget: My boss, because he'd hear it from other people.

Coach: What would he be hearing?

Bridget: He'd be hearing from the other directors. He'd be hearing them talk about the programs they'd been on. He'd hear them talk about how brilliant the programs have been for their people. It could be the induction and how good it was for the engineers who'd been through it, or the latest leadership program. And instead of me asking for his support, he would be saying to me, "Look, how about this?" I'd be getting more suggestions from him about training courses. Instead of it always being me justifying the budget, he would actually be saying, "Here's the budget." That's the difference, it would be a fairer discussion about budgets.

Coach: He'd be supporting you from the outset?

Bridget: Yes, he'd be a lot more supportive. He'd understand training more. He'd understand that it costs money.

(Depending on the length of time for the coaching session, there might be a more comprehensive or even exhaustive description of the future perfect. In this session, we move on.)

Coach: OK, let's look at a scale here, from 0 to 10, where 10 is all of those things that you've just described are happening—so you're getting those emails in, the team are working well together and with you, they're coming with new ideas, you're getting a good response to the training itself and the feedback is good. The boss is supportive and forthcoming with ideas and budget to help develop this training. All of that happening is 10. None of it happening at all is 0. Where would you say you are now?

(The coach defines both ends of the scale, in relation to what has been said during the outcome discussion.)

Bridget: Between 3 and 4.

Coach: 3 to 4. More 3 or more 4?

(A little more time for thought, a greater degree of (apparent) precision.)

Bridget: Actually, maybe more 4.

Coach: More 4, OK. What's happening at the moment then that's lifting it to 4?

(Looking for know-how that supports the scale figure.)

Bridget: We are a good team.

Coach: Good team, what's good about the team?

Bridget: They are skillful in in-house design, they know their jobs well. I'm very fortunate to have a good administrator. I know people live or die by their administrator—she is good, she deals with the changes very well. My team are credible, in the main—one of them has an

engineering background, which is good. The others come through
HR so they are credible in that way.

Coach: The spread of skills, a history to them, and they're a good team?

Bridget: Yes, they work OK together.

Coach: What else?

Bridget: They work well with me.

Coach: They work well with you? How do you achieve that?

(Seeking the performer's contribution to the useful interaction.)

Bridget: Well, I make time to spend with them and sit down with them
and talk to them. I'd like to think I communicate with them well.

Coach: What else is getting us up to a 4?

Bridget: I'm invited to some directors' meetings and I do get to put my
case forward and I deliver things. I do deliver. I've been here two years;
I must be doing OK, because I'm still here.

Coach: What's talked about as one of your successes from these two
years?

(A question to unearth the most relevant know-how—what has she done
that works well in this setting?)

Bridget: We had a computer system put in, a new supply chain system
that was highly technical, and it didn't work. They hadn't involved me
and my people in it at all, and it didn't work because people were shy
of the system. I heard about this and spoke to the operations director.
I said I wonder if it's because people using the system don't understand
the big picture, what the system is all about. We set up some meetings
to look at the big picture with them, the whole business, and what this
system might mean for the whole business. From that, we got an
external consultant to come in, and we designed a really good training program that involved using plastic bricks and all sorts of toys,
which taught people the big picture of how the company worked and
where the supply chain fitted. It got everyone involved and the engineers were now better able to understand the problem areas.

Coach: And that training program brought you more credibility?

Bridget: It did. It made a big impact on the bottom line of the business.
It stopped the money going out the back door, so to speak.

Coach: And this was important to the directors?

Bridget: It was very important to them. Strangely enough, it was important to the marketing people, because they had a particular issue with the overseas offices.

Coach: What else is in place already that's getting us up to this four?

Bridget: We keep good records, so we know who's done what. What else? We have a good set of core programs: presentation skills, basic management skills. We get enough sign-up for those and people come along. They seem to think our courses are OK. We've tried a few new things, like computer-based training, with varying degrees of success, but they're open to us trying things.

(As with the description of the future perfect, the elicitation of know-how could be more elaborate, given more time. In this case, the coach affirms some of the important points and asks about action.)

Coach: It seems to me, from what you've told me, that there is a lot in place. You're very keen to work with your team. There's an ear at director level—you've got some credibility there, you've shown you can make an impact, get results; with that IT issue, for example, that spread all the way through to marketing. You've got foundation programs that are working well and are getting a good response, and that you can build on; also some new ideas. So I'm wondering, what might you do that would take you just one point up the scale—to a really solid 4, or to a 4.5—that you might like to do?

Bridget: It was interesting thinking about the marketing, about the supply chain thing. I'm not sure specifically, but there's something there about looking into the business. Because what happened there was I didn't say "This is what we're doing"; that was the one time when I saw an issue and stepped in.

(Bridget does not answer the question directly, but has sensed an area in which she might make more of the sort of impact she wants.)

Coach: Rather than telling them what you wanted to do, you saw something they were...

Bridget: I saw a business need—the need for development. We were working backwards to tie in with that need. Maybe it's about tying things that don't appear related to business needs at the moment. There is something about making that link for them because when they do, it seems to work.

Coach: So, just one point up the scale, what might you do to advance that?

Bridget: Well, I think I'll go back to some of these people. The R&D person... if I went and spoke to him and asked him a bit more about where he sees his business going, what are some of his key business needs, and then link that back with people challenges, I might get some insight from him from that conversation. I don't want to just wait—I want to connect with his biggest business needs.

Coach: Suppose you did that, how might that work out well?

(By speculating on the beneficial consequences of a proposed small action, we can increase the level of detail that can later be recognized as that action working well (and the motivation to take that action), or can allow a shift to an action that the performer likes even better.)

Bridget: If I sat down with him and had that conversation and it was about him and what he wanted, I think that might help him see that that's what we're there for. It will give me a lot of information that I can give back to him when we start to do any programs... I might start with someone easier. I might start with the operations director. Then I'd get the information and there might be overlaps between it. I hear about some of these things in the management meetings, but I'd get a bit more depth about their wants by speaking to them individually. I would like to find out what's important to them.

Coach: Clarify where you would start.

Bridget: I would start with the operations director.

Coach: When are you going to do this?

Bridget: I'll have the opportunity to do that tomorrow. I can speak to him tomorrow and arrange a meeting about when we're going to do that.

Coach: And what are you going to say?

Bridget: I'm going to sit down and speak to him. I'm looking at development needs and just say to him I'm looking at what important business needs are coming up in the next six to twelve months and we can sit and look how that fits in with the future development of his people. So, developing his people in line with his business needs.

(Bridget speaks purposefully and confidently about what she wants to do. The coach thanks her and leaves her to get on with it.)

Coach: OK, enjoy it. Thank you very much.

(Bridget and the coach meet again almost one month later. Here is the "R"—review—part of that conversation.)

Coach: What's better?

Bridget: A lot, actually. There's been quite a change in things. Last time we talked we discussed what I could do. I made the connection that it was about how I was talking to people, about business as opposed to training. I did go away and I spoke to quite a few people and it was absolutely fascinating: We were almost thinking the same things. Well, they were thinking the same as me.

(It sounds as if Bridget has done considerably more than the small action she proposed. Whether one thing led to another or it happened some other way does not matter here—the point is she can credit herself with progress and continue to take well-chosen, useful steps.)

Bridget: I collected all this information and I started feeding it back. They came to me with a lot of requests, like a leadership program, which I've been desperate to get off the ground. We discovered that through the conversations there's a whole gap in succession planning, for example. They were delighted to find someone who would support them with this.

Coach: And with your team?

Bridget: I'm working with one of my team on it because it's such a big thing. It's very exciting. And my team are happier.

Coach: How's your administrator?

Bridget: Oh, she's a lot happier (*laughs*). There's still chopping and changing, but she's still doing the job. They're all still there. They were getting very frustrated but slowly it's filtering through and they're feeling a lot better. It will take a bit of time, I mean, this is a big change—especially at the top level.

The role of the coach—optimism and pessimism

Some people argue that the role of the coach is to act as a neutral source of questions and "describer of reality." As you'll appreciate from the above example, solutions-focused coaches may be far from neutral.

Martin Seligman describes the results of his 30 years of research into the differences between optimists and pessimists.[1] Seligman writes that optimists take credit for their successes and ascribe failures to circumstances outside their control or to things that can be changed. Pessimists, on the other hand, tend to describe their successes as flukes and take full personal responsibility for the times things went wrong. They say, "I'll never get the hang of this" or "I'm just not cut out for this kind of work."

As a coach, part of your role may be to nurture optimism, to help performers to take the credit (or at least a share of it) for their successes. Develop your skill at letting performers know what you are impressed by in their performance.

At the end of a coaching session, consider:

- ✔ Saying what's impressed you about the performer during the session.
- ✔ Describing what has impressed you about the performer's efforts so far; this may include personal qualities such as tenacity and resourcefulness as well as progress made.
- ✔ Offering your views on how this particular performer's own efforts have contributed to the progress.
- ✔ Describing your grounds for optimism for further progress.

AFFIRM

Many people need to practice this part. While it does not always come naturally, affirming is a skill that can be refined and improved until the performer takes the compliments as "real" and "genuine."

Sometimes you are faced with a self-critical or pessimistic performer, ready to take the blame for their perceived poor performance. You can make use of this responsibility to point out that if they are to blame for what went wrong, they must also take the blame for any progress. This can help to nudge them to a more optimistic view.

Remember that this applies to coaches too. If you sometimes feel yourself partly responsible for your performers' lack of progress, make sure you award yourself an equal (modest) amount of credit for the aspects that are going well now and that improve over time. You can also check any such personal negative tendencies by taking a solutions focus to reappraise all the possibilities you and the performer are exploring to find the performer's route to success.

Once action is under way, your role as coach may change more to that of cheerleader. You spend future sessions primarily assessing what has happened, and are particularly interested in what has improved. "What's better?" is the main thrust of these encounters.

What's better may be different from what anyone expected. Yet whatever has happened is fresh information about the territory. As you know, everything is a useful gift, so you sort through the best of these gifts in order to amplify positive changes.

Some of the improvements could be accidental. But chance improvements are fine—as long as you capitalize on them or "select" them. So resist dismissing them as accidental. Instead, ask "How did you do that?" or "How did that happen?"

As a coach, use whatever presence and authority you enjoy to endorse the performer's positive change. The performer often has those "Aha!" moments of insight as you help them think through the ways they engendered improvements.

One consultant learning to deploy the Solutions Focus was uncomfortable with the title "cheerleader," saying that while she understood the concept, it had negative connotations for her. We agreed that her preferred metaphor was a British spectator offering a polite nod of affirmation and an occasional round of applause.

The example of Bridget above follows the OSKAR process step by step, but it would be a mistake to think that the process itself is what is most important. While it is generally advisable to stick to a process—

particularly while learning enough about it to make it work for you—it is just as important to remain flexible and to listen carefully to the answers you are getting, so that you can respond to what's there.

11

Managers Coach Their People to Solutions

Imagine a manager who keeps catching their staff doing things right: a manager who takes every opportunity to note anything that is going well, how the plans are fulfilled and what a great contribution everyone makes. And any time a member of their team is in difficulty or feels ready for a new challenge, that manager is promptly available for a supportive coaching conversation that leaves staff inspired to take useful action that will help get what's wanted or needed.

Many organizations are now taking an interest in their managers being solutions-focused coaches to their staff—to direct reports and also as a service to any other colleagues. They offer this coaching both one to one, which is the main topic of this chapter, and as team coaches, described in Chapter 12. Why are they doing this?

Managers using the Solutions Focus

James, a production manager in a components factory, was getting increasingly frustrated by the faults of his second-in-command. He felt irritated and let down, and at times assumed that his deputy was aiming to sabotage all of his initiatives. Before the relationship reached a point of no return, James learnt the solutions-focused coaching approach and held a conversation with his deputy about his resources and skills. They both enjoyed the conversation and discovered that the deputy had a talent and an ambition for strategic planning. With a minor adjustment of responsibilities between them and a third manager, they were able to realign the deputy's job to use his capabilities and satisfy his ambition, which not only improved his performance but also rescued the relationship.

Tanya, an account director at a major advertising agency, needed Fiona, one of her team, to give more presentations to clients and potential clients. Fiona was reluctant, as she had previously had a bad experience with one of these presentations and was now understandably nervous. Tanya set aside 30 minutes to coach Fiona, and they agreed what a good presentation would be like; the standards were clear. Fiona also shared three methods by which she thought she could control her nerves. The breakthrough was when Tanya asked when else Fiona had given good presentations: Fiona realized she actually enjoyed making presentations within the agency to colleagues, and decided she would take the same approach to her next external presentation. She did so, with great success.

Bill, the human resources director at a local authority in the UK, changed the authority's induction process to include coaching sessions for each new recruit. During these he concentrated on what each candidate already knew about working in a local authority, rather than assuming they were empty slates who had to be told everything (which was the tenor of the previous induction process). Because most had some good, relevant experience, they got up to speed in about half the time it used to require.

In all of these cases, there were instant results in the form of improved performance. And in each case, the coach also reported that communications improved as well—with better day-to-day contact on any issue. Their staff were having more constructive conversations with the coaches and with their colleagues. In the organizations where solutions-focused coaching was spreading, people were also picking up the common language of coaching and OSKAR, talking to each other about outcomes and scaling, even during meetings and informal dialogues.

Coaching for excellence, not for punishment

The ethos in coaching organizations changes to one where people are expected to find more answers for themselves, albeit with the support of those around them. For organizations attracted to empowerment or greater delegation, adding coaching skills to the managers' repertoire might be one answer.

Coaching now comfortably straddles sport and industry, and most people in organizations are familiar with the concept. When it is pointed out to them that no high-performing tennis player or athlete would contemplate their profession for long without a personal coach, employees and managers often find the idea of a coach most appealing.

The emphasis is on improving performance and getting better results, lacking any hint of the remedial that has historically accompanied seemingly similar services such as counseling or therapy. With coaching, it's more a matter of prestige. And the rise of the manager-as-coach reflects this perception, while recognizing that not everyone can afford a personal external executive coach. And of course, many of the benefits of a coaching approach can be reaped when your existing managers act more as coaches.

Taking solutions-focused coaching into training programs

Coaching to win at Walkers

Walkers Snackfoods was looking for a program to develop coaching skills for managers as a core competence, to help people learn faster through sharing knowledge and experience, and to improve the organization's ability to manage during an ambitious program to grow market share.

The company was attracted by the flexibility of the solutions-focused approach, which promised a process that each manager could use to some extent in their own way, and particularly by OSKAR's ability to bring in knowledge sharing as an explicit part of the process.

The basic program was a two-day training course in solutions-focused coaching for up to 24 participants at a time. The managers on the course learnt about the Solutions Focus and OSKAR. They discussed when to coach and when not to, and watched expert coaching in action. There was little theory, and they swiftly began practicing and preparing to coach their direct reports.

The program was supported by every member of the executive team, who attended the training first as a participant and then as a supporter to introduce the training to a later cohort. Each also set aside time every month when anyone in the organization could book a coaching session directly with them.

The training was supplemented with follow-up sessions, attractive notebooks for keeping a coaching log, cards with reminders of the key concepts, coaching mouse mats and screensavers.

From the outset, the intention was to spot internal facilitators who would eventually run the program themselves, and we engaged in coach talent spotting every time we ran the course.

As coaching took hold and results began to improve, Walkers' parent company PepsiCo studied the process and asked us to train its own trainers in the same program.

Leadership and coaching with CEL

Another organization, the Centre for Excellence in Leadership (CEL)—in partnership with the Solutions Focus—took the support process even further in a wide-ranging program of training managers within higher education colleges, the police force and with budding entrepreneurs.

Using what program director Shaun Lincoln describes as "triple-loop learning," each participant manager is allocated one or two colleagues to coach. They also enjoy the services of an external coach for six sessions, during which they are coached on any issues that may be useful to them (including how well they are doing with coaching their colleagues).

The CEL Leaders as Coaches program enables managers to use a coaching leadership style at work, first by introducing them to coaching skills in a three-day workshop, and then sustaining and developing their ability to use these in both formal and informal coaching situations over a six-month period. Managers learn in three different ways, integrating their internal coaching of colleagues with coaching from a CEL leadership coach and group supervision. At the end of the six months, managers then decide whether to use these coaching skills within their own teams or more widely in their organization, or both.

Shaun says, "When designing this program, we were looking for a coaching approach that was simple to pick up, brought immediate results, and could be used both inside and outside line management. OSKAR fits the bill perfectly, with managers especially appreciating the opportunity it affords them to share their own know-how and expertise. An unexpected bonus has been its flexibility, and we are now using this not only in the learning and skills sector, but also with great success in police and prison services."

Results have been impressive, ranging from helping key staff to cope with demanding new roles to changing how managers work together— for example middle managers are now more likely to present their boss with a range of possibilities, where before they came looking for answers. In particular, it is clear that once managers experience the benefits of OSKAR and SIMPLE at first hand, these tools are then used outside coaching. For example, one organization now uses OSKAR to structure its board meetings and enable the team to reach solutions more directly. Another finds scaling invaluable in staff reviews.

"Our clients are recognizing that OSKAR is more than a simple coaching tool," concludes Shaun, "and for many it represents an opportunity to change not only leadership but also culture. So much so that we now use this with our own staff."

Introducing a coaching program to an organization

At Walkers it was important that the program began with a presentation to participants outlining the compelling reasons for the program and asking them what benefits they thought they might gain from learning coaching skills. It was stressed that coaching skills were an addition to the managers' repertoire. The degree to which they introduced and used the new skills as part of their own work with their reports would be up to them. They enjoyed just as much flexibility as before in how they chose to manage and to achieve their results. This was never coaching for its own sake, always coaching for performance.

The quick wins associated with solutions-focused coaching were a great help. Most participants were invited to take a small action overnight between the first and second days of the training course as part of OSKAR practice. Returning the next day with a clear desk, a memo that had at last been written, a productive conversation with a spouse or a child, many participants were impressed with the impact on themselves and those closest to them.

Unlike some coaching models that claim greater psychological depth, OSKAR can be grasped quickly and used immediately. Managers and their staff also enjoy it, because rather than delving into unpleasant problems, they concentrate straightaway on the search for solutions and the recognition of their talents and resources. Remember that the Solutions Focus approach has been shown to be effective even in tackling extremely serious mental health issues—its simplicity and directness are important benefits, not compromises.

While conventional coaching may start from what you are doing wrong, with your coach typically taking time with you to analyze the barriers to better performance, a solutions coach begins with what's working well. This principle can apply not only to each individual coaching interaction, but also to the design of a project—it makes sense to find out what is already happening in an organization that a coaching program can build on.

In the training itself, it helps if participants briefly experience both approaches—problem focused and solutions focused—and explicitly discuss the differences. It's not that there's anything inherently wrong with exploring problems, it's just that doing so is not usually necessary in order to find a solution, nor is it the quickest route to a solution.

There is frequently an "Aha!" moment for a participant on a training course, when this potentially life-changing realization kicks in. Part of the facilitation effort is to appreciate that that moment occurs to different people at different times. One of the pleasures of these programs is to see everyone "get it" to some extent, irrespective of the varying levels of skill with which they then apply the concept as coaches.

How much expertise does the coach need in the performer's topic?

The Solutions Focus approach builds on the existing skills of each coach and performer in any coaching interaction. While it clearly makes a difference to have a more skilled coach, it is possible to get good results with relatively inexperienced coaches—a patient listener armed with a couple of solutions-oriented questions and a beginner mind can go a long way. We found that in an organization where managers typically remained in one role for less than a year, it was helpful for them to realize that they could confidently place responsibility for expertise in the hands of the performer, with the coach being expert in coaching, not necessarily in the topic.

One issue in many organizations is that managers have less functional expertise than their staff, yet are still expected to coach. The Solutions Focus coaching process works whether or not the coach knows precisely how to do what the performer is aiming to do.

This contrasts with the usual relationship between a sports coach and a performer, in which the performer expects a great deal of functional expertise, and looks to the coach both for analysis of technical problems and for the tips to solve them.

Making use of the manager's expertise

If the manager-as-coach does have the technical expertise, then they might operate more like a conventional sports coach. When Paul, for example, was receiving tennis coaching, he appreciated technical tips. The prompt "bring your left hand across your body when you play a forehand, Paul" proved a quick way to improvement.

Similarly, the Solutions Focus model also allows the performer's search for expertise to include the coach's functional expertise, in the radically useful guise of know-how. Here, the coach might be asked to transfer pertinent knowledge, rather than "telling the performer what to do" as in much physical skills training or conventional management by command.

The differences are:

❏ The performer decides when to ask for know-how from the coach.
❏ The coach offers the know-how as a "gift" rather than as a "must-do" instruction.

During the Walkers program, for example, coaches practice the art of telling stories. They ask if the performer would be interested in hearing how the coach or perhaps a colleague they both respected had gone about the issue. Then they might share a story related to, say, time management or decision making, and invite performers to extract the helpful elements for themselves.

In a series of interviews after the coaching program had been running for three years, executives at Walkers summarized its main benefits. They said:

✔ This is about solving real business issues before they happen, not diagnosing them after they happen.
✔ It's made "sharing know-how" part of our business—it's OK to ask for help, we don't need to reinvent the wheel. We have greatly increased the amount of know-how sharing within and across functions.
✔ Coaching wasn't in the culture before, and it is now. Hundreds of people have been through the program and the model is being used, the terminology is being heard. Coaching is regarded as a legitimate process and an essential tool for the development and growth of the company—growth of people and growth of profit.
✔ We gave our managers simple tools and concepts that they can quickly and easily use to coach their people day to day. We like the simplicity of the approach.

✔ We have made a shift in mindset from tell to coach; from feedback after an event to coaching before an event; from the manager taking ownership of the problem to the manager enabling their team to solve their own problems.

✔ It helps build self-belief within an individual and "instilling self-belief" is one of our values.

✔ We have moved our organizational health survey scores on coaching significantly, demonstrating that more coaching is happening and having an impact on our people.

Contrasting internal managers with external coaches

While there are some particular considerations for managers acting as coaches (as distinct from external coaches), they are surprisingly few.

The "contracting" will be different, because the manager-as-coach has an existing relationship with the performer. This appears to bring in issues of hierarchical authority, confidentiality and the scope of the coaching. Yet the existing relationship means that there is already an implicit (and perhaps also an explicit) contract between the manager and the direct report that covers this. All that changes might be that the manager starts asking one or two rather different questions and gives the performer more leeway to make certain decisions. It is the external coach who generally must spend more time at the start, explaining and agreeing their role and methods.

Topics for coaching range across the entire spectrum of a performer's responsibilities. Typical topics include reaching the standards demanded by a particular task or project, time management, delegation and project planning. A good manager may also coach their direct reports into better roles inside or even outside the organization.

One particular consideration for any manager changing to a more coaching-oriented way of managing is to decide when to coach and when to manage by any of their other, traditional means—telling someone directly what to do, for example. Our view is that managers are paid precisely to make these judgments. A manager often expects that while coaching will bring long-term benefits, they may get faster results by telling someone what to do. Their task then is to make sufficient time for coaching, and they will perhaps be amazed at how fast it does bring the desired results. (The improvement in morale and motivation often more than makes up for any initial skill deficiency.)

If the risk associated with a particular issue is high and the time is extremely limited, then it may make sense for a manager to tackle the task personally rather than coach a subordinate to take it on. If it is a question of gross misconduct or responding instantly to an emergency alarm, then this is probably not the moment for coaching.

Coaching lends itself readily to performance issues—when the manager wants to get an improvement, and the performer has the capability to deliver it.

Coaching also fits well with performance management. In the Nationwide bank, for example, the Solutions Focus was introduced as a performance management tool, teaching managers to have these kinds of conversations during appraisal interviews.

Deft use of the coaching tools

Let us consider how a manager-as-coach can make deft use of each of the OSKAR steps.

Outcome

Managers usually need their staff to perform well. They have responsibility for the achievements of their direct reports, and they use all sorts of methods to encourage, help or force those people to get results. If the direct report does well, the manager gets a degree of the credit, and vice versa.

So when a manager chooses to coach rather than issue a direct order, the manager still has a stake in the outcome. This is different from an external coach, who may have a desire for the performer to do well, particularly in terms of self-development, but whose future does not hang on the immediate handling of the organization's issues. The coach may lose a client, the manager may lose their job.

Yet the manager is taught as a coach to encourage the performer to set the outcome—to establish their own platform and describe their own future perfect. Many times this is likely to consist of what the manager wants to hear, the performer raising the bar for their own results and generating sound ways to move forward. But what if the outcome described by the performer falls short of what the manager wants, goes excessively (and in the manager's opinion unrealistically) beyond it, or fails to match it at all?

The answer is that managers have every right to add their own view about the platform and to contribute information about their vision of the future. The difference is more in the degree of subtlety with which this is done using solutions-focused methods. For example, the direct report may describe what to the manager is an incomplete future perfect. The manager might ask for a fuller description, by asking what other stakeholders would notice: "What will our customers see?" or, a little more directly, "What do you suppose I'm expecting to see?" At this point, the performer may guess accurately what it is the manager wants, or the manager might wish to add some detail offered as information (not a command).

If the manager-as-coach is primed to look for overlaps between their own desires and those of the reports, rather than the differences, then the conversation will be easier. When those aspects are encouraged, the performer is likely to be taking steps toward achieving shared goals. Later, the situation can be revisited to find out what else needs to be done. Cooperation and support take the place of argument and motivation-sapping standoffs.

Coaching in action: Robin's office

In this example, Margaret (the manager using coaching) is helping Robin (her direct report), who wants to improve his organization of the office administration team.

Margaret: Robin, suppose that tonight you go to bed and go to sleep as usual... and during the night a miracle happens and you suddenly become able to organize the office administration team as well as you'd like to. But you're asleep, so you don't know that the miracle has happened. When you come into the office tomorrow morning, what will first tell you that the miracle has happened?

Robin: (*pauses*) Umm... that's a hard question.

Margaret: Yes, it's important, take your time.

Robin: The first signs... OK, I'll be feeling really positive when I get to the office. I'll want to get in and get on with my work.

Margaret: OK. What else?

Robin: Then, when I get to my desk, I'll know what everyone in the team is doing—all the schedules for today's tasks and meetings, and all my paperwork is stacked and tidy. The most important parts are all accurately entered into the computer on the shared database.

Margaret: Great. And how will the other people in the office know that it's different today?

Robin: Oh, I'll be first to arrive, so they won't know to start with!

Margaret: Excellent! How will the security guard on the front desk know about your positive feeling?

Robin: (*pauses again*) Hmm... I guess he'll see me walking quite fast and bouncily, and smiling at him, saying "Good morning," and I'll have my security pass at the ready, not be standing there trying to find it.

Margaret: And when you get to your desk, suppose I left a video camera running and recorded you arriving. What would be on the tape?

Robin: My desk would be tidy and organized. I would switch on the computer and then open my briefcase—oh, by the way, the briefcase would *not* have any work in it, just my lunch and my golf magazine—and get my diary out. You'd see me checking today's appointments, making sure the diary and the computer agree, and then ensuring that the papers were all there in the files. Then you'd see me quickly checking my emails and getting rid of them all—by replying and doing what's required there and then. I really *hate* having a full inbox!

You can see here how Margaret has helped Robin to describe his future perfect in small, detailed and observable words by taking other viewpoints. Note that these can either be real people (like the security guard) or artificial (like the imaginary video camera). This "inbetween" view reveals potential interactions between the performer and other people and even the environment. In thinking about how others will know about his positive feeling, Robin may also be helping himself by translating his ideas about the positive feeling into actions he can do—thus lending himself greater influence over the outcome. Margaret should probably continue to help Robin unpack more and more details about this future perfect.

This is all splendid, but Margaret also wants to hear something about how Robin proposes to improve the poor performance of Arthur, a junior member of the team.

Margaret: And how will the team know—Arthur, for example?
Robin: I'll be having a much more effective conversation with each of them. I'll be well prepared for the weekly briefing, and Arthur will know exactly what I'm expecting from him. There's time for a one to one with each of them, too. And no room for misunderstandings and excuses. Even Arthur has a very clear picture…

As with Margaret and Robin, any coaching conversation gets off to a great start if it includes an early, clear description of the future perfect from the performer. A vivid description:

- ✔ Provides a series of hooks from which to hang conversational threads about know-how.
- ✔ Makes it easier for the coach to spot opportunities to affirm the performer.
- ✔ Stimulates the minds of both manager and staff to see the actions that are likely to lead toward a future perfect.

Other coaching methodologies—for example John Whitmore's GROW model (Goal, Reality, Options, Will)[1]—focus the goal exclusively on the performer. This can miss the benefit of thinking about a future perfect from the viewpoints of others involved.

Scaling

Many solutions-focused coaches ask the performer to scale their confidence of achieving their goal, or to rate the chances of a course of action being fruitful. A scale is also often used to rate current performance, where 10 is the future perfect and 0 is "as bad as it's ever been" or some such opposite. As an effective tool for discovering what's happening and what might happen next, scaling combines simplicity with subtlety.

Gauging progress is nothing new. Any project manager will tell you about the importance of milestones, the steps along the way to completion. Often such milestones are identified and agreed at the start of the project with all parties, though they may change. The scaling tool, however, offers a strikingly simple method for engaging subjective and objective viewpoints to build progress.

We are often asked if it matters whether the scale starts from 0 or 1. Not really—it seems to be more a matter of personal preference. The way we use scales means that this end of the scale is not an important feature: It matters as the counterpart to 10, not as a detailed description.

Questions for scaling

All of the tools in the solutions kit can be applied with variety as well as precision. Here are some of the scaling variants with which to approach your issues as a solutions-focused coaching manager.

- ❑ On a scale of 0 to 10, with 0 representing the worst that it has ever been and 10 the future perfect, where would you put the situation today?
- ❑ You are at n now, what did you do to get you that far?
- ❑ You are at n now, what stops you from slipping back to $n-1$?
- ❑ You are at n now, what would take you to $n+1$?
- ❑ How would you know you were at $n+1$? How would other people know?

❏ What would be a high enough level for you to be satisfied?
❏ What do you think would be a high enough level for me (the manager) to be satisfied?
❏ On a scale of 0 to 10, how confident are you that these actions will take you in a useful direction?
❏ On a scale of 0 to 10, what's your commitment to taking these actions?

Let us return to Margaret and Robin to see an example of scaling in action.

Margaret: Robin, on a scale from 0 to 10, where 10 is the day after the miracle and you are organizing the team really well and 0 is complete disorganization, where do you put things now?
Robin: Hmm… 7.

Scaling, as we use it, differs from milestones. People make subjective and personal responses to scaling questions. In managing someone through a project, a description of 10 on the scale can set powerful expectations. If 10 represents a project completed on time, on budget, with everything going just as the performer wants it, then the notion of 10 automatically tends to draw a performer toward achieving it. Because the performer takes the lead in defining a 10, if they can safely call their current position on the scale without criticism then 10 is likely to be highly motivating.

Even if the manager decides to offer their description of a 10 to the performer, this can add a lot of clarity about expectations, still without the manager insisting on what the performer is to do.

In this conversation, Robin has taken a moment to assess some quite complicated thoughts, maybe imagining an aspect of the future perfect and adding to his own ideas about it, and then assessing his personal standing with respect to this. And he says it's a 7—not an 8 or a 6, but a 7.

Margaret knows nothing of what may have gone on for Robin to arrive at this point. So, she accepts his 7 and makes use of what's there.

Margaret: 7. OK. And what's happening already that's getting you up to a
   7?

Note what else Margaret could have done here, but wisely chose not to.
She could have argued with Robin's 7—either that it was too high
(because he's "clearly hopeless" at getting the best from his team), or that it
was too low (as he's patently a talented guy with many good strategies). She
may think either of these, but she doesn't say. She accepts Robin's score.

   She could have given her own view of Robin's position on the scale.
But that risks taking away Robin's own responsibility for his perspective.
Scales are highly personal and subjective, and so it is simplest to work
with whatever answer the performer offers. The number *per se* actually
tells us little, but it is an important stepping-stone to the next part of the
discussion.

   For a manager in an organization, one of the most important considerations is to avoid confusing scaling with other measures and figures. All
kinds of performance measures might already be in place when a manager begins to use coaching. There may be financial targets, production
figures, or numbers of people to recruit or retain.

   Scaling in a coaching conversation is different. The other figures are
measurable by anyone who has access to the information. Profits either
have reached 80 percent of the target or they haven't. Leaving aside the
practical difficulties of measurement and the true usefulness of many
organizational numbers, they are at least in this sense objective.

   Scaling is by contrast a subjective figure, set by the performer, belonging to the performer, with which the manager is ill advised to argue (even
if it is tempting to do so). For the performer the scale soon starts to take
on an objective quality, as the detailed descriptions of various points along
it fall into place. The figure *n* is where we are now. The future perfect is
10. There are interesting points called "the highest it has ever been for
you," "one point up the scale," "the figure you would aim to reach," and
so forth.

   The idea behind the scale is to inculcate the possibility of progress, not
to provide a stick with which to beat someone for being lower than the

figure the manager would like to see. We have encountered one or two figure-obsessed managers who have not succeeded in grasping that distinction, and for them we recommend coaching without scaling (there are plenty of other coaching tools they can use instead to get the results that they and their direct reports require).

Know-how

In this example, their coaching session might continue with a search for know-how that relates to days like the one Robin has described. Perhaps he backs up his assessment of a 7 with an example of a rare day that has gone exactly as described and the more frequent occasions when some of the future perfect has been in place. He could well realize as he speaks that indeed he does possess all the self-discipline and logistical skills to arrive at his office with everything organized the way he wants more often than not.

Robin: What's already happening? Well, I do get to most of my meetings on time, and my briefing sessions are pretty well organized. Most of the team spend their days very productively—and that must be something to do with the way I organize the rotas and negotiate the targets.

Margaret: What is it about the way you organize the rotas that's useful, do you think?

Note how Margaret, having found a trace of useful know-how, wants to encourage more reflection by Robin about what exactly he's doing that is helping. This may be directly useful to apply to the situation, or it may illuminate what the team finds useful and so lead indirectly to more ideas.

Expertise and beginner minds

It is commonly accepted that problems are the domain of the expert. All around us are experts who know about our problems, and are keen to show us their skills in solving them. With solutions-focused coaching, however, we generally suppose that solutions are personal and context specific. So what looks like the same "problem" can have as many different solutions as there are customers for change. The same solution may fit several customers, but you don't know until you try.

Likewise, every scale and every scaling are different. The performers—who create the scale—rate themselves in a personal way. The evidence they then offer to support their view is also personal, but is more open to discussion, clarification and elaboration.

If when coaching you are offered a surprising score on a scale, it's an opportunity to use your beginner mind. Some people who appear to be in great difficulty nonetheless rate themselves 8 out of 10. Others who have apparently made outstanding progress score themselves at "only" 4. The process for the coach is the same for all: accepting the score, enquiring about how the performer has got that far and enabling them to identify plausible prospects for progress.

Not needing to know a person's precise meaning frees the scaling process considerably. Instead of sticking to aspects of the organization that can be measured in (seemingly) objective ways, the customer for change can select topics that are personally meaningful, about which they care and are motivated to do something.

Affirm

 When a manager is used to offering praise, the affirming part of solutions-focused coaching comes naturally. The manager might use an affirm at any part of the conversation. It is simply a matter of listening out for what is going well or sounds useful, and reflecting it back to the performer.

For managers less used to offering praise, it is a formal step in the process to ensure that they at least make an effort to do so, as the affirm may have a powerful and motivating effect on the performer while they are deciding what to do next. In either case, the affirm should be genuine and based on evidence from the conversation.

Margaret: I'm impressed with your ideas on organizing these guys even better. You seem to me to really want to improve the situation, and you are a very conscientious manager where your team is concerned. It's clear you have given it a great deal of thought, and have even come up with a couple of ways of getting the best out of Arthur. You say you are currently at a 7 on the scale, what do you think you might do to make that an 8?

Action

Most people in organizations are already familiar with action plans, action points, SMART objectives and so on. Organizations tend to be action oriented, with everyone expected to "do" things, and often an expectation that people will tell one another what they are doing. A project plan might be thought of as a summary of what everyone is going to do and when.

For the manager-as-coach, one consideration is how to make the action in an OSKAR session a particularly well-chosen one—personal to the performer, and capable of generating progress for them and for the organization.

On the other hand, it may also be worth taking some pressure off the action in a coaching conversation. For progress to occur (which is the point of the coaching), it is neither here nor there whether it occurs as a result of a particular action chosen by a performer. All sorts of factors may lead to progress, and this action may or may not be part of it. In a complex setting, we are not going to waste time looking for causes, and the performer will not be tested on whether or not they completed the action or on what its consequences were.

There is a subtle difference here if "responsibility" is perceived to be an issue in the organization or for that performer. Then it might make perfect sense for the performer to choose an action to demonstrate how responsible they can be, and for subsequent actions to be reviewed.

In any case, the manager will hold staff accountable in various ways, whether for actions taken or for results achieved. What's important is to be clear about whether a particular conversation is "coaching"—in which the action is simply part of the conversational process—or "planning"—in which case the actions are agreed and testable—or both, combining all these attributes.

Review

As we have discussed, the point of a review is not to establish what happened to the action, but to seek progress. The key question is, "What's better?" It is fine to speculate on what might account for the progress, and a good coach will ask the performer to consider what they did to contribute to the progress.

The next part of the review is to explore how progress might be maintained or improved. All the OSKAR tools might come back into play, with the coaching as an iterative process.

With an external coach, a given number of sessions are probably scheduled (say, six sessions). With a manager-as-coach, there is likely to be more of a continuing relationship. The former lends itself well to coaching through a particular project. The latter lends itself to a whole range of issues, often hinging on steadily improved performance, with the coaching becoming more and more informal and even invisible over time.

What the organization needs to consider when introducing coaching

All sorts of factors influence the degree of success of any cultural change or training program within an organization.

At Walkers, the director of human resources, Sarah Miles, identified from staff interviews and a survey that the people in the organization were asking for coaching, and this need was then not surprisingly an important factor in the success of the program.

"We knew we needed to create a compelling employee proposition, and lack of coaching was identified as a big gap. We also believed that given the age and service profile across our management population, sharing know-how would have huge competitive advantage," she said.

"The Solutions Focus approach also fits with our culture—for example we say 'no weakness—just opportunity,' but the program also challenged us, as we have had a culture of feedback—people were used to saying, 'Let me tell you what you should do!' We liked the new concept of helping people find their own solutions."

Attention to this kind of detail in the design phase is important, to reassure the client that their expectations stand a chance of being met and to be ready for the onslaught of a rolling program every few weeks.

Equally, it is useful to remain flexible within each running of the course, and to be ready to redesign both between programs and even on the fly. On every run of the Walkers' program, for example, at least one character emerged with a question or a case scenario we hadn't seen before.

It can help to strike a balance between ambition and realism. If you are teaching managers to coach, it is probable that learning coaching for them is going to take less time and less focus than a full-time coach might devote. It's important, therefore, to allow them a degree of flexibility and to take a more relaxed view toward mistakes. In any case, the manager-as-coach is playing a longer game than they were playing before. It takes time for their staff to get results, which means time for the manager to get results. Ensure that there's no pressure or expecting everything to be solved with a single conversation each time.

It's advantageous for managers if their colleagues are using coaching too. Opportunity arises for formal and informal support if there's awareness throughout the organization that this is the preferred approach.

Above all, the success of a project hinges on taking a positive, solutions-focused view from the outset, confident that:

✔ Participants will lend themselves willingly to becoming better coaches.
✔ The organization is committing itself to supporting the program.
✔ There will be sufficient coaching expertise within every cohort to demonstrate good practice that can spread readily to every participant within the short space of a training course.

12

Team Coaching

By now, you have probably started to come up with your own solutions-focused ideas for finding ways forward with groups and teams. In this chapter we'll examine how working with groups offers additional challenges and possibilities to individual work, and look at practical ways to use our six solutions tools with groups and teams. We will also look at solutions-focused reflecting teams, a format for group wisdom sharing and solution building.

When Hopi Indians prepare to go hunting they don't discuss a strategy, splitting the problem up into parts. They sit down together and as a group imagine good hunting. This is like a different grammar of time.

What's your role in the team?

You can use the concepts in this book from any position in the team—that's part of the beauty of taking an interactional view. You may be the team manager or leader, keen to help your people make progress. Or you may be a facilitator, conjuring up useful processes for the teams you work with. You may even be a member of the team, fed up with problem-focused discussions and seeking to nudge things toward more productive territory.

As a manager

If you are the manager, you might want first to focus quietly on solutions for yourself. You'll gather experience that puts you in good stead when you start explicitly working with your team. If some team members are slow to latch on to a solutions-focused way, you may need to be patient and gently nudge conversations in the direction of solutions. Remember, make use of what's there.

As a coach

If you are a coach or facilitator, you will be seeking processes to engage the team in solutions-focused discourse. The six solutions tools can form the basis for great team discussions and actions. You will be facing the additional aspect of dealing with multiple voices—different people with differing views. Working with these multiple voices is a key part of team coaching.

As a team member

As a team member, you may still be able to suggest processes or pose questions for your colleagues. However, even if you don't feel comfortable doing this, there is an alternative course of action for you, "guerrilla SF." There will be more on this later in the chapter.

Working with teams

The key (and obvious) difference between working with individuals and teams is precisely that: The single voice of the individual is replaced by the multiple voices of the group. We saw previously the importance of careful listening and responding to the language of the performer. Now, the "performer" constitutes several people, all with their own views, words and opinions.

Useful differences

As a coach, it can be tempting to view these differences as a nuisance, something to be minimized and overlooked in the interests of making

When everybody thinks alike, nobody thinks much.

progress. "If only they'd all agree," we sigh to ourselves, "we could all get on with the job in hand." This might look like a sensible hope, but it misses the point and the power of groups. It is the differences—in outlook, desired future, hope, concern, priorities—that make groups and teams so powerful.

A key role for coaches working with groups is to ensure that these multiple voices are heard, and heard in a useful way. Therefore, the ways in which you respond to differences are crucial. If you respond with impatience, dismiss some of the views or criticize people for their contributions, you are unlikely to promote further participation. If you respond with interest and take differences seriously, you may start to discover useful ideas and momentum for moving forwards.

This is where a Solutions Focus approach can start to pay real dividends. Any differences over what the problems are, the causes of the problems, the "real" problems, who is to blame and so forth can just be taken, accepted, and then gently left behind as discussions move toward what everyone wants to have happen.

Choosing a useful perspective

There are many ways to look at any given team situation, and no one perspective is more "correct" than any other. Be careful about what one member or faction claims to be the facts, particularly if there is a dispute. The six blind men who encountered an elephant and all felt a different shape were talking about the same animal.

In taking a Solutions Focus within the group, beware your own "knowledge" of the situation. The only exercise you get may be jumping to conclusions.

Too much time is wasted in disputes about perspectives. Different people talk about the same thing in different ways and then argue about it. While we debate whether the glass is half full or half empty, the level of liquid remains the same, or even slowly evaporates. It is often better to start to agree on what we want to have happen.

If you are facing disputes between members of a group when detailing a preferred future, you may allow the argument to run its course, then seek the shared ground. Or you could acknowledge the difference and seek agreement on a few first signs. Or take the focus off the team and move it onto the interaction between the team and other stakeholders—how would the customers or the support staff know that a miracle had happened overnight? If the existing perspectives have not so far offered one that allows a solution, then another perspective may be in order. You can often open up a whole new set of ideas fast.

Finding common ground

Differences within "solutions talk"—about what the members of the group want, what is already helping and so on—can again be accepted and held on to, as something that might help everyone toward a better future. Rather than seeking a compromise, one tactic for the solutions-focused coach is to start to seek common ground, the part that everyone can agree on.

A problem-focused way of finding common ground might be carefully to examine all the disagreements in the group, the causes of the disagreements and the underlying value differences behind them. However, you may remember the advice of William James at the beginning of this book: The art of being wise is the art of knowing what to overlook. So here, while it is important not to dismiss any disagreements, you may find it worth keeping the spotlight firmly on finding things that everyone can rally around and work with.

Sometimes it can be useful to focus on really big things as a source of common ground—the end results, or the purpose of the team. On other occasions more traction can be gained by looking at very small details—the first signs of progress, for example. And if one of these tactics does not provide some movement, you can always try the other.

The voice of the team leader

You may be a manager or team leader looking to use the Solutions Focus ideas in working with your team. This can sometimes feel like a rather awkward situation. On the one hand you want to act as a facilitator and encourage participation, allowing the voices of your team to be heard and useful ideas to be produced. On the other hand, you are being paid to manage these people and get results from them, and you have a clear idea of the performance that is required. So what are you to do?

Work with an outside coach

One idea is to work with an outside coach. The coach will look after the process of the sessions, leaving you free to deploy your own voice as you see fit. You will know, of course, the risks of stifling debate—or encouraging it—by taking a position or by being visibly open to ideas.

There is no one right way here. It was famously said of former British Prime Minister Margaret Thatcher that she would state her position at the start of a discussion, and then almost dare people to challenge her. This is rather the opposite of the facilitative style that is currently promoted by many people, but for Maggie, in the context of British politics in the 1980s, it seemed quite successful. We raise this not because we are enthusiasts for the Thatcher mode (far from it), but to point out that different styles can work for different people in different contexts.

Use your own voice

If you are going to work with the team yourself, you will nonetheless need to use your own voice. Take care to work out when to use it, and how to do so for the best. Some ways to do this might be:

✔ Setting the context—if certain results are required of you or desired by you, letting people know early on might be better than keeping this information up your sleeve and hoping that the team will miraculously match your expectations on their own.

✔ Owning your statements—by clearly preceding them with "In my view..." or "It seems to me that..." rather than stating your own views as unchallengeable facts.

✔ Listening very carefully to what's being said—and responding constructively. Using affirms can be very useful in letting people know that you have heard what is said.

Platform with teams

As with any other application of Solutions Focus ideas, building the platform is very important. The key question with platform is again:

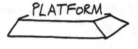

"Who is a customer, and for what?"

With teams, the degree of "customership" and perceptions about the key issues may differ, and so the preparation becomes even more important; it is possibly best done in advance of any team workshop or meeting. The way people are invited to get involved with any piece of work can also prove crucial.

One starting point is for the team members to agree their aims. Often these are assumed, but they are worth making explicit. One group all agreed that they knew what their goals were, absolutely no question about it. When a volunteer was asked to describe the goals they were all agreed on, however, the others shouted him down.

In building a platform with a team, it will usually be necessary to listen to the issues, gripes, moans and general problems afflicting the team. Remember that you are listening here not with a view to finding out more about the problems, but with a view to clarifying what everyone wants. Alongside the usual ground rules for running team workshops—

clarifying expectations, establishing goals for the process and so on—there are many ways to approach this. Here is a small selection.

Hot topics

Swiss coach Daniel Meier, author of *Team Coaching with the SolutionCircle*, suggests using the hot topics process when there may be a diversity of views among the team about issues and priorities. Every participant writes down on cards a few notes on unsatisfactory, suboptimal or otherwise disturbing situations they have experienced. These are displayed on a wall.

The group is given the opportunity to clarify the meanings of individual cards. As these are all personal experiences, there is no need to agree or disagree; justifications or apologies are not necessary. Daniel suggests that this discussion be kept "as long as necessary and as short as possible."

The cards are then clustered, either by the group or possibly by the coach, and each cluster given a heading. From these, a list of hot topics is developed. Each team member can decide which of the topics is really important and sign their name to it. This provides various groups to work on various topics—perhaps on the same day, in the same session, with processes from the same coach.

This process has the definite benefit of really allowing every team member a choice in where to put their energy on the day. We find that this can be very beneficial in terms of commitment and quality of work.

What's helped us before?

Another way of helping to build a firm platform comes from British consultant Jim McLaughlin.

"Large groups have a habit of focusing on problems and describing them in some detail, thereby sapping the energy that could be useful in solving them. They tend to talk about the failure patterns of the organization with frustration. As an antidote, I develop and run staff conferences with a solutions focus. The atmosphere is light-hearted and I try to help people who want to discharge frustration to make the next step—into positive solutions.

"One way we do this is by getting people to identify how changes actually come about in their organization. Groups get together and examine specific examples of how successful changes have happened, giving as much detail as possible. What was it that helped in the past? We then put these on the wall, to act as a stimulus and checklist for the team in whatever's coming next."

Future perfect with teams

Jointly describing a future perfect can be an excellent way to get teams working together and focusing on solutions—the things they want—rather than problems and causes. This first example show one use of a future perfect as the basis for progress with a team.

Don Coles, in Australia, was asked to run a workshop for a group of physio-therapists, occupational therapists and speech therapists on work with "frustrating families," where the professionals felt frustrated about the families' various ways of blocking their work.

After the group talked for a while about their frustrations, he asked them about their future perfect:"Let's imagine that, as a result of this two-hour workshop, you went through some sort of miraculous transformation, and the problem of getting frustrated with clients or families was solved for you, but somehow you weren't aware that this transformation had taken place... When you next go to see a client or family, what would tell you that this transformation had occurred? What would you look for?"

They discussed their answers, interviewing one another in pairs, and then asked each other questions about ways they were already acting consistently with such a transformation. How are things different when this happens, for themselves and for their clients? This produced good, detailed feedback about steps. It also promoted discussion about factors that were within their control with families and factors out of their control.[1]

Leapfrogging the problem with a time quake

British consultant John Henden was asked to work with a team who wanted remotivation. Following ten years of success, their organization had suffered setbacks—a financial backer had withdrawn, contracts were postponed and the workforce reduced, a shock to staff and management alike.

In the end, the company shrank to around one seventh of its previous size. "The factory was like a ghost town," recalls John. "Managers and staff could be seen ambling around looking downcast and disinterested, trying to keep up their own morale. Another difficulty was the organization's traditional method of dealing with problems: calling a lengthy meeting to analyze the problem, assign blame and work out whose job it was to sort it out. These meetings tended to leave people sapped of energy and creativity."

John was asked to lead a workshop to start the process of remotivation. Having built a platform by discussing people's hopes and expectations, gripes and complaints, and also starting to notice strengths, he announced that it was time to "leapfrog" the problem and start to look at how things might be. He posed this question:

We are going to set up an imaginary meeting like this in six months' time. Things will have improved considerably in the meantime. Our purpose at that meeting is to find out:

❑ What is better?
❑ How do we notice things are better?
❑ What are you most proud of?
❑ Where do you stand on the progress scale?

The group split into two and began to pile up details on flipcharts. More and more emerged about the future perfect description. John allowed 25 minutes for this process, with the participants "jetting themselves forward" into a different future and describing it in detail.

"The result of Time Quake was to give real hope and optimism," he recalls. "I noticed that two participants in particular who started the meeting looking almost clinically depressed were much brighter."

John followed up the Time Quake by stepping back and having the group start to look for things that were already working well (counters) and small steps. "The team were greatly remotivated by the workshop. I was told later by the general manager that they had gone on to develop many revenue-earning projects to get through the tough times, and had succeeded in regaining financial backing after a difficult 11-month period. The company is now almost back to full strength."[2]

What difference would the miracle make?

Sometimes the future perfect can lead very quickly to changes in perception and action, not only in describing it, but in looking further at what differences it would make to the people concerned. This can be a great help in getting a closer fix on what people want and helping them to focus on it.

Waiting for the move

A small work team was waiting to move into a new office building. The building was delayed, they didn't know when the move would take place, and the team were not working well.

When asked about their future perfect—how would it be next week if a miracle happened—they said, naturally enough, that they would have moved into the new building. When asked what other differences that would make, they said they would set up a project to investigate new opportunities for the team, make contact with funding bodies, and a group would consider flexitime work options.

A long list appeared. Then one of the team said, "Just a minute, we don't need the new building to do most of these." She was right—many parts of the future could be fast-forwarded before the move. Somehow the move, over which the team had little control, had overshadowed everything else. By attending to what they could do and change now, the team made immediate progress.

Scaling with teams

10 ⊤ S Scaling is an effective way to develop a discussion about
    C what's already helping, and what might be small (and quickly
    A do-able) next steps. This is as true with teams as with
    L individuals.
    E
1 ━   Because scaling is a subjective process, everyone can have
his or her own, equally legitimate, view. So if someone thinks that the
current situation is a 4, and someone else says it's a 7, that's just fine. The
person scaling 7 may believe we're closer to perfection than the 4 scorer.
Or they may be more easily impressed. It doesn't matter.

Make use of what's there by examining what is supporting each
rating.

Ask the 7 scorer:
❑ How come you've scaled it as a 7? What's making it that high?
❑ What would it take to make it an 8?

Ask the 4 scorer:
❑ What have you noticed that your colleague may have missed?
❑ What would it take for you to raise your rating to a 5?

Ask them to compare notes on what each has seen that the other has
missed or valued differently.

From their answers you can reap the benefits of multiple perspectives,
while discovering aspects of each personality that may help in the next
steps. Perhaps one is more skeptical and would enjoy checking claims, and
the other's more optimistic disposition would suit an exploratory discussion with a new third party. They would be finding their appropriate roles
for this particular task while working on the early stages of the task, without the time and expense of a more formal "team roles" assessment or
other intervention.

Walking the scale

In Germany, solutions consultant Peter Röhrig enjoys using scales with groups.

"I was working with quite a large group—around 100 people—from a trade association. Their line of business suffers from rather a poor public image, and they wanted to explore ways to improve their standing in the community. I asked them each to rate individually, on a scale of 1–10, how well they personally were contributing to the good image of their business nationally. I then set up a scale along the room, with 1 at one end and 10 at the other, and asked everyone to stand at the point they had scaled. Everyone could see who was scaling what right away.

"Then I 'interviewed' people at different points on the scale, asking how come they had put themselves at that point: What were they already doing, and what was helping to enhance their image? After we had heard from people at different points along the scale, I asked everyone to move to a position reflecting where they wanted be in 12 months' time: How would they then be contributing to enhancing public perception? Again, everyone moved and could see where their colleagues were rating. We then split into a number of groups, with neighbors identifying the steps needed to get them there."

Multi-scaling

One interesting possibility with a team is to use multi-scaling. This is where a group decides to work on several different topics at once, with small subgroups tackling each area. Scaling can be used as a process to help each group move along together, with moments for the different subgroups to interact and share their findings and work to date.

One such process was devised by Björn Johannson and Eva Person of Solutionwork in Sweden. Different topics are selected and people volunteer to work for a while on each one. The facilitator or manager then takes all the groups through this multi-scaling process:

❏ What are you trying to reach? What will you be doing then, in detail? A short period of solo thinking, then discuss in groups of four or five and create a future perfect scenario (six minutes). Remember—do *not* consider what we should do to get there yet.

❏ Scale—on a scale from 1–10 where the future perfect is 10, where are we now? (One minute)

❏ What are you doing already? (Eight minutes)

❏ What of that can you do more of in the next two weeks? (Five minutes)

❏ Share, add, reflect—in plenary, one group at a time. The other groups hear what has been discussed and offer further ideas and input.

❏ Is that enough? On the basis of doing "what you can do more of," is that sufficient? (For each group)

❏ If not, what else?

The short timescales for each phase are quite deliberate. They help the subgroups to stay focused on the question at hand and gently keep them from wandering off into problem talk.

Counters with teams

 The team gathering of counters, or know-how as we refer to it in the OSKAR model, can be an interesting and exciting process. The original definition of counters—examples and signs of the solution happening already, and resources connected to it—can be extended beyond the original customers for change, and toward a wider search for relevant know-how. In the Solutions Focus approach, this know-how is naturally connected to the things you want, not the problem or any causes that may be attracting your attention.

Wider know-how

Sometimes a little lateral thinking is helpful in unearthing counters. They may lurk in related circumstances, rather than in the prime position of the situation under discussion.

The Solutions Focus is about finding what works *for you*. Sometimes you make the discovery by looking inward at the organization. Other times it may be productive to turn outward for sources of differences that make differences. This may mean that the "fit" with your organization is less sure, but there are certainly some powerful lessons to be found.

Pit stops for aircraft

Southwest Airlines in Dallas had the problem of planes that were on the ground for 40 expensive minutes of refueling. They asked, "What's the problem? Why are the planes spending so long on the ground?"

They knew downtime was expensive, and they knew why it took as long as it did. But perhaps the costs were not really a problem, in that the causes seemed reasonable. They even tried benchmarking against their competitors, only to find they were already one of the leaders.

The quantum leap came when they rephrased the question to a more solutions-focused "How can we get the planes to spend less time on the ground?" They adopted the pit-stop turnaround process from Formula One racing—the fastest refuelers in the world—and reduced their refueling time to 12 minutes.

Setting a clear goal for a radical improvement led to a search for what was working well elsewhere in refueling. This gave them new thoughts, enabling them to unpick and unpack their own old practices.

A new face for computer security

Computer passwords pose people great difficulties. Many of us can't remember a long string of letters and numbers, particularly if they change with any frequency. One company realized this was a problem and wondered what they might do about it.

They could have asked lots of questions about the problem: Why can't people remember long lists? What gets in the way of them remembering changes to passwords?

Instead, they asked in a solutions-focused manner how they could make a more memorable—and hence reliable—computer access system: What do people remember and recognize easily? The answer was not strings of letters and numbers, but faces. The company experimented with showing people five faces—their password faces—from a wide range of possibilities.

When you logged on to the computer you saw nine faces, and had to spot the position of your first password face. Increased levels of security were generated by having multiple screens—the second screen featured your second face, and so on.

The solution used our innate ability to recognize faces instantly, and the whole password system became faster and more reliable. Trials showed that the system worked well, and calls to the helpdesk regarding forgotten passwords reduced substantially. The Real User company introduced the system worldwide—check it out at www.realuser.com.

Affirms with teams

AFFIRM

Affirms can be used in all kinds of ways in solutions-focused processes. Strengths can be noticed along the way, grounds for optimism can be summarized, positive qualities can be acknowledged.

With teams, the simple use of affirms and discussion of strengths can lead to extremely useful and productive steps. If you point out strengths, people may be encouraged to notice and use those strengths to make progress and to perform better. This is a far cry from some of the "team-building" methods popular in decades gone by, where weaknesses were relentlessly revealed, analyzed, probed and dissected, and which certainly produced reactions, albeit not always useful ones.

One example of a simple and effective team activity based on affirms comes from Evan George and the Brief Consulting team in London. Team members in pairs are asked to address the question: "What is it that makes you a valuable member of the team?" They are then asked "What else? What else?"—up to 15 times! For maximum effect 'What else" should be asked gently and interestedly, rather than in a demanding way—this is not an interrogation. This can be supplemented by questions such as:

❑ How does that show?

❑ What is the smallest sign of that?

❑ What do others appreciate?

These build and amplify each piece of useful know-how toward forms where people can be more aware of what they do that has impact on others, and even how they can do more of it.

This is a fascinating exercise to carry out for yourself. In our experience people sometimes know the first few things that make them a valuable member of the team, and then start having to think a little harder and more widely. These latter answers can easily lead to new and useful discussions about the way the individual functions within the team. It's easy to see how this kind of exercise could be extended, perhaps to the whole team offering their ideas about the valuable contribution each member makes.

Small actions with teams

The focus on small actions is as useful with teams as it is with individuals. The advantage when working with teams is that the team members can interact while the actions are being carried out, to notice and react in vari- ous ways. Sometimes this can simply mean noticing and responding positively whenever people see a colleague doing something useful, capitalizing on what's happening inbetween the team members.

A slightly more elaborate version is for members deliberately to keep their useful action secret. In Finland, psychiatrist and author Ben Furman tackles actions within a group by "positive paranoia."

Within a given period, say the next week, each member of a team has to do something beneficial for another member or for the team as a whole, but without saying what it is going to be—and without even announcing when they've done it or what they've done.

Everyone tries to spot when the beneficial actions are taken. All will be revealed at the end of the week, when they meet again with the organizer, facilitator or team leader. Meanwhile, it creates an atmosphere of people spotting colleagues doing useful turns for each other. When people are hunting for what they want—especially in a charged atmosphere of expectant uncertainty—they stand every chance of tracking it down.

Guerrilla SF

You may be thinking that this Solutions Focus business is all very well for consultants, facilitators and managers. After all, they are there to ask questions and get people thinking, they have a role to play in doing that. But what if you are just a member of the team? Up to a point you can ask questions, but starting to give the team processes to follow might be seen as unhelpful by your manager. Or you may be a member of a board, wishing to nudge things in a more solutions-focused direction. How can you help your colleagues to act and discuss things in a solutions-focused way?

One possibility is for you to employ guerrilla tactics—to use Solutions Focus ideas in an undercover way to nudge the meeting in a more productive direction. One way to do this is to make solutions-focused statements, rather than ask solutions-focused questions. Think of the question you would like to ask the team and then answer it yourself out loud. This method

"Be the change you wish to see in the world."
Mahatma Gandhi

is similar to one used in improv theater, where momentum in a scene is generated better by statements (to which the others can respond) that move the action along than questions (which have the effect of holding up the scene until an answer can be found).

For example, suppose your team meeting has spent ages analyzing what went wrong. You would like to move the discussion on to more productive territory. So rather than asking about what went well, you might say: "One of the things I thought went well last time was..." This encourages other people to join in, to add their own views about what went well, and generally to change the emphasis of the conversation.

Another possibility might be for some closet platform building, something like: "So, what we're saying is that next time we would like (*x*, *y* and *z*) to happen." Again, people may agree or disagree, but you have at least nudged the discussion toward solutions, not problems.

Similarly, you can lead off a search for counters by noticing: "It seemed to me that what helped us tackle this before was…"

Affirms can be very useful here. These usually take the form of statements anyway, and you can always be impressed with something that someone has done and name some useful resources that they seemed to you to show. In our experience this can lead to all kinds of positive changes in the direction of the conversation.

> *"Machines can be controlled. Human beings can only be disturbed."*
> *Fritjof Capra, author of*
> The Tao of Physics[3]

Finally, you can reinforce and join in with any traces of solutions-focused talk around the table. Remember the assumption that "change is happening all the time," notice any small, useful changes and seek to amplify them by joining in, helping to expand and draw more attention to what we want, what's working already and so on. The objective is to nudge the conversation gently in the direction of productivity, not push it or drive it there. Make a gentle disturbance.

Celebrating success—what's better and why?

After a period of working well together, celebrate success. The Solutions Focus, with its emphasis on what is going well, means that celebration plays an important part in:

✔ Acknowledging changes.
✔ Valuing the contributors.
✔ Maintaining a thrust toward even more progress.

Our final example of solutions in action with groups and teams comes from Australia. Alison Lewis-Nicholson and her colleague Monica Hingston from Connections (Geelong) were asked to facilitate a celebration evening to mark a year's work promoting rural health. Members of the consortium of health service providers joined members of the local communities who had participated in defining and using the services. The facilitators were instructed that the focus should be on the achievements of the community, rather than the infrastructure of support.

"We were faced with the challenge of how to elicit the very individual stories of the different communities in a way that was respectful of the participants, and draw these diverse strands of stories into one whole that could be celebrated by the constituent parts, and the consortium as a whole."

They also had to deal with observers in the form of "chiefs" from the participating health organizations, who wanted to pick up ideas for working with these now established community consultations.

The evening was planned from a solutions-focused perspective, and took four main parts.

Getting to know you

"A warmup session was undertaken whereby words describing community interests were pinned randomly on all the individuals' backs. The participants were instructed to form four groups, each of which contained the requisite community interests. Groups comprising a mixture of consortium and community members were then asked to interview their members, and present in song, word, dance or mime to the whole group with a short explanation as to why each of the participants had joined the consultation. This enabled participants to mix with members of other communities and other consortium members, in a way that did not embarrass participants by requiring them to perform an individual presentation about their neighbor on the left."

Follow the yellow brick road

"In their community groups, community and consortium members made a time line from yellow string to represent their project. Then the community members 'led' a blindfolded consortium member through the timeline. This symbolized what was happening in practice, the community leading the process and the consortium responding to their direction.

"Each group then presented their findings to the other groups, using furniture and people as props.

"Three different stories—of times of failure, encouragement and success—were graphically described. One group had the consortium member crawling under a table through the tunnel of despair. This led through many deviations in the form of chairs and corners to the success of buying a new podiatrist's chair for the health center. Volunteers enjoyed acting out the counters, showing how they overcame the odds, and presenting the signs of success. Each group expressed a great sense of pride in their achievements."

The fishbowl

"With the group arranged in two concentric circles, the inner circle of community members listened without comment to the discussion of the outer circle of consortium members and then vice versa.

"This enabled the professionals to hear the story 'as it was' without an obligation to try elaboration or justify positions, and it gave the community members an opportunity to hear, perhaps in a new and amplified way, what the professionals thought of their achievements, without the structures and organizational mechanisms getting in the way.

"The facilitators asked the community members:

❑ What went well?

❑ How did you achieve it?

❑ How were the consortium members helpful to you?

❑ How were you able to sustain your involvement?

❑ What surprised you?

❑ What next?

"This was then reversed so that community members could reflect back their impressions. It proved particularly powerful when the health professionals talked about the strengths and competencies of community members, who were amazed to hear that the 'experts' had been impressed by and had a great deal of respect for the community members' abilities."

A look at the future

Finally, the participants playfully created three sentences to describe their preferred future for their community and community activity. The limitation on the number of words helped the groups identify the essentials quickly.

You probably recognize the parts of the process that are particularly solutions focused. Although the activities described are quite complicated and require skill to facilitate, they are also SIMPLE. We hope that you can discover ways to help yourself and your teams by adding SIMPLE touches to whatever you are already doing.

Applying SIMPLE principles to coaching

We have derived all of the coaching tools and ideas from the six SIMPLE principles that serve as guidelines for a solutions-focused approach to issues in organizations. Let's look at how a coach might take nourishment from these principles.

Solutions, not problems

In using the Solutions Focus as a coach, remember to keep the conversation focused on solutions, not problems. This does not mean refusing to discuss problems, but deploying any "problem" discussion to discover what the performer wants to do, learn about their commitment and passion, and perhaps unearth initial evidence of skills and resources they are already using. You can then progress to discussing the future perfect, a much more goal-oriented area.

Of course, encouraging a performer to concentrate on goals in coaching is nothing new. But in taking a solutions focus, there is rarely any sense of emphasizing a problem or starting with what's wrong, an approach favored by those who hold the theory that it is necessary to "talk through the problem" in order to make progress.

Inbetween, not individual—the action is in the interaction

Each time you coach someone you are jointly creating a new interaction. Likewise, each time the performer performs, they are creating another set of interactions with their workmates, customers and others. As a coach you are on the lookout for helpful interactions—from any parties—as clues to the ways forward. Help the performer assess how they can use their behavior to help others to respond helpfully, whatever "helpful" might mean in your context.

Make use of what's there, not what isn't

In making use of what's there, notice evidence of helpful behavior, results and counters in your performer. This is a rather more focused method of working than simply helping your coachee talk through their performance. You can point out these counters to bring them to the performer's attention. You can also prompt them to find counters elsewhere in the organization, in their life experience or from wider fields.

Possibilities—past, present and future

As a coach, one of your principal aims is to help generate a sense of possibility. There may be evidence from the performer's past that can help to shape the future. You can use resourceful words easily in the context of conversations focused on solutions, and highlight good aspects of performance by offering compliments. And by acting as if progress is not only possible but inevitable, you can help to generate that vital ingredient, hope, for the performer.

Language—clear, not complicated

One duty of a solutions-focused coach is to release the performer from the snares of unhelpful $5,000 words.

You can avoid introducing any of your own, resisting for example temptations to smuggle in previously unmentioned concepts of "self-actualization," "disempowerment" and "cross-functional operational mindsets."

And you can accept and restate the performer's words in describing their performance, maybe using the scaling tool to elicit simple, shared descriptions of what's going on and what might happen next.

You also play a part in performers choosing helpful labels for themselves ("on the way to...," "almost" or "potential") and avoiding negative tags ("nowhere near...," "failure" or "hopeless").

Every case is different, beware ill-fitting theory

Make sure that each coaching assignment is fresh, so that you help each performer reach more of their potential. You will grow more expert, not so much in your technical area of skill, but in finding out what's special about each coachee and how that is material to their progress. And you can definitely remember to be solutions focused, not solutions forced—if the performer is convinced that something else is a good prospect, then let's allow that too.

13

Organizational Solutions

We now move from working with individuals and teams to the wider world of organizational solutions. From the many possibilities in consulting, we select the main options for using Solutions Focus ideas in organizational change.

In this chapter we talk about consultants as coach to the organization. However, if you are a manager inside an organization wanting to change it, then do read on. What follows will apply equally to you and your situation. One of the implications of the interactional view on which the Solutions Focus is based is that change can be started from anywhere—top or bottom, inside or outside—and then spread like ripples around the organization and its environment.

Suppose we want something different in our organization. There are several different ways to proceed, which we might call consulting models.

Consulting models

One interesting way to classify consultancy forms was presented by Ed Schein in his classic book *Process Consultation*.[1] Schein splits the consulting world into three.

The purchase of expertise model

The purchase of expertise model is where the organization buys the expert services of an outsider to do something. We sometimes call this the "plumber" model. When your pipes are leaking, it makes sense to call a plumber to fix them. Likewise, if you want to set up an emergency data-recovery system or revamp your product packaging, you may decide to call on experts in the field to do the job for you. The final decisions are of course yours, but the expertise is with the external provider—that's why you hired them.

This model often works perfectly well. Its success requires the organization's managers to work out what they need, come to the correct decisions, communicate the needs to the consultant, and assess the consultant's skill at meeting those needs. If one of these steps is executed incorrectly, the project may turn out much less successful than everyone hoped. In particular, if the managers' initial diagnosis is wrong, the whole affair may prove a dead end.

The doctor–patient model

In the doctor–patient model, rather than precisely specifying what needs to be done, the manager—aware that something may be amiss with the organization—calls in the consultant to carry out the diagnosis. The doctor/consultant then arrives, checks you over and tells you what to do.

The difference to the previous model is that the diagnosis rests with the consultant, albeit with the consent and possibly help of the manager. This model places a great deal of power in the hands of consultants as they take on both the diagnosis and the prescription, which may (in Schein's words) account for its popularity with consultants. It can work, but its success depends largely on the managers' acceptance of the diagnosis. Consultants are still producing lengthy, expensive reports that are ceremonially presented and then linger unread in a drawer.

This model does not sit happily with a solutions-focused approach. One of the central tenets of the Solutions Focus is that the steps to take are best discovered by examining the solution—what you want—rather than the problem—what's wrong. Our mental health colleagues have discovered the limitations of treating psychological issues on this basis, and the same is true in organizations. The model also limits the degree of collaboration between consultants and managers.

Process consultation

Process consultation, Schein's third form, has gained popularity and acceptance since he first named it some two decades ago. He describes it as:

> a set of activities on the part of the consultant which help the client perceive, understand and act on the process events that occur in the client's environment in order to improve the situation as defined by the client.[2]

As you can see, this is much more akin to the kind of work that a solutions-focused consultant might do. This is a model of joint effort between manager and consultant, with the manager providing their experience and input and the consultant working to help the manager figure out what to do.

But wait, even process consultation can be problem focused. Indeed, Schein himself makes this quite explicit. He states:

> Managers often do not know what is wrong and may need special help in diagnosing what their problems actually are.[3]

In other words, the consultant still has a role in uncovering the problems and presenting them to the managers. Schein goes further, stating,

> No organizational form is perfect; hence every form of organization will have some weaknesses for which compensatory mechanisms must be found.[4]

The consultant's role here seems to be to find problems and weaknesses, and to address them.

Solutions-focused process consultation

Many of the examples we offer in this chapter are about consultants using process consultation ideas in a solutions-focused way. As you may expect, this will not be fundamentally about helping managers to discover problems and weaknesses. It will instead be about discovering what people want, when that happens already, relevant strengths and small steps to take. Unless weaknesses are directly interfering with progress, it is preferable to leave them and concentrate on developing strengths instead. What makes organizations—and people—into world-class performers does not lie in their (mended) weaknesses but rather their (developed) strengths.

So a solutions-focused process consultant will aim to use the principles and tools in this book to help managers and clients to perceive, understand and act by recognizing what they want and doing more of what works to deliver it. This may well be different in each case, which means the processes may need to be adjusted to fit each time. This, then, is the consultant as coach to the organization.

Appreciative inquiry

Another strand of positive process consulting, appreciative inquiry (Ai), can be traced back to David Cooperider and Suresh Srivastva in 1980, who themselves built on the social constructionist approach. Invited to contribute to an analysis of "what's wrong with the human side of this organization," Cooperider was amazed at the level of positive cooperation, innovation and egalitarian governance he saw. Over the years, he, Srivastva and others have developed their insights into a way of working with organizations.

Cooperider and Srivastva argue that organizations are not "problems to be solved" but centers of infinite human capacity, ultimately unpredictable, unknowable, or a "mystery alive." They offer the hypothesis that human systems grow in the direction of what people study, therefore we should search for the true, the good, the better and the possible in human systems.

Cooperider and Diana Whitney define Ai in these terms:

Appreciative Inquiry is about the coevolutionary search for the best in people, their organizations, and the relevant world around them. In its broadest focus, it involves systematic discovery of what gives "life" to a living system when it is most alive, most effective, and most constructively capable in economic, ecological, and human terms. Ai involves, in a central way, the art and practice of asking questions that strengthen a system's capacity to apprehend, anticipate, and heighten positive potential.[5]

Ai is usually presented with four distinct, practical stages, the 4-Ds model:

❏ Discovery—appreciate "what is."
❏ Dream—imagine "what might be."
❏ Design—determine "what should be."
❏ Destiny—create "what will be."

There is now a large Ai community around the world, with many books and resources available. Ai has often been used to take on large-scale organizational challenges, with the deliberate involvement of many people in interviewing and building change, though this emphasis is shifting to include work with teams, individuals and leaders.

When we are asked whether the Solutions Focus is the same as Ai, we reply that there are many similarities and some differences. The similarities lie in the interactional, constructionist underpinnings of the approaches and in the view of the power of the positive. Also, affirming what is going well is part of both approaches. There are some differences stemming from their respective origins—wide-scale organizational change (Ai) and individual and small-group change (Solutions Focus). However, the most significant differences appear to us to lie in the language chosen by practitioners to describe their work. Ai uses terms like systematic discovery of what gives "life" to a living system when it is most alive; the more minimal Solutions Focus favors "find what works and do more of it."[6] These seem to appeal to different constituencies.

Finally, it appears that positive approaches—of all types and traditions—are coming to the forefront of organizational work. There is much to learn from all of these different methods.

Finding what's working in organizations—every case is different

In solutions–focused process consulting, our objective is to make progress by finding what works and doing more of it, in the specific case in question. The consultant's expertise, therefore, is more in finding what works here than in remembering what worked in previous cases. This is a novel mindset, and one that requires the consultant to be particularly alert to notice useful counters. There is an interesting parallel here with the world of medicine, in the use of phage, the virus that cures.

Every case is different—the strange story of phage

The development of antibiotics was one of the outstanding achievements of the twentieth century. These drugs—each of which can wipe out many kinds of disease-causing bacteria—have revolutionized our ability to save lives. Now, in the early years of the twenty-first century, the use of antibiotics is so widespread that certain viruses are becoming immune to their effects. This is potentially serious: What can be done when the major weapon against infection and disease is rendered ineffective? One answer lies in using the power of selection.

Phage—viruses that infect and kill bacteria—were discovered during the First World War. They were widely and effectively used in the 1920s and 1930s, until the development of antibiotics led to phage work being shelved. Scientists in the Soviet Union kept the work going, and results from the Bacteriological Research Institute in Tblisi, now part of the independent state of Georgia, are attracting renewed attention in the West. The first well-documented case of an antibiotic-resistant infection being cured by phage was in 1999 in Toronto, where a female heart patient, dying from a strain of staphylococcus aureus that resisted all the available drugs, was given an experimental treatment.

Phage work in a different way from antibiotics. While one antibiotic can kill many different strains of virus, each strain of phage attacks only one particular strain of virus. The phage seeks out its target, attaches itself to the bacterial cell and injects it with viral DNA. Within minutes, hundreds of new phage grow inside the cell until the target is burst apart and killed, allowing the new phage to search for remaining target cells. In this way, even a small dose of phage can eliminate a large bacterial infection in a few hours.

Given that each phage has a specific target, it is clearly critical to select the right phage to tackle the infection concerned. At the institute in Georgia, when a new phage is needed, the staff bring to bear the power of selection—using raw sewage as their starting point! Rich in viruses and biological matter, a good bucket full of sewage contains vast numbers of different organisms, including (apparently) the required phage. The question is, how to get it out? Staff at the institute grow the target bacteria on dishes in their laboratory, and smear liquid from the sewage onto the dishes. They then wait, and in time note that although the bacteria have multiplied on some dishes, on others they have reduced or disappeared. Samples from these dishes are grown on other bacteria-infected dishes to refine the resulting mixture. Eventually, they isolate the relevant phage ready for the treatment.[7]

There is a close parallel between the antibiotic and phage approaches, and conventional and solutions-focused methods in organizations. Just as antibiotics attack many strains of virus, popular business and organizational theories work quite well in many cases. In both the phage and solutions-focused approaches, the solution that fits the situation is uniquely and efficiently selected from the whole swirling complexity of the starting point, be it the organization wanting change, or the bucket of sewage.

Phage are selected by matching them against the target and seeing which works. In the Solutions Focus, you sort out what's working by means of questioning, acting and observing.

In both cases, our intention is to select the useful bits from the rest—and that's all. Each case requires a fresh platform to work on and another trawl through the bucket to find what works in this particular case.

Note that nothing is "changed" here; the process is more one of identification, selection and allowing nature to take its course. But the effect is decisive. Similarly, you can view the Solutions Focus as being a means of shifting with very little "change"—in fact, we often advise people to see how little they have to change to get results.

Notice how what works in these next two examples turns out to be much more significant than what doesn't, and how in both cases the idea of simple language helps keep matters on track.

A new leaf for an old plant: When the "culture" was right all along

On an industrial site in the UK, the managers had struggled for many years to get the workers to follow the latest operating procedures. The plant was complex and most of the workforce had been employed there for a long time. They knew the plant well, and operated it effectively and safely.

Difficulties arose, however, when managers changed the operating procedures. The revisions were carefully planned and the plant operating manuals were always updated with each revision. Due to the complexity of the plant, the manuals were large—many heavy volumes—and so were stored in central locations such as the control room. The need to ensure comprehensive and reliable updates meant that only a known, limited number of the manuals existed.

Few members of staff chose to visit these volumes. Instead, most carried a small notebook in which they collected information on the practical ins and outs of how to work the plant. These were individual, personal documents, built up over a working lifetime—but the problem was that there was no consistent updating procedure when processes or regulations changed.

The managers discouraged the notebooks, viewing them as unreliable and unofficial. "If only the culture could be changed to one where people referred to the official manuals," said one manager, "then the plant would be a safer and more profitable place."

They spent years trying to ensure that this happened by issuing orders and instigating formal processes, but to no avail. At last, thinking along solutions-focused lines, someone asked a crucial question: "When do people around here read instructions?" To which one answer was, "When the instructions are in their pocket books." This proved a key to finding a solution.

The plant managers printed looseleaf pocket books, sized to fit in an overall pocket, containing the most useful information that people really wanted, and nothing else. These were the key operating points—brief checklists, simple diagrams—that related to common operating errors and also to revisions of existing procedures. As these books were now part of the official plant documentation, updates could be controlled and issued regularly, in the confident expectation that everyone would receive them.

One might suggest that the "culture" had been right all along. It was just that in their enthusiasm to ensure that the plant was operated correctly, managers had lost sight of how that was being achieved already. In fact, in days gone by, the do-it-yourself notebooks had started precisely because all the clutter in the large manuals was preventing people finding the sections they needed, even in instances when the information was there.

Getting unstuck with a Solutions Focus: The Combe Down Stone Mines

The village of Combe Down, where Paul used to live, is built over and around the mines that provided the limestone that built the nearby World Heritage city of Bath. Early in the 1990s, the local authority saw an opportunity to fill the gradually deteriorating mines with a concrete mix, which would have handily disposed of an immense quantity of industrial waste. The scheme was so full of technical, environmental, political, legal and financial flaws that it rapidly got nowhere. Nonetheless, the village was blighted by the publicity the scheme received, and something still needed to be done to rehabilitate the stone mines.

The new project started to progress only when a positive vision—based on a Solutions Focus process about "what the community wanted"—replaced the negative vision of "trouble with the mines." The new picture of a preferred future began to generate energy and enthusiasm in council and villagers alike.

The new Combe Down project was described as "a flagship partnership project for B&NES (the local authority) that aims to apply best practice in the management of geological hazards in Combe Down." The key objectives were to:

❑ Ensure Combe Down is a stable, prosperous and accessible community.
❑ Help realize the potential of Combe Down to contribute to the sustainable economic development of B&NES as a whole.
❑ Rehabilitate the mines.

❏ Make best use of the area's historical, geological and environmental
   significance.

From these clearly solutions-focused goals, the project generated first steps,
including recognizing the mines as an asset, strengthening the road network
and preserving and enhancing the archaeology and wildlife of the area.

The plan drew on the existing resources, prompted by the counters question, which asked: "What reasons are there to have confidence in the Combe
Down area?" The answers included good employment prospects, as new firms
were moving in, and the opening or refurbishment of a number of local shops.
Parts of the desired future were already happening, including new building
developments, a new doctors' surgery, and an influx of people buying houses in
the village—in full knowledge of the circumstances.

Growing and expanding businesses

Entrepreneurs, business owners and chief executives around the world are
discovering the power of taking an explicit Solutions Focus for growing
and expanding their organizations. The two cases that follow show different ways to do this, starting with high-flying Japanese entrepreneur
Masanori Kanda, who turned his own business around after discovering
the Solutions Focus.

Part of the company credo

Organization is an eternal challenge for the entrepreneur. When your attention
is on building the business as fast as possible, things can get confused and
chaotic. Masanori Kanda of Almac Inc., Japan was in just this situation. He discovered the Solutions Focus and now uses the approach as part of his company
credo.

"My marketing consultancy was growing rapidly from a $3 million business
to a $6 million business. At that time I didn't know much about management,
and everything was completely chaotic and disordered. We struggled to send
out our products to the customers, the clerical and logistic side was terrible, and
people were stressed out, sometimes to the point of sickness.

"I came across the Solutions Focus approach, and started to try asking some of the Solutions Focus questions around the office. This was a very different kind of method from the analytical and logical way I was taught in business school, and I felt at the time that it was really a breakthrough. So I started to ask future perfect questions of my staff—and things started to go more smoothly! They began to think and come up with the steps for themselves; this is a big benefit of using this approach. I then experimented with other questions and processes.

"On one occasion, there was a mistake in our accounting department. A $100,000 transfer was messed up, with confusion between us and the bank. The employee concerned was very deflated. I would usually have addressed this by trying to find the cause of the problem, but decided to use a Solutions Focus instead. I asked the employee a future perfect question, and she started to describe it. Then we did some scaling—she was at 3 or 4 then, found small steps and gradually developed a way forward. Within a month everything was sorted out—we got back most of the money and moved on.

"Three months after the event, she confided to me that if I had tried to find out the cause of the problem and accused her, she would have resigned. That employee is now my chief operating officer! We have found many ways to use Solutions Focus methods in getting the management team to take up the reins of responsibility and create systems as we have grown. People still forget to do it sometimes though! So every month we remind ourselves and share the different ways we have used it. Two recent examples are with customer complaints and in changing management systems. The approach helps our staff to think for themselves in a focused and useful way.

"The Solutions Focus approach is so effective, and Japanese people seem to find it particularly useful. We like harmony, and the Solutions Focus offers some very constructive ways to make progress in very difficult situations without resorting to conflict."

Solutions-focused strategic planning in Canadian television

The Solutions Focus is a complete approach, and it can also add impetus to other methods. In this example from Canada, an entire strategic planning process is reinvigorated when an external consultant deploys Solutions Focus questions and processes at each step.

Alliance Atlantis of Toronto is a successful film and television business, which has changed its core strategy several times over the past 25 years. Now, as a specialty broadcaster and owner of the CSI—*Crime Scene Investigation*—television franchise, the organization was in the final stages of transition from its former entrepreneurial approach to a more structured, shareholder-held corporate business. It wanted to further improve its strategic planning method.

Alan Kay of the Glasgow Group was asked to bring an external facilitator's view to the planning, to design the process, advise on preparation work for the project, and facilitate the planning off-site sessions.

He began by interviewing the executive team using Solutions Focus questions to find what did not need to change and what had worked well in previous planning work. Although previous planning efforts sometimes stumbled into unproductive discussions, the team nonetheless was able to derive action-oriented plans. The second step was for core members of the management team to take an active part in preparing the plan, particularly to develop a solutions-focused view of the desired post-planning successes. They were also keen to get middle manager input to the plan.

Questions addressed in designing and executing the project were:

❏ How would participation by the mid-level managers in the pre-session planning work enhance post-plan alignment and implementation?
❏ How would it be useful if we asked our consumers and distributors about their needs?
❏ What difference would it make if the planning work was a visible stake in the ground, took root and sustained?

Answers to Solutions Focus questions like these helped the team see what kind of planning elements were needed to advance the planning process.

The planning process sequence was:

❏ Interview executive management—assess what's working plus past planning successes.
❏ Form a core team to design the planning activity and develop their post-planning preferred reality—the future perfect.

❏ Conduct mid-level management roundtables (participative dialogue sessions) about "What do we admire about our company?" "What could we do differently?"

❏ Conduct roundtables with the cable companies distributing Alliance Atlantis shows—"To be even more successful, what does your business need from partners like us?"

❏ Have the core team and chief executives prepare a key issues and opportunities assessment.

❏ Conduct the planning off-site workshop using the key issues presentations ensuring a solutions-focused dialogue about the key issues. At the planning session, discussions about the future of each aspect of the business were structured around: "What are we already good at in this area and in 2007 what will we be doing even better?" Here they created a vision statement and chose their strategic priorities. Finally, the team had a roundtable discussion on how successful plan implementation would work for the staff.

❏ Conduct a post-session core team review to discuss what's different since the planning event.

By layering Solutions Focus questions into each of the standard elements of the planning process, Alliance Atlantis took a more optimistic view of its current situation and created clearer possibilities for the future. Norm Bolen, executive VP for programming, said afterwards: "The Solutions Focus planning approach proved to be a highly useful and effective methodology. It helped the organization fulfill its potential and the planning resulted in clear stretch strategic objectives fleshed out with practical action plans. The outcomes were extremely positive for the organization and for the management team."

In this case, rather than rush in with his Solutions Focus toolkit, Alan took time to learn from the client organization what it had already done in strategic planning that worked well, and was careful to build the project on this. It can be easy to get overenthusiastic about using solutions tools, and to start using them irrespective of the fit with the case. Here, while using some of the tools, Alan also applied a Solutions Focus twist to existing strategic planning ideas and formats. The result was a more effective and focused piece of work, and a satisfied customer.

Building solutions between organizations in conflict

So far we have considered examples of solutions within organizations. But you can also apply the Solutions Focus in even more challenging situations—when there is conflict between organizations or groups.

Flying foxes: A complex multi-stakeholder problem

Flying foxes are fascinating creatures. Larger cousins of bats, Pteropus scapulatus live high up in the trees in the tropical rainforests of northeastern Australia. They hang upside down from trees to roost, and can grow to wingspans as wide as two metres. They find fruit, their preferred food, with their eyes rather than the echo-location systems of bats.

And fruit is the source of the problem. Northeastern Australia is also home to many (human) fruit growers. In 2002 they were up in arms about the quantity of crops lost to scavenging flying foxes and were taking direct action to deal with the creatures, including shooting them. Arrayed against them were conservation groups and scientists, who wanted to see this interesting and endangered species protected. The farmers were taken to court and banned from shooting the flying foxes. They felt aggrieved at being prevented from protecting their crops and livelihoods.

The Queensland government set up a trial working party to address the issue and got nowhere—the rival parties simply could not work together. Miles Shepheard of the Synergia consultancy was asked to run a workshop to get things moving. Miles knew that the issues were not new, and that the various parties held long-established views that could easily lead to deadlock. A debate had already been raging in the press, adding to the tension. "The two parties were at war," says Miles. "They were hurling their differences at each other. As soon as one side said 'black' the other said 'white.' I was asked to come in and facilitate."

 Miles started by building the platform—asking what the various parties wanted from the day and requesting them to list the issues. He accepted all the suggestions and put the list on the wall for reference. Continuing with his platform building, he split the workshop into "mixed" groups—participants from different sides working together—and asked them to define the five or six problems that, if solved, would make the most difference. Interestingly, no group came up with more than four key problems.

The time was now right to jump to the future perfect. Miles did this by posing the question: "Suppose, in five years time, this is all sorted out. What does it look like? What's going on? No 'how we got there'—only 'what is happening.'"

FUTURE
PERFECT

Miles still smiles at what happened next. "They had no trouble at all in working together to produce a detailed description of how things would be—cooperation started to break out." This list included:

❏ All fruit growers across Queensland have implemented effective, affordable, humane and sustainable integrated crop-protection systems on their properties after assessing the risks and choosing from a range of options.
❏ Flying fox management considerations rank alongside other pest management decisions and growers have identified a level of damage that they can viably sustain.
❏ A consensus has been reached about flying fox population sizes, trends and dynamics. With a clearer understanding of viable population sizes, a sustainable rate of culling in fruit orchards has been identified that supports a damage-mitigation framework.
❏ Flying fox populations have stabilized, the threats to habitats and populations have been minimized, and there are no flying fox species on a national or state threatened species list.
❏ Adequate habitats are preserved to provide for the conservation of flying foxes and to ensure abundant natural food supplies. Flying fox populations are in balance with available habitat area.

Miles then continued to build both the level of detail in the future perfect and the cooperation in the group by a process he calls "back-casting"—getting more information about the implications of this new world of flying fox sustainability and fruit production. He asked the group: "Suppose all this is happening. What else is in place to support the situation?"

The group continued to unpick the details, and came up with more information to support their future perfect, including:

❑ A comprehensive and well-resourced research program.
❑ A flying fox management and conservation plan, including population monitoring.
❑ A choice of crop-protection systems that are effective, affordable and sustainable.
❑ Strong partnerships between growers, researchers, regulators and conservationists.

AFFIRM

Miles now wisely resisted the temptation to start planning a strategy to deliver this future. Instead, he stopped and moved the discussion back to the present, affirming to the group that there seemed to be little difference between them on what they wanted. He asked them to think about very small things they could start to do, to work together on small projects that would begin to move things in the right

SMALL

direction—small actions.

Again, the group were able to produce practical ways to go forward together, including:

ACTIONS

❑ Prioritize research needs and identify funding opportunities through an iterative process between the group and key members of the research community.
❑ Strengthen communication links between Queensland, New South Wales and Victoria to stay better informed of progress and possibly to seek development of joint approaches.
❑ Improve the communication among the group and all stakeholders, including industry, conservationists and other interested people in the community.
❑ Have the Environmental Protection Agency develop guidelines for the damage mitigation permits for the next harvest season.

This would continue to promote practical cooperation and give the parties something to do instead of "hurling rocks at each other," as Miles puts it. They continued to work together, and the tensions between the stakeholders were replaced by cooperation and progress.

In this example, Miles managed to avoid getting bogged down in the problems during the platform building, and jumped straight to developing a detailed future perfect. He skillfully overlooked the history of the problems and the possible dire consequences, and focused on the "solution"—what people wanted. Having defined it, he then also avoided the trap of trying to make a strategy to deliver. Instead, he focused on small steps that could be taken quickly and together, building momentum without diverting energy and attention to complex and unknowable futures.

The Solutions Focus is as much about what is *not* done as what *is* done. This example shows both of these applied simply and with skill in an inflammatory situation. It also illustrates that you do not need to use all the solutions tools all the time. There is no one right way to apply solutions-focused ideas, and simply using the parts that seem to make sense in a given context is a useful way to proceed, particularly in organizational settings.

Positive deviance

Positive deviance is a fascinating new approach to organizational change that has much in common with the Solutions Focus. Originating from community problems such as malnourishment and HIV/AIDS, this approach involves identifying "positive deviants," people who are finding better solutions to pervasive problems than their neighbors despite having access only to the same resources. These "uncommon behaviors" can then be spread and adopted more widely by the community.

Taking responsibility for nutritional development in Vietnam

An early example came from Vietnam in the 1990s. Aid NGO Save the Children (SC) had received an invitation from the Vietnamese government to implement a program to address childhood malnutrition; at the time, 60 percent of children were estimated to be suffering. It was clear to all the stakeholders that the traditional approach—providing supplementary food—was unsustainable.

Despite the high prevalence of malnutrition, SC noticed that a small minority of poor families had children who were well nourished. How come? These families had no special access to food or other resources, and yet they seemed to be coping in a remarkably different way. A positive deviance investigation revealed that these families were feeding their children on free or inexpensive tiny shrimps and crabs found in rice paddies. These were not traditionally fed to small children. They also fed the children more frequently during the day.

Building on these successes, SC implemented a program enabling villagers to take responsibility for their own nutritional development, where this new practice of feeding children was learnt and spread through the region. The community developed and managed this program themselves, with the help of outsiders. The program has now reached a population of 2.2 million inhabitants in 250 Vietnamese communities.[8]

Key aspects of the positive deviance approach are:

❑ Although most problems have complex, interlinked underlying causes, the presence of positive deviants demonstrates that it is possible to find successful solutions *today*, before all the underlying causes are addressed.

❑ The assumption is that there is useful know-how waiting to be discovered.

❑ The know-how, being rooted in the context, automatically has a good fit and is therefore acceptable and relatively easy to spread.

❑ The focus is on changing the practice rather than the knowledge of those involved. The positive deviance website observes that "it's easier to act your way into a new way of thinking rather than think your way into a new way of acting."

❑ The knowledge comes from the specific context, the community or group in question, rather than from external experts. It's also important to repeat the inquiry within each community, as otherwise the approach simply reverts to "experts tell you best practice," a very different paradigm.

The positive deviance approach is now also reaching the business world,[9] with companies including Goldman Sachs and Hewlett-Packard using it in both management and technical challenges. Experience shows that the power of positive deviance, as with the Solutions Focus, lies in facilitating the people involved to discover, learn about and amplify the useful change that's already happening. The power of making things concrete—dealing directly with specific issues in simple language rather than with meaningless abstractions—is also visible in both cases.

More ways to find counters in organizations

Given that organizations are bursting with interactions, the relevant counters will often be close at hand, if only you can find the right questions to unearth them.

Sometimes counters lurk slightly further away, requiring different searches. This section describes seeking counters at random, and by doing something deliberately different.

Random counters

Nobel prize-winning physicist Murray Gell-Mann, in his book *The Quark and the Jaguar*, postulates that the world around us is the result of the laws of physics and a whole set of "frozen accidents."[10] The fact that all the cars of a certain model look basically alike is not random—the cars were made from the same design. But the fact that a particular design was chosen was (in the wide scheme of things) an accident.

Accidents that are "frozen" or selected have an important place in evolutionary change. In applying the Solutions Focus, you are on the lookout for "happy accidents," random occasions when, for no very good reason, circumstances conspire to produce an event that is useful, positive, part of the preferred future.

You are interested in this kind of event because it shows one way in which this can happen. It provides clues about how to have it happen more. No matter whether the positive result was intended or not, it is a

useful element to know about, to reflect on, to watch for again or deliberately to set about engineering in the future.

Many great discoveries have been made by accident. Alexander
Fleming noticed that the mold on his dirty lab dishes was killing other
bacteria, and discovered penicillin. X rays were accidentally discovered by
Wilhelm Roentgen in 1895 when he noticed that an early fluorescent
screen, by chance close to his electrical apparatus, emitted light when the
equipment was switched on.

If you watch out for and successfully identify such useful occurrences,
you can make a great impact by capitalizing on them. If they are not spotted, or are written off as flukes or irrelevancies, they are rapidly lost for
ever. Adopting the Solutions Focus helps you to be aware of the importance of these events, to search for them, to notice when they happen,
and to use the results to construct new and better futures.

Note how this process works in reverse too. If you study the times
when things go wrong, you become expert in how to do things
wrong—but perhaps less informed than you think about when matters
go right.

Sometimes people ask us if, by focusing on what's better, we're ignoring what's bad. Not at all. Our objective is to replace what's bad with
something better. This may happen in a disciplinary situation at work, for
example. Someone may be on course for dismissal if they persist, and we
need to make sure that they know that. And at the same time, we can
search for counters to help move the future in a different direction.

Do something different—evolving change

Our description of the course of change in organizations—changes
created by small actions that are prompted by desired futures—closely
parallels the way evolution works.

Small changes—mutations—are happening all the time. The question
is which are selected and carried on. In evolution, the selection is at the
mercy of the environment. In the Solutions Focus, by focusing on what
you want and then seeking to discover it, selection is intentional.

It is surprising how often people set out to aim for one notch up a scale, then find themselves in an evolutionary spiral that takes them three notches or all the way to the top, as obstacles are swept away or side-stepped. This is partly because success breeds success, and perhaps also because you—having constructed a detailed picture of the future perfect—can now readily recognize it and more easily aim for it as it unfolds.

Probes

Organizational solutions evolve in this real sense out of huge numbers of interactions, most of which were happening to some extent already. As Daniel Dennett puts it in his book *Darwin's Dangerous Idea*, evolution is random things happening plus selection.[11] So, consider generating new possibilities by doing something different, then selecting from the results.

Businesses can try doing something different in a relatively cheap and effective way by using "probes." You may be familiar with the idea of a probe from *Star Trek* or from information on real-life space exploration—a small instrument launched to gather information from a distant place.

In the business context, a probe is a kind of experiment, done quickly and cheaply to test an idea and gather information from the world around us. In their book *Competing on the Edge*, Shona Brown and Kathleen Eisenhardt discuss the use of low-cost, numerous and highly varied probes to inform a corporation about what works.[12] These include experimental products and trial alliances.

Brown and Eisenhardt note the advantages of probes as effective ways to learn. They are hands on rather than vicarious, so the learning takes place in the world rather than in the managers' heads.

It reminds us of the two managers who wanted to find out about possibilities of international cooperation. One manager stayed in his office and read the *Financial Times*, seeking to identify targets for an approach. The other manager boarded an airplane, headed off to a likely spot in eastern Europe and asked questions. Soon he had contacts, knowledge of the situation on the ground and several offers of contracts.

This focus on testing in the world and getting feedback, rather than musing in your head and appreciating more about what you are thinking, is the pragmatic heart of the Solutions Focus.

Another advantage of probes is that they provide options for the future. A variety of possibilities, all tested and explored, give a good basis for choosing further action.

Don't expect all probes to succeed. You want sufficient variety to assure yourself you are exploring widely. Concentrating on only one area or one type of probe leaves organizations open to changes in other areas. For example, probes that target only existing customers can leave a gap where new market entrants might find a whole new vein of sales potential.

Brown and Eisenhardt conclude:

> *The best probes reveal the unexpected, the unanticipated, and the previously unknown. Probes insert an element of randomness that freshens thinking. After all, why investigate what is already known?*
>
> *When probes surprise, they stimulate creative thinking. From a competitive point of view probes that surprise can reveal frame-breaking ways to compete that alter "the rules of the game." Probes take creative thinking beyond the limitations of an office-bound brainstorming exercise to possibilities that managers simply cannot imagine on their own.*[13]

Note the emphasis on doing something differently—rather than just thinking, not doing and then feeling surprised that nothing happened.

When you apply the Solutions Focus, you are acting in this same spirit—to discover what happens, to gather more information about what works, and sometimes about what doesn't.

You act hopefully, of course, but success is not guaranteed first time. What is guaranteed is a better chance of finding something that works, if not first time then second or third.

Toward the solutions-focused organization?

Having read this far, you may be thinking, "That's terrific. What I need to do now is have everyone in my organization working like this. Let's be a solutions-focused organization!"

We applaud your aspirations and expect you to make good progress along this road. But first consider the talking trap.

The talking trap

People in organizations achieve an immense amount by talking. It is a skill that allows us to say anything from describing the weather to vocalizing our innermost thoughts. Often our first attempts to resolve issues at work are by talking. For example, we ask people to behave differently. We talk to our boss, our colleagues, our subordinates, anyone who will listen. And we remain undaunted by those who won't.

> *"We are supposed to preach without preaching, not by words but by our actions."*
> Mother Teresa *(cited on a plaque at the Martin Luther King Centre for Non-Violent Social Change, Atlanta, Georgia)*

Yet sometimes, even then, nothing happens. We may be falling into the talking trap. We understand that talking to people ought to work, and in any reasonable circumstance it surely would. But we have found that it doesn't in this case. So stop doing what doesn't work and do something else.

When the various forms of talking fail to resolve a problem, it is time to act. Note, too, the difference between acting while you announce your action, and simply acting.

Acting is often more powerful than talking. And before you act, you may want to listen to this advice from experienced solutions consultant Michael Durrant:

1 *If you set out to "change the organization to Solution Focus" you will most likely learn a useful lesson about how to manufacture resistance.*

Anything that gives staff the impression of "starting next week, you are all going to change the way you think and act" is almost guaranteed to provoke a range of responses from "oh, no, we're not" to "yeah, just try and make us." It's natural, of course—if we start to tell everyone that they've got to start working differently, they naturally assume that we are criticizing the way they've been working up until now.

2   *Organizations who've made progress didn't set out to impose (or even encourage) the adoption of a particular framework or model. They worked hard to identify the kind of place they wanted to be, including what they were already doing that was working, and began from a consideration of the kinds of values they wanted to demonstrate. Once you identify the kinds of values the people in the organization want to reflect (and they are usually "empowering," "working cooperatively," etc.) and then really begin to figure out what difference these values might make to how we do things (so, what will "empowering people" really look like? What kinds of things will our customers notice different about us? etc.), then the staff are most likely to come up with some of the kinds of things you're wanting. If they have helped build the direction (goal) they're more likely to want to go there!*

3   *I don't set out to "sell" Solutions Focus to people. I am conscious of trying to demonstrate the process by the way I encourage them to focus on some of what they were already doing that was working and where they wanted to go. In the end, I can maybe present Solutions Focus to them as something that might be helpful and might fit with the direction in which they were wanting to go. That is, adopting Solutions Focus can be a consequence of their change in direction rather than the impetus for it.*

4   *Once they'd clarified their goals and identified Solutions Focus as a means for helping get there, then further training etc. was able to be more purposive and definitive.*

Conclusions

The examples of coaching, team building and wholescale organizational change by no means exhaust the potential applications of the Solutions Focus. Indeed, many of its most obvious uses are in contexts of personal development, close to the method's sources in counseling and psychology. It can prove remarkably effective for workers in organizations in both one-to-one settings and as a self-help technique.

In the next chapter, you'll read ideas about how to apply the process as an art and as a science.

14

The Solutions Artist and Scientist

"I know that most men, including those at ease with problems of the greatest complexity, can seldom accept even the simplest and most obvious truth if it be such as would oblige them to admit the falsity of conclusions which they have delighted in explaining to colleagues, which they have proudly taught to others and which they have woven, thread by thread, into the fabric of their lives."

Leo Tolstoy

The key to applying the Solutions Focus is keep things as simple (and SIMPLE) as possible. Simple, however, does not always mean easy. There is definitely a deal of skill in using the Solutions Focus effectively.

Sometimes you are an artist—creatively, flexibly and intuitively wielding your solutions tools on each new project. At other times, you work as a scientist—probing, observing, taking meticulous care with language, waiting for the results of your experiments before calculating the next step.

The solutions artist

It is easy to create the impression that there is a fixed sequence for applying the Solutions Focus to your circumstances of change. This book, like any explanation, follows a certain order. And while there is a logic to that order, it would be a mistake to imagine that the order must be adhered to rigidly. If the overriding principle is to do what works, there will be times when a different order will work better.

Sometimes you will reshuffle your solutions pack, and on other occasions you will drop some of the cards altogether. It all depends. What you have here is a kit to adopt and adapt with discretion and finesse.

Just as Monet painted 24 pictures of haystacks and all of them were different, so are 24 solution-focused projects in the same organization, 24 teams seeking to improve their performance, or 24 different performers being coached to similar goals.

Your awareness counts. It keeps you responsive to minute and subtle changes in the responses of the people you work with. Who has an impact on whom? Is there a sense that the step proposed is of the right size? These are the nuances with which you deal, retaining your sense of immediacy, of being in the here and now.

Personal styles vary, but you will not go far wrong if your style includes a foundation of respect. The people you work with will trust you when you show respect, and this will lead toward your guidance being valued, good results and plenty of engagements in the future.

In the practical world of companies, you are searching for usefulness rather than truth, better rather than right. The Solutions Focus is the process of co-constructing "better" (rather than right, wrong, good, bad).

Each organizational quest is an exploration of the relative. It is finding out what better looks like and what change seekers are up to when they are doing it. It is about discovering what's there when the problems are not there for a while, or not there any more.

The solutions scientist

Along with flexibility of interpretation and individual style, there are aspects of applying the Solutions Focus more often associated with the cool and sober style of the scientist.

You adopt a beginner mindset when examining what's happening. This means avoiding prejudgment of what's important. If you are following up your prefigured expectations and hunches, the vital information about what works can be streaming over your head, out of the window, and into oblivion.

Sometimes the search for solutions, or evidence of possibilities and counters, is almost forensic. The difference, for example, between "He never does that" and "He hardly ever does that" is potentially enormous. There is a world of possibility to prise open from the knowledge that there are rare occasions when he does.

So, avoid treating the Solutions Focus as a formula. If one aspect of the approach turns out to be inappropriate, you can readily try something else.

If, for example, someone reacts to compliments as a debilitating experience, switch tack. Maybe try "not-compliments," such as "Mmm, I'm not sure whether you are up to this." The response may be more constructive than you expect.

> "I tend to find that when Solution Focus isn't 'working' it's actually because I have (imperceptibly) stopped really using it."
> Rayya Ghul, Canterbury Christ Church University College

Some executives are suspicious if it appears too easy for them to reach their desired future. Perhaps the good results are only temporary. In these cases, a colleague's pessimistic demeanor can lead to greater determination and confidence.

Others are reluctant to engage with strengths unless equal justice is done to weaknesses. Naturally with such people you examine and acknowledge weaknesses, although at least taking pains to reframe the weaknesses as characteristics that they would like to do something about.

Even with the most straightforward cases, consider how you propose to overcome obvious obstacles on your route to the future, particularly once you have found a way ahead that seems to be paying off.

Keep on keeping on

Many people have a natural affinity for the Solutions Focus: As they learn about it, the new behavior is embedded quickly. And because the Solutions Focus is a method of bespoke solutions construction—the solution is tailored to fit the customer—it comes as no surprise that the customer for change is generally comfortable with it.

Once a solution has been found, it usually slots easily into place and all concerned can continue with their (now slightly different) lives. Not much is "changed," but there can be effects far beyond the original purpose of the solution. In fact, the Solutions Focus is effective precisely because of the focus on using what's there. Sometimes we caution overeager managers to change as little as possible. Concerns about a "quick fix" can be seen in this context: Nothing is really fixed, it is simply allowed to function as it always has, but within some slightly different context.

If keeping on track does not always prove easy, remember what works for you and keep doing it. Simply remembering what works and then not actually doing it is usually insufficient! Each reapplication of what works is also an opportunity for new learning and experimentation.

And as our friend, colleague and top learning consultant Dave Meier says, "The learning is in the 'wobbles.'" Each time you work harder to stay SIMPLE and discover what works in a particular case, the more you'll learn.

And finally...

Remember that the Solutions Focus is about finding what works and stopping doing what doesn't work. The ideas in this book are meant to be simple, practical and effective. Believe the world rather than the model, and if it doesn't appear to be working, do something different.

15

How We Reached Here

We have developed the ideas in this book from many strands of thought and practice. The main precursors include:

❑ The systems thinking and communication research of Gregory Bateson.
❑ The psychotherapeutic genius of Milton Erickson.
❑ The "interactional view" developed by John Weakland and co-workers.
❑ The shift from problem to solution focus led by Steve de Shazer and Insoo Kim Berg.

This chapter sets out the story so far, positioning *The Solutions Focus* in its proper context, clarifying the links, similarities and differences to its related disciplines.

Anthropology and systems

On the East Coast of the US in 1947, the ideas eventually known as systems thinking were formed in an intellectual ferment. Following the Second World War, the first computers were developed hand in hand with mathematical and philosophical breakthroughs.

One of the leaders of this systemic revolution was English anthropologist Gregory Bateson. Before the war he was noted for his research in the South Pacific islands with his then wife Margaret Mead. They became immersed in the new concepts of cybernetics—the science of communication and control systems in living organisms and machines—and how these applied to group processes. Their daughter, Mary Catherine Bateson, recalls Norbert Wiener, now known as the "father of cybernetics," visiting frequently, "smoking smelly cigarettes, pouring out his latest idea ... without being much interested in the response."[1]

One day Bateson was puzzling over an equation sent to him by Warren McCulloch, the neurophysiologist who first developed mathematical models of neural networks. The phone rang and the slightly nervous young man on the line introduced himself as John Weakland, a student of cultural anthropology who was interested in Bateson's work. When he mentioned he had formerly been an engineer, Bateson interrupted him, said "Come right over," and solicited his help in understanding McCulloch's equation.[2] This began a relationship that would have a profound effect on the social sciences, and on groups, families and organizations into the twenty-first century.

Bateson proposed a research project examining how disrupted, confused and paradoxical communication might give rise to some of the patterns of behavior called mental illness. In 1952, he raised a grant from the Rockefeller Foundation and, over a celebratory dinner at Peter's Back Yard restaurant in Greenwich Village, offered Weakland a job on the project.[3]

Paradoxes in communication

Weakland moved to the West Coast with Bateson and they set up shop in the Veteran's Hospital at Menlo Park, California. Bateson had also recruited Jay Haley and William Fry, and together they examined paradoxes of abstraction in human communication. It was varied work: They introduced the novel practice of taping interviews with schizophrenics at the hospital and studied their conversational patterns. They were all interested in film criticism and compared notes on Chinese, German and American movies. They went to the zoo and observed animals communicating. Their first important publication was "Toward a Theory of Schizophrenia."[4]

Enter Milton Erickson

Bateson also introduced his team to doctor and psychotherapist Milton Erickson, who already had a reputation for achieving startling results with his clients through his use of language. Weakland and Haley visited Erickson regularly for 17 years. Haley recalled[5] that Erickson helped to keep them in the real world, in contrast to Bateson's thoughts and abstractions; a prime case of Occam's Razor, perhaps.

Haley says: "I remember talking to Erickson about a case I had of a patient, one of those in our project [at the hospital] who had the idea that his stomach was full of cement and that was very painful for him. And he kept objecting to this cement. I was trying to get him over this idea by making interpretations about mother's milk, that sort of thing, and I went to Erickson, and I said, 'What would you do with this patient who got this idea he's got cement in his stomach?' And Erickson said, 'I would go to the hospital dining room and see how the food is.'"

The Mental Research Institute

In 1959 Bateson's team founded the Mental Research Institute in Palo Alto, California, to continue their study of communication in groups and to extend their work with families. Under Don Jackson, the group developed the revolutionary conjoint family therapy approach, observing and interacting with whole family groups rather than just the "patient." The nearby Stanford University had a Center for Advanced Studies in the Behavioral Sciences and this provided a source of interesting ideas and new recruits.

Early research associates included Paul Watzlawick, an Austrian and a professor at Stanford, Richard Fisch and Virginia Satir, later to make her own name in family therapy. Scottish psychiatrist RD Laing was also a visitor.

The MRI approach of exploring how communication—in the broadest sense—between people could create and maintain problem behavior grew in influence. The first training program began in 1962, and co-directors Weakland and Fisch founded the Brief Therapy Center in 1967, maintaining their links with Bateson and Erickson.

When Don Jackson died in 1968, aged just 48, Weakland said, "The most basic contribution Jackson made was to be among the first to see things in terms of what people are doing between each other in the present, rather than get stuck on the idea that behavior just depends on something that comes from the inside and has no relationship to the world people live in."[6]

The MRI's basic philosophy of change[7] can be stated thus: People have difficulties all the time. They routinely resolve these difficulties as part of everyday life. Occasionally, a difficulty is mishandled; the attempts to resolve it fail. If this happens repeatedly and the people concerned have no better alternative solutions, then a problem is created and they seek help. As the problem is the result of continued misapplication of the wrong attempted solution, our job is to have them stop doing that and do something else. Once they have found what works, they simply need to do more of it. In short:

1 If it ain't broke, don't fix it.
2 Stop doing what doesn't work and do something different.
3 Once you know what works, do more of it.

When Mark visited the MRI in 1994, he was delighted to find the operation still in full swing. In the modest building in Palo Alto sit the results of thousands of hours of observation by the team, now expanded and augmented. John Weakland was weak from illness and sadly died in 1995. Dick Fisch still directs the Brief Therapy Center, while Paul Watzlawick, who is 85 as we write, remains active as a teacher and faculty member. Thinking about all the different approaches and people who had passed through this place was tremendously exciting, and to find the originators ready and willing to talk about their work over a pizza was a valuable and welcome discovery.

The roads from Palo Alto

In the early 1970s, the original MRI approach was taken up and adapted around the world. Jay Haley wrote his book on Erickson, *Uncommon Therapy*, in 1973 and founded the strategic therapy school. In Italy, Mara Selvini Palazzoli and co-workers founded the Milan school of systemic family therapy.

Meanwhile, Bateson took an interest in the work of a neighbor, Richard Bandler, and his colleague John Grinder, then a young linguistics professor at Stanford. The two were interested in therapy and change work and Bandler was running a Gestalt group. Bateson introduced them to Erickson, setting in train the events that led to neuro-linguistic programming (NLP). Bandler and Grinder also observed Virginia Satir and (on tape due to his demise) Gestalt therapist Fritz Perls. Their conclusions about the linguistic patterns utilized by these master therapists were published[8] before they coined the NLP name.

Since the 1970s NLP—usually defined as the study of the structure of subjective experience—has developed into an increasingly complicated collection of models, theories and schools. It is now widely known as an approach to therapy and personal development. Sue Knight's book *NLP at Work*[9] is one of the more practical offerings aimed at people in an organizational context.

From problem to solution

In the mid-1970s two fresh faces arrived at MRI: Steve de Shazer, a keen saxophonist and home brewer interested in language and philosophy, and pharmacologist-turned-therapist Insoo Kim Berg from Korea. Together, they founded the Brief Family Therapy Center in Milwaukee in 1978, using their house as collateral. Wally Gingerich, Eve Lipchik and Alex Molnar were key members of the team.

As de Shazer and Berg refined their practice, they "serendipitously"[10] realized that the MRI approach could be made even simpler. They figured that no people "problem" happened consistently all the time. There were moments when it was not happening or happened less—when times were better. The easiest key to progress was to discover when and how this occurred and encourage more of it. This reversed two of MRI's principles of change, giving us:

1 If it ain't broke, don't fix it.
2 Once you know what works, do more of it.
3 Stop doing what doesn't work and do something different.

This seems a modest adjustment. However, the kind of conversation you have when searching for times when matters are better is very different from an apparently similar conversation searching for previous failed solutions.

De Shazer and Berg's solution-focused brief therapy clients also produced other useful ways of defining and discovering progress. The "day after the miracle" and scales are examples of ideas that clients proffered, Berg picked up and used, and de Shazer noticed and captured.[11]

De Shazer spotted connections with Ludwig Wittgenstein's linguistic philosophy, a fascinating parallel that often helps people to understand some distinctive aspects of solutions-focused work.

Philosophically minded readers may know that Wittgenstein's work is generally seen as falling into two phases. His early work, published as the *Tractatus Logico-Philosophicus*, broadly sought to put "problems" of language, and hence philosophy, on a firm, logical basis. The second phase, from the 1930s to his death in 1951, recognized the futility of the first endeavor and took a more pragmatic stance, investigating how we use language in terms of games with rules created as we go along.

Although these two efforts are different, they have a core of common ideas, and this book includes quotations from both phases of Wittgenstein's work.

Solutions spread

The Milwaukee ideas spread around the world. De Shazer and Berg continue to publish books on their approach.[12] Other authors, including Bill O'Hanlon, Brian Cade and Michelle Weiner-Davis, were reaching similar conclusions based on their own experiences with Erickson and the MRI. With the deaths of both Bateson and Erickson in 1980, the torch passed to the next generation.

The solutions-focused approach is now spreading rapidly, not only through the "people professions" but in many situations where progress is wanted. We know of applications and conferences relating to education, conflict resolution and mediation, prison, self-help, parenting and occupational therapy, for example.

While writing the first edition of this book, we made contact with other organizational consultants and coaches who were finding their own ways to use solutions-focused ideas in their work. Eager to discover even more connections and ideas, we and our Bristol Solutions Group colleagues decided to host a conference. We invited anyone in the world using these ideas in organizations to join us for a three-day event in Bristol, to be known as SOL 2002. We expected about 30 people to attend. In the event, more than 80 practitioners from nine countries found their way to the UK's West Country to participate.

SOL (Solutions in Organisations Linkup) has now become an annual conference, and has recently spawned a summer university residential program. SOL 2003, also in Bristol, led to the production of a series of articles published as *Positive Approaches to Change*.[13] SOL 2006 in Vienna attracted participants from 20 countries. Workshops addressed all manner of organizational contexts, from coaching to conflicts and learning to leadership, with many international authors and presenters adding their knowledge to the mix. For information about SOL events, visit www.sol-world.org.

We have also been introducing these ideas within companies around the world, and have been struck by how much support and how little disagreement we have found. From workers at the sharp end to leaders in the boardroom, we meet people wanting to grasp these ideas and start to use them. We know of organizations helping themselves to better performance via leadership development, coaching, teamworking, appraisal, meetings, questionnaires, strategic planning, competence management, training, creativity, feedback, outplacement and even health and safety—all using a solutions-focused twist to help them on their way.

Research findings

A growing canon of research is proving the effectiveness of solutions-focused approaches in a wide variety of settings, including mental health, school behavior problems, anger management, family and marital therapy, occupational health and rehabilitation, problem drinking and prison.[14] There are more than 40 studies, including controlled randomized studies, which assess the effectiveness of the Solutions Focus methodology. Clients reported improvement in 60–80 percent of cases, figures as good as or better than comparative treatments, and mostly achieved in between one and five sessions. Interestingly, in many of the studies the work was implemented by relatively inexperienced workers, often just recently trained. For an annually updated summary of research, visit the website of EBTA president Dr Alasdair Macdonald at www.psychsft.freeserve.co.uk.

Mark McKergow

Mark's first inkling of solutions-focused work came during an MBA degree course with the Open University. As a reformed physicist turned manager in the electricity industry, he was keen to find helpful new ways of thinking and acting. He spent time learning to apply neuro-linguistic programming (NLP) to his work, as a scientist being interested in the ideas and philosophy behind it, and discovered the work of Gregory Bateson and Milton Erickson.

A chance encounter with philosopher James Wilk introduced Mark to solutions. Mark liked the clarity and simplicity of this line: sharper, less theory burdened, easier to learn, pragmatic and focused on results for an individual.

For the next year or so between consulting assignments, he trained with key figures such as Steve de Shazer and Bill O'Hanlon. He was struck by the way in which the ideas of the Solution Focus were being applied in a huge range of circumstances, from difficult psychotherapy cases to social work, family and child protection, and workplace counseling. And these were experienced, feet-on-the-ground professionals dealing with their most challenging situations.

At around this time Mark chanced on a copy of M Mitchell Waldrop's *Complexity: The Emerging Science at the Edge of Order and Chaos*. Waldrop described the development of complexity science—a descendant of chaos theory—in which economists, biologists, mathematicians and others were grappling with systems that, although simple in essence, produced complex, beautiful and unexpected results. Even if all the properties of the system were known, there was no way, short of having a go, to calculate how the overall interactions would turn out. The reflexive and systemic nature of such systems has strong resonance with the development of cybernetics some 40 years earlier.

The striking aspect of all of this was a link backward and a link forward. During his PhD research, Mark had carried out computer simulations of hydrogen in metals. At low temperatures, hydrogen atoms can form themselves into ordered structures in the gaps between the metal atoms. These were, had the term been coined then, complex systems. A full calculation of the ways in which model hydrogen atoms interacted was impossible, and Mark had spent months performing Monte Carlo computer simulations, starting from a random arrangement and seeing how things resolved each time.

The link forward was to solutions. Here again were the same ideas: simple interactions leading to complex and unpredictable phenomena, the primacy of "what happens" over theory, the focus on describing events in as simple a way as possible without ignoring the vital factors. Since then the application of complexity ideas to management has become a hot topic, but often in hotly debated terms of applying a general "theory" to a general "organization." Mark liked the way that the Solutions Focus was different each time it was applied, so the fact that different things happened in different places was not only unsurprising, it was normal.

Mark quickly realized that these ideas would take their place in his own fields of consulting, facilitating and training in organizations. In particular, he appreciated how solutions were rooted in interactions between people, rather than starting in the unknowable and indescribable world of guessing about what goes on inside people's heads. Seeking a way forward, he and fellow Bristol-based solutions enthusiast and counselor Harry Norman founded the Bristol Solutions Group, the world's first cross-disciplinary solutions-focused network and support group.

Paul Z Jackson

A year or so later, Mark introduced Paul to the Solutions Focus. Paul had graduated to consultancy and training from the diverse careers of newspaper journalism and making radio comedy programs for the BBC. He had spent a parallel ten years training three groups of performers—in Cardiff, Manchester and the southwest of England—to deliver hundreds of improvised comedy shows on stage.

These were intensely practical efforts, with instant measurements of success—either members of the audience laughed or they didn't. And if they did, the question was whether you could make them laugh more.

Paul distilled the mechanisms of laughter through improvisation and began teaching spontaneity, adaptability and creativity to members of the public and to teams within organizations. The emphasis was always on what worked, with new ideas added to the stockpile if and only if they proved their usefulness.

He was immediately impressed by the simplicity and power of the solutions approach, and devoured a bookshelf of solutions-focused literature, attended courses and conferences, and began applying the Solutions Focus in his consultancy work.

One great attraction was the derivation of solutions from the participants' own resources, their skills and successes rather than failures and deficits. Working with comedians, actors and writers in radio, television, and theater, he had always been struck by how much better they responded to praise, encouragement and a view to the future than to criticism and retrospective analysis.

Almost all of Paul's creative work involves collaboration, which fits well with the co-construction—inbetween—aspects of solution building. These elements of joint creative effort are as important and effective with leaders and managers, office and factory workers, as they are with more obviously artistic talents.

He also liked the pragmatism, having benefited from many quirky examples of what worked as keys for getting results in pressurized situations—such as improvising comedy in front of a live audience. While one performer might need an intensive group warm-up, another would do better with a quiet drink alone in a bar, then both would deliver the goods. It was possible to find some commonalities, but the main lessons were about diversity and how it was impossible to predict what would suit the next candidate.

Each solution is unique and fresh, yet here was a method offering a robust, logical set of principles, which could enable skilled yet skeptical individuals or groups of players to reach amazingly high levels of performance. The methods, themselves flexible, deliver us to the point from which an on-the-day "what works" can be applied, enjoyed and relied on.

The Solutions Focus, as you may have discovered in this book, chimes with many aspects of improvisation. In impro, one of the key techniques is to respond to suggestions with the words "yes" and "and." The "yes" directly parallels the solutions requirement of accepting what the customer for change tells you. Then we are ready together for the "and," which is about proposing the next step forward.

In any drama, convincing an audience depends on performers staying "here and now," in a state of responsive alertness. In the Solutions Focus, instead of arriving with a theory, a consultant or facilitator arrives with an interest in what's happening here and now. We work with these people, in their present circumstances, aiming to help them achieve their objectives.

We also know that they have a problem or are stuck in some way, and that it will be a rewarding process to help them get out of it.

We need to remain alert primarily because "everything is a useful gift"—a key tenet of improvisation and a direct inheritance from the Solutions Focus's therapeutic great-grandfather, Milton Erickson, who called it utilization. The idea is to welcome the new, unusual, peculiar or even problematic aspect and use it, to the full. That is often what creates the magic in an impro scene: the mistake, the audience suggestion, the novelty. And it is often the key to the solution in an organization.

Acknowledgments

We acknowledge the writings and speakings of our friends and colleagues in the world of solutions. We must first pay tribute to Steve de Shazer and Insoo Kim Berg, founders of the Brief Family Therapy Center in Milwaukee, without whom none of this would have been the same. Then there are our Bristol Solutions Group colleagues: Harry Norman, Jenny Clarke, John Henden and Kate Hart, and Ron Banks.

The people we have trained with and learnt from include the Brief Therapy Practice in London, in particular Harvey Ratner, Evan George and Jane Lethem; Bill O'Hanlon, Brian Cade, Paul Watzlawick and Dick Fisch. The discussions we've had with Matthias Varga von Kibèd, Rayya Ghul, Jonathan Prosser, Alasdair Macdonald, Harry Korman, Michael Hjerth, Gale Miller, James Wilk, Janine Waldman and Michael Durrant (over a curry) have all been most illuminating.

We thank the participants on the Solution Focused Therapy listserv (SFT-L) and the Solutions in Organisations listserv (SOLUTIONS-L), and delegates at the 1997, 1999 and 2000, 2001, 2002, 2003 and 2004 European Brief Therapy Association conferences in Bruges, Carlisle, Turku, Dublin, Cardiff, Berlin and Amsterdam respectively (sorry, we missed Salamanca 1998). We have greatly enjoyed and valued all the learning, connections and conversations at the SOL conferences: 2002 and 2003 (Bristol), 2004 (Stockholm), 2005 (Interlaken), 2006 (Vienna); and the SOL Summer Universities, 2005 (Venice) and 2006 (Prague). Thanks also to those who have helped us to spread the word around the world with their energy and industry in promoting open workshops: Alan Kay (Canada), Edwin Tan (Singapore), Debra Knox (New Zealand), Solutionwork and FKC (Sweden), Anna Nöst (Austria), Coert Visser, Gwenda Schlundt Bodien and Louis Cauffman (the Netherlands).

Particular thanks to all those who gave us their ideas and case examples; your names are in the text. And our many clients, who helped us form our ideas and allowed us to put them into practice.

References

Chapter 2

1 Reported in Paul Watzlawick, *How Real Is Real?*, Viking, 1977.
2 Wally Gingerich & Sheri Eisengart, "Solution-focused brief therapy: A review of the outcome research," *Family Process*, 39: 477–98, 2000.

Chapter 3

1 Aryeh Keshet, of Haifa, Israel, interviewed Turku, Finland, August 2000.

Chapter 4

1 At the World Conference for Systemic Management, Vienna, May 2001.
2 See Mitchell Resnick, *Turtles, Termites and Traffic Jams,* MIT Press, 1994.
3 Reported in the *Guardian,* 17.8.99.
4 Steven Rose, *Lifelines,* Allen Lane/Penguin Press, 1997, p 93.
5 *Ibid.,* p 140.
6 At a meeting of the Cheltenham Festival of Literature, 1997.

Chapter 5

1 Bill O'Hanlon and Michelle Weiner-Davis, *In Search of Solutions,* Norton, 1999, p 15.
2 Jeffrey K Zeig and W Michael Munion, *Milton H Erickson,* Sage, 1999, p 42.

3 Noel McElearney, based on "Under stress and M&S: Helping the real experts to take charge," *People Management*, 30 September 1999, pp 34–5.

Chapter 6

1 *Independent on Sunday*, 13 December 1998.
2 A fuller version of the Frito-Lay story is told by Peters and Waterman in *In Search of Excellence*, HarperCollins, 1982.
3 *Independent on Sunday*, 17 October 1999.
4 Steven Rose, *Lifelines*, Allen Lane/Penguin Press, 1997, pp 291–2.
5 "Pigeonholed," *New Scientist*, 30 September 2000, pp 38–41.
6 Robert Rosenthal and Lenore Jacobson, *Pygmalion in the Classroom*, Irvington, New York, 1968, expanded 1992. See also Robert T Tauber, *Self Fulfilling Prophecy: A Practical Guide to its Use in Education*, Praeger, 1997.
7 Referred to in "Pygmalion in the classroom," *National Teaching and Learning Forum*, 8(2), 1999.
8 Martin Seligman, *Learned Optimism*, Random House, 1991.

Chapter 7

1 John Heaton and Judy Groves, *Wittgenstein for Beginners*, Icon Books, 1994.
2 Prof Andrew Derrington, professor of psychology, University of Nottingham (from "Psych yourself up," *Weekend FT*, 29 January 2000).
3 Solutions Focused Therapy listserv, 2 April 1998.

Chapter 8

1 For an example of spirited debate between physicists and economists, see M Mitchell Waldrop, *Complexity*, Viking, 1993, pp 136–43.
2 Story from Judy, Solutions Focused Therapy listserv, 26 October 1988, who attributes it to the mystic and sage Gurdjieff.
3 Karl Popper, *Conjectures and Refutations*, Basic Books, New York, 1963, recounted in Bill O'Hanlon and James Wilk, *Shifting Contexts*, Guilford Press, 1987.

4 Paul Z Jackson, *Impro Learning*, Gower, 1998.
5 John Ziman, *Reliable Knowledge*, Cambridge University Press, 1978, p 8.
6 Professor Andrew Derrington, professor of psychology, University of Nottingham, commenting on the aspects of solution-focused work that most impressed him (from "Psych yourself up," *Weekend FT*, 29 January 2000.

Chapter 10
1 Martin Seligman, *Learned Optimism*, Random House, 1991.

Chapter 11
1 John Whitmore, *Coaching for Performance* (3rd edn), Nicholas Brealey Publishing, 2002.

Chapter 12
1 Don Coles, on SFT listserv SFT-L, 9 March 2000.
2 John Henden, in Mark McKergow and Jenny Clarke (eds) *Positive Approaches to Change: Applications of Solutions Focus and Appreciative Inquiry at Work, Solutions Books*, 2005, pp 39–51.
3 Fritjof Capra, speaking at the OD Network Conference, Montreal, Canada, October 2002.

Chapter 13
1 Ed Schein, *Process Consultation*, Addison–Wesley, 1988.
2 *Ibid.*, p 11.
3 *Ibid.*, p 10
4 *Ibid.*, p 10.
5 David L Cooperider & Diana Whitney, "Appreciative Inquiry," Berrett-Koehler Communications, 1999, www.bkcommunications.com.
6 For a detailed comparison of the Solutions Focus and Appreciative Inquiry, see Kendy Rossi, Tricia Lustig and Mark McKergow, A Comparison of Appreciative Inquiry (AI) and Solutions Focus (SF),

Appreciative Inquiry Commons website, 2003, http://appreciative-inquiry.cwru.edu/research/bibPapersDetail.cfm?coid=3231a.

7 Clive Cookson, "Introduction to germ warfare," *Financial Times*, 30 October 1999.

8 For more details on positive deviance methods see www.positive deviance.org.

9 Richard T Pascale and Jerry Sternin, "Your company's secret change agents," *Harvard Business Review*, May 2005.

10 Murray Gell-Mann, *The Quark and the Jaguar*, Abacus, 1994, p 228.

11 Daniel Dennett, *Darwin's Dangerous Idea*, Penguin, 1996.

12 Shona L Brown and Kathleen M Eisenhardt, *Competing on the Edge*, Harvard Business School Press, 1998.

13 *Ibid.*, p 151.

Chapter 15

1 Mary Catherine Bateson, *With a Daughter's Eye*, William Morrow, 1984.

2 Wendel Ray and Steve de Shazer (eds), *Evolving Brief Therapies: In Honor of John H Weakland*, Giest & Russell, 1999.

3 John Weakland, in Wendel Ray and Steve de Shazer (eds), *Evolving Brief Therapies: In Honor of John H Weakland*, Giest & Russell, 1999.

4 Gregory Bateson, Don Jackson, Jay Haley, and John Weakland, "Toward a theory of schizophrenia," *Behavioral Science*, 1(4), 1956.

5 In Wendel Ray and Steve de Shazer (eds), *Evolving Brief Therapies: In Honor of John H Weakland*, Giest & Russell, 1999.

6 On the Don Jackson memorial website, www.dondjackson.com.

7 Summarized by Paul Watzlawick, John Weakland, and Richard Fisch, *Change: Principles of Problem Formation and Problem Resolution*, Norton, 1974.

8 Richard Bandler and John Grinder, *The Structure of Magic I*, Science and Behavior Books, 1975; *Patterns of Hypnotic of Milton H Erickson MD*, Meta Publications, 1975.

9 Sue Knight, *NLP at Work*, Nicholas Brealey Publishing, 2002.

10 Steve de Shazer and Insoo Kim Berg, "The brief therapy tradition," in John Weakland and Wendel Ray (eds), *Propagations: Thirty Years of Influence from the Mental Research Institute*, Haworth Press, 1995.

11 Harry Norman, Mark McKergow, and Jenny Clarke, "Paradox is a muddle: An interview with Steve de Shazer," *Rapport*, 34: 41–9, 1996.

12 Steve de Shazer, *Keys to Solutions in Brief Therapy*, Norton, 1985; *Clues: Investigating Solutions in Brief Therapy*, Norton, 1988; *Putting Difference to Work*, Norton, 1991; *Words Were Originally Magic*, Norton, 1994.

13 Mark McKergow and Jenny Clarke (eds) *Positive Approaches to Change: Applications of Solutions Focus and Appreciative Inquiry at Work*, Solutions Books, 2005.

14 Wally Gingerich and Sheri Eisengart, "Solution-focused brief therapy: A review of the outcome research," *Family Process*, 39:477–98, 2000.

Bibliography

The Solutions Focus in business and organizations

Mark McKergow and Paul Z Jackson, *Solutions At Work: An Introduction to Solutions Focused Consulting, Coaching and Facilitation*, Solutions Books, 2005. Audio CD featuring a carefully crafted dialogue between the authors.

Mark McKergow and Jenny Clarke (eds) *Positive Approaches to Change: Applications of Solutions Focus and Appreciative Inquiry at Work*, Solutions Books, 2005. Leading SF practitioners apply these ideas to coaching, team remotivation, performance management, strategic planning and other areas.

Daniel Meier, *Team Coaching with the SolutionCircle: A Practical Guide to Solutions Focused Team Development*, Solutions Books, 2005. SF ideas applied specifically to working with teams.

Insoo Kim Berg and Peter Szabó, *Brief Coaching for Lasting Solutions*, WW Norton, 2005. Detailed exposition of solutions-focused coaching; companion DVD available.

Jane Greene and Antony M Grant, *Solution-Focused Coaching*, Momentum, 2003. Including solutions-focused ideas alongside cognitive behavioral and other coaching methods.

Origins

Gregory Bateson, Don Jackson, Jay Haley and John Weakland, "Toward a theory of schizophrenia," *Behavioral Science*, Vol 1, No 4, 1956 (reproduced in Gregory Bateson, *Steps to an Ecology of Mind*, Ballantine Books, 1972).

Mary Catherine Bateson, *With a Daughter's Eye*, William Morrow, 1984.

Wendel Ray and Steve de Shazer (eds) *Evolving Brief Therapies: In Honor of John H Weakland*, Giest & Russell, 1999.

Robert Rosenthal and Lenore Jacobson, *Pygmalion in the Classroom*, Irvington, 1968, republished by Crown House Publishing, 2003.

Steve de Shazer and Insoo Kim Berg, "The brief therapy tradition," in John Weakland and Wendel Ray (eds), *Propagations: Thirty Years of Influence from the Mental Research Institute*, Haworth Press, 1995.

Paul Watzlawick, Janet Beavin Bavelus and Don D Jackson, *Pragmatics of Human Communication*, Norton, 1967.

Paul Watzlawick, John Weakland and Richard Fisch, *Change: Principles of Problem Formation and Problem Resolution*, Norton, 1974. A key point in the writing on change, practical steps toward taking an interactional view and understanding instances of spontaneous change occurring in situations that appear hopeless.

Paul Watzlawick and John Weakland (eds) *The Interactional View*, Norton, 1977.

Solutions-focused and other brief therapy

Insoo Kim Berg and Peter de Jong, *Interviewing for Solutions*, Wadsworth, 2001.

Brian Cade and Bill O'Hanlon, *A Brief Guide to Brief Therapy*, Norton, 1993.

Jenny Clarke, "Occam's razor as a therapeutic tool," dissertation, National College of Hypnotherapy, 1994.

Michael Durrant, *Creative Strategies for School Problems*, Norton, 1995.

Ben Furman and Tapani Ahola, *Solution Talk*, BT Press, 2001.

Wally Gingerich and Sheri Eisengart, "Solution-focused brief therapy: A review of the outcome research," *Family Process*, No 39, pp 477–98, 2000, www.gingerich.net.

Jay Haley, *Uncommon Therapy*, WW Norton, 1973.

Linda Metcalf, *Parenting Towards Solutions*, Prentice Hall, 1996.

Linda Metcalf, *Teaching Towards Solutions*, Center for Applied Research in Education, 1998.

Linda Metcalf, *Solution Focussed Group Therapy*, Free Press, 1998.

Gale Miller, *Becoming Miracle Workers*, Aldine de Gruyter, 1997.

Scott D Miller and Insoo Kim Berg, *The Miracle Method*, Norton, 1995.

Bill O'Hanlon and James Wilk, *Shifting Contexts*, Guilford Press, 1987.

Bill O'Hanlon and Michelle Weiner-Davis, *In Search of Solutions*, Norton, 1989.

Bill O'Hanlon, *Do One Thing Different*, William Morrow, 1999.

Harry Norman, Mark McKergow and Jenny Clarke, "Paradox is a muddle: An interview with Steve de Shazer," *Rapport*, No 34, pp 41–9, 1996.

John Rhodes and Yasmin Ajmal, *Solution Focused Thinking in Schools*, BT Press, 1995.

Steve de Shazer, *Keys to Solutions in Brief Therapy*, Norton, 1985.

Steve de Shazer, *Clues: Investigating Solutions in Brief Therapy*, Norton, 1988.

Steve de Shazer, *Putting Difference to Work*, Norton, 1991.

Steve de Shazer, *Words Were Originally Magic*, Norton, 1994.

Fritz B Simon, *My Psychosis, My Bicycle and I*, Aronson, 1996.

Michelle Weiner-Davis, *Change Your Life and Everyone in It*, Fireside/Simon & Schuster, 1995.

Complexity science and interactions

Per Bak, *How Nature Works*, Oxford University Press, 1997.

John D Barrow, *Impossibility: The Limits of Science and the Science of Limits*, Oxford University Press, 1998.

Arthur Battram, *Navigating Complexity*, Industrial Society, 1997.

John L Casti, *Complexification*, Abacus, 1994.

Richard Dawkins, *The Blind Watchmaker*, Penguin, 1986.

Daniel Dennett, *Darwin's Dangerous Idea*, Penguin, 1996.

Murray Gell-Mann, *The Quark and the Jaguar*, Abacus, 1994.

Kevin Kelly, *Out of Control: The New Biology of Machines*, Fourth Estate, 1994.

Donella Meadows, Dennis Meadows, Jørgen Randers and William Behrens, *The Limits to Growth*, Universe Books, 1972.

Mitchel Resnick, *Turtle, Termites and Traffic Jams*, MIT Press, 1994.

Steven Rose, *Lifelines*, Allen Lane/Penguin Press, 1997.

David Ruelle, *Chance and Chaos*, Penguin, 1993.

Karl Sigmund, *Games of Life*, Penguin, 1995.

M Mitchell Waldrop, *Complexity*, Viking, 1993.

John Ziman, *Reliable Knowledge*, Cambridge University Press, 1978.

Language

Richard Bandler and John Grinder, *The Structure of Magic 1*, Science and Behavior Books, 1975.

Richard Bandler and John Grinder, *Patterns of the Hypnotic Techniques of Milton H Erickson MD*, Meta Publications, 1975.

Sue Knight, *NLP at Work*, Nicholas Brealey Publishing, 2002.

Mark McKergow and Jenny Clarke, "Occam's razor in the NLP toolbox," *NLP World*, Vol 3, No 3, pp 47–56, 1996.

Alan Sokal and Jean Bricmont, *Intellectual Impostures*, Profile, 1997.

Robert Tauber, *Self-Fulfilling Prophecy: A Practical Guide to Its Use in Education*, Praeger Publishers, 1997.

Paul Watzlawick, *How Real Is Real?*, Vintage, 1977.

Paul Watzlawick (ed.), *The Invented Reality*, Norton, 1984.

Ludwig Wittgenstein, *Philosophical Investigations*, Blackwell, 1953.

Ludwig Wittgenstein, *Tractatus Logico-Philosophicus* (trans. D F Pears and B F McGuiness), Routledge, 1961.

Business

Shona L Brown and Kathleen M Eisenhardt, *Competing on the Edge*, Harvard Business School Press, 1998.

Clay Carr, *Choice, Chance and Organisational Change*, Amacom, 1996.

Paul Z Jackson, *The Inspirational Trainer*, Kogan Page, 2001.

Paul Z Jackson, *58½ Ways to Improvise in Training*, Crown House Publishing, 2003.

Peter Senge, *The Fifth Discipline*, Century, 1990.

Patricia Shaw, *Changing Conversation in Organisations*, Routledge, 2002.

Ralph D Stacey, *Complex Responsive Processes in Organizations: Learning and Knowledge Creation*, Routledge, 2001.

Appreciative inquiry

David Cooperider, Peter Sorensen, Diana Whitney and Therese Yaeger, *Appreciative Inquiry: Rethinking Human Organization Toward a Positive Theory of Change*, Stipes, 1999.

Sue Annis Hammond and Cathy Royal (eds), *Lessons from the Field: Applying Appreciative Inquiry*, Practical Press, 1998.

Diana Whitney and Amanda Trosten-Bloom, *The Power of Appreciative Inquiry: A Practical Guide to Positive Change*, Berrett-Koehler, 2003.

Positive psychology

Marcus Buckingham and Donald O Clifton, *Now, Find Your Strengths*, Simon and Schuster, 2001.

Mihaly Csikszentmihalyi, *Flow: The Classic Work on How to Achieve Happiness*, Rider, 2002.

Martin Seligman, *Learned Optimism*, Random House, 1991.

Martin Seligman, *Authentic Happiness*, Nicholas Brealey Publishing, 2003.

Index

$5 words 11, 92–3, 95, 101, 102
$5,000 words 11, 92–3, 96, 99,
    102, 199
4-Ds model 205

A

accidents
    frozen 219
    happy 219–20
    helpful 44–5
accusatory explanation 72, 74–5,
    87
actions 138–9, 143–4, 145, 151–2,
    169, 175–6, 193–4
    small 19, 95, 105, 106–11, 125,
    129, 134, 135–6
affirm 19, 72, 80–1, 87, 129, 132,
    134, 138–9, 142, 144, 146, 151,
    154, 169, 174–5, 192–3, 195,
    216
Alliance Atlantis, 211–13

anthropology 230–1
appreciative inquiry 204–5

B

Bandler, Richard 234
Bateson, Gregory 15–16, 230–2,
    234, 236
Bateson, William 59
Bavelas experiment 13–14
beginner mind 14–15, 117,
    119–20, 125, 163, 173–4, 228
Berg, Insoo Kim 27, 92, 230,
    234–6
bespoke solutions 11, 229
Brief Family Therapy Center 234
Brief Therapy Center 233
Brown, Shona 221–2
Buckingham, Marcus 56
Butterfly Effect 16

C

Cade, Brian 236
Capra, Fritjof 195
causes 54, 76
    of problems 47–9
    of solutions 75
celebrating success 195–8
Centre for Excellence in
    Leadership 160–1
change 15–16, 111
    customer for 21, 28–30, 35, 60,
    78, 96, 112
    resistance to 6, 59, 63, 65–6, 68
Clifton, Donald O 56
coach
    as facilitator 138
    external 165–6, 182
    manager as 157–77
    role of 154–6
coaching 136
    conversation 137 145–53,
    167–9, 173, 175
    for performance 162, 166
    framework, OSKAR 138–53,
    158, 159–60, 161, 162, 166–76,
    190
    introducing to organization
    176–7
    skills 159–61, 162, 163–5,
    166–76
    solutions-focused 137–225
    team 178–200

to organizations 201–25
Coles, Don 185
Combe Down stone mines
    209–10
common ground 181–2
complex systems 16, 39, 40–2, 76
complexity science 10, 37
compliment fish 80
compliments 80–1, 87, 129, 132
conflict between groups 214–17
consequences, unintended 44–5,
    76
consulting models 201–6
conversation, coaching 137
    145–53, 167–9, 173, 175
cooperation 63, 65–6
Cooperider, David 204–5
counters 11, 18, 19, 58–62, 68, 95,
    111–12, 128–9, 131, 133, 142,
    148, 155, 190–2, 195, 199, 206,
    219–21, 228
    questions for 59–60
culture 100–101
customer for change 21, 28–30,
    35, 60, 78, 96, 111
cybernetics 231

D

de Shazer, Steve 103, 230, 234–5
Dennett, Daniel 221
Derrington, Andrew 95, 123
design 205

destiny 205
deviance, positive 217–19
difference that makes a difference
    15–16
differences, useful 180
discovery 205
doctor–patient coaching model
    202–3
dream 205
Durrant, Michael 223–4

E

Eisenhardt, Kathleen 221–2
emergence 37, 39–42, 49–50, 54
Erickson, Milton 57–8, 82, 230,
    232, 234, 236
every case is different 11–12,
    103–25, 200, 206–10
    benefits of 104
everything is a useful gift 56–7,
    68, 96, 155, 240
expectations 84–5, 87, 228
expert mind 14–15, 122–3, 125
explanations
    accusatory 72, 74–5, 87
    helpful 85–6

F

first signs of progress 93–4, 100,
    108

Fisch, Richard 232–3
fit 105–6, 125
Fleming, Alexander 220
flying foxes 214–17
Forrester, Jay 39
frozen accidents 219
Fry, William 231
Furman, Ben 73, 74, 193
future perfect 3, 4, 18, 19, 22,
    31–4, 35, 78, 83–6, 94–5, 107,
    128, 130, 132–3, 134, 138–40,
    147–9, 151, 167, 169–70,
    171–2, 185–7, 198, 212,
    215–17

G

Gandhi, Mahatma 194
Gell-Mann, Murray 219
genes 52
George, Evan 192
gift, everything is a useful 56–7,
    68, 96, 155, 240
Gingerich, Wally 234
Goldman Sachs 219
Greenfield, Susan 52
Grinder, John 234
GROW model 169–70
growing businesses 210–13
guerrilla SF 179, 194–5

H

Haley, Jay 231–2, 234
happy accidents 219–20
helpful accidents 44–5
Henden, John 186–7
Hewlett-Packard 219
Hingston, Monica 195–8
hot topics 184

I

ideas 1, 2
inbetween 10, 36–54, 64, 169,
    198–9
    benefits of 37–8
interaction, between people 42–3,
    198–9
interactional
    systems, organizations as 43–7
    view 10, 36–8, 42–7, 54, 66, 99

J

Jackson, Don 232
James, William 181
jargon 11
Johansson, Björn 189–90

K

Kanda, Masanori 210–11
Kay, Alan 212–13
Knight, Sue 234
know-how 138–9, 141–2, 146,
    149–51, 164, 169, 173–4,
    190–2, 218

L

Laing, RD 233
language 11, 77, 88–102
    benefits of simpler 89
Lewis-Nicholson, Alison
    195–8
Lincoln, Shaun 160–1
Lipchik, Eve 234
Lotka-Volterra cycles 46

M

make use of what's there 1, 11,
    55–68, 199
    benefits of 55–6
managers-as-coaches 157–77
McCulloch, Warren 231
McLaughlin, Jim 184–5
Mead, Margaret 231
Meier, Daniel 184
Mental Research Institute 232

metaphors 15, 53, 98
Miles, Sarah 176–7
milestones 170–1
Miller, Gale 99
mind
    beginner 14–15, 117, 119–20,
    125, 163, 173-4, 228
    expert 14–15, 122–3, 125
Molnar, Alex 234–5
more with less 2
multi-scaling 189–90

N

Nationwide 166
neuro-linguistic programming
    (NLP) 234
not-compliments 228

O

O'Hanlon, Bill 236
Occam's Razor 12–13, 91, 232
optimism 154
organizational development 136
organizations
    coaching to 201–25
    solutions-focused 223
Ormerod, Paul 40
OSKAR coaching framework
    138–53, 158, 159–60, 161, 162,
    166–76, 190

outcome 138–9, 145, 147, 149,
    158, 166–70

P

Palazzoli, Mara Selvini 234
paranoia, positive 193–4
PepsiCo 160
performance, coaching for 162,
    166
Perls, Fritz 234
Person, Eva 189–90
perspective, useful 180–1
pessimism 154–5
phage 206–7
pitfalls, potential 1, 21, 27–9,
    31–2, 47–9, 51–2, 63, 64–5, 66,
    74, 82–3, 89, 90–1, 95–8,
    99–101, 104, 105, 112–4
platform 11, 18, 22, 27–8, 34, 35,
    128, 130–1, 138, 140, 144,
    145–6, 147, 167, 183–5, 194–5,
    207, 214–15, 217
platform-building questions 28
plumber coaching model 202
positive
    deviance 217–19
    forces 2
    paranoia 193–4
    power of 205
    thinking 2, 77
possibilities 11, 69–87, 107,
    119–20, 199, 228

possibilities (*cont.*)
  benefits of 71
  future 69, 70–1, 83–6
  past 69–70, 72–7
  present 69–70, 71, 77–83
potential pitfalls 21, 27–9, 31–2,
  47–9, 51–2, 63, 64–5, 66, 74,
  82–3, 89, 90–1, 95–8, 99–101,
  104, 105, 112–4
power of the positive 205
presupposition 77–8
probes 221–2
problem focus 2–3, 5, 59, 63, 126,
  162, 181–2, 203
problem talk 10, 16, 21, 23–5, 27,
  35, 81, 190
problem-free talk 138–9, 145
problems 1, 3–4, 140–1, 174, 180,
  198, 203, 204
  solvable 21, 31, 34–5, 97
  underlying 53
  unsolvable 31, 34–5
process consultation 203–4
  solutions-focused 204
progress, first signs of 93–4, 100,
  108
psychotherapy 137, 140–1
purchase of expertise coaching
  model 202

reification 99–100
resistance to change 59, 63, 65–6,
  68
resourceful words 82–3
resources 62–4, 81–3, 87, 128–9,
  131, 134
  questions for 82
review 138–9, 144–5, 153, 176
Roentgen, Wilhelm 220
Röhrig, Peter 189
Rose, Steven 48
Rosenthal, Robert 84

S

Satir, Virginia 232–3, 234
Save the Children 217–18
scaling 19, 89, 94–5, 102, 130,
  133–4, 138–9, 141, 149, 158,
  161, 170–3, 174, 188–90
  questions for 170–1
Schein, Ed 122, 201–3
Seligman, Martin 154
Senge, Peter 38–9, 41
Shepheard, Miles 214–17
SIMPLE model 9–19, 126, 161,
  198
  applied to coaching 198–200
simplicity, power of 12
skills 62–4, 128–9
  coaching 159–61, 162, 163–5,
  166–76
  for questioning 2

R

Real User 192

small actions 19, 95, 105, 106–11, 125, 129, 134, 135–6

small steps 2, 139, 143–4, 152, 153, 188, 193–4, 216–17, 220-1

social constructionist approach 204

solution forced 105, 123–4, 125

solution-focused
  brief therapy 234–6
  change 1
  coaching 137–225
  organizations 223
  process consultation 204

Solutions Focus in action 2–3. 5, 8, 22–3, 26–7, 30, 31, 38, 43–4, 51, 58, 60–2, 63–4, 65, 67, 71, 75, 82, 83, 90, 93–4, 108, 112, 119, 121–2, 159, 162, 198–200

Solutions Focus
  benefits of 6–7
  compared to appreciative inquiry 205
  precursors 230–6
  ways to use 7

solutions 1, 4, 8, 141, 147
  artist 226–7
  bespoke 11, 229
  not problems 10, 21–35
  scientist 226, 228–9
  talk 10, 21–5, 35, 79, 82, 181–2
  tools 9, 15, 17–19, 126–36, 178, 179

solvable problems 21, 31, 34–5, 97

Southwest Airlines 191

Srivastva, Suresh 204–5

steps, small 2, 139, 143–4, 152, 153, 188, 193–4, 216–17, 220-1

stories 72–3, 78
  organizational 72–3
  personal 73

success, celebrating 195–8

systemic approach 10, 36–7, 38–42

systems
  dynamics 39, 54
  synthesis 42–7

T

talk
  problem 10, 16, 21, 23–5, 27, 35, 79, 81, 190
  problem-free 138–9, 145
  solution 10, 21, 23–5, 35, 79, 82, 181–2, 195
  video 34

talking trap 223–4

team
  building 82, 136
  coaching 178–200
  leader 182–3

Teresa, Mother 223

Thatcher, Margaret 182

theories, ill-fitting 112–17, 125

theory of no theory 7

time quake 186–7
tools, solutions 9, 15, 17–19,
  126–36

U

underlying problem 53
unintended consequences 44–5,
  76
unresourceful words 82–3, 87
unsolvable problems 31, 34–5
utilization 56–8, 240

V

video talk 34

W

Walkers Snackfoods 138, 159–60,
  161–2, 164–5, 176–7
Watzlawick, Paul 232–3
Weakland, John 230, 231–3
Weiner-David, Michelle 236
what works 1, 2, 4, 6, 16, 103,
  107, 162, 205–10, 229
White, Theodore 2
Whitmore, John 169–70
Whitney, Diana 205
Wittgenstein, Ludwig 21, 91, 235
words
    $5 11, 92–3, 95, 101, 102
    $5,000 11, 92–3, 96, 99, 102,
    199
    resourceful 82–3
    unresourceful 82–3, 87

About the Authors

Mark McKergow PhD MBA is a scientist by training and by nature, who continues to seek simplicity and reliability in learning and change. His influences range from systems thinking and brain research to language, narrative and philosophy.

Mark has pioneered the use of solutions-focused methods in organizational and business contexts. He has presented the Solutions Focus on every continent except Antarctica, and is in demand as a keynote speaker. He now runs **sf**work—The Centre for Solutions Focus at Work.

Mark was instrumental in the founding of the SOL (Solutions in Organisations Linkup) conference series, is a member of the SOL international steering group, and founded Solutions Books with Jenny Clarke in 2005. He has been elected to membership of Jack Canfield's Transformational Leadership Council, the only British-based person to be so honored.

Find out more about Mark and his latest work at www.sfwork.com.

Paul Z Jackson is an inspirational consultant, who devises and runs training courses for corporate clients and public organizations. As a journalist, a senior producer with BBC Radio, and the founder of the More Fool Us improvisation comedy team, he has prompted a lot of laughter, on stage and off, mostly intentionally.

As a consultant, trainer, facilitator, coach and speaker, Paul has introduced the Solutions Focus ideas and methods to hundreds of people within organizations.

A graduate of Oxford University (MA, Oxon) and contributor to scholarly publications, Paul's other books include *Impro Learning*, *58½ Ways to Improvise in Training*, and *The Inspirational Trainer*. His personal website is www.impro.org.uk.

Mark McKergow   Paul Z Jackson
sfwork—The Centre for   The Solutions Focus
        Solutions Focus at Work   34a Clarence Road
15 St Georges Avenue   St Albans
London N7 0HB, UK   AL1 4NG
mark@mckergow.com,   UK
        mark@sfwork.com   paul@thesolutionsfocus.co.uk
Tel +44 (0)8453 707 145   Tel +44 1727 843820

www.thesolutionsfocus.com

Our website has information on the solutions-focused approach, examples of the Solutions Focus in action, book lists, news of upcoming events, and links to solutions-focused practitioners around the world.

You may also be interested in our audio CD, *Solutions at Work: An Introduction to Solution Focused Coaching and Consulting*, available via the website.